V&R Academic

Research in Contemporary Religion

Volume 21

Vandenhoeck & Ruprecht

Hans-Joachim Sander/Kaspar Villadsen/
Trygve Wyller (eds.)

The Spaces of Others – Heterotopic Spaces

Practicing and Theorizing Hospitality and Counter-Conduct beyond the Religion/Secular Border

Vandenhoeck & Ruprecht

With 5 Figures

Bibliographic information published by the Deutsche Nationalbibliothek
The Deutsche Nationalbibliothek lists this publication in the Deutsche Nationalbibliografie; detailed bibliographic data available online: http://dnb.d-nb.de.

ISSN 2198-7556
ISBN 978-3-525-60455-7

You can find alternative editions of this book and additional material on our Website:
www.v-r.de

Typesetting by Konrad Triltsch GmbH, Ochsenfurt
Printed and bound by Hubert & Co GmbH & Co. KG, Robert-Bosch-Breite 6, D-37079 Göttingen.

Printed on aging-resistant paper.

Preface

This is a book that is squarely rooted in many years of research cooperation. The three editors met in another context than the preparation of this book, drawing on their common interest in spaces for others, Foucault, the welfare state and hospitality. This interest then developed into the present book as a common project. We have shared workshops, seminars and excursions to many of the five cases analyzed and included. Professor Anne Birgitte Pessi, Helsinki, was part of the project during the first stage, but could not continue because of (very positive) family commitments. Thanks to her for hosting one important initial workshop in her location.

PhD student Kaia Schultz Rønsdal has been with us most of the time (thanks for your contributions and participation!), others have been part of the group for a shorter period. Meeting Professor Bryan Turner, New York, and having him become part of the book and the last part of the project has definitely been an experience of a very competent contribution to the important interdisciplinarity we try to pursue. Turner is one of those very good scholars, where standards are set, something that is always very helpful and important for us.

Coming from different disciplines and even confessions, there are still basic things that unite us: the ambition to research a better fundament for what a space *for* others and spaces *of* others might look like. Instead of writing one more book on the importance of otherness, we wanted to do a book on how to theorize the practices of the spaces for others. We hope that our readers will share our interest and follow the discussion many of us belong to and are committed to.

There are many people and institutions to thank. First of all, we are more than grateful to all the participants we have met in the different projects we write about and interpret. Without their hospitality, and the hospitality of their leaders, this book could not have been possible. This also goes for the trust they have shown, not only by inviting us in, but also your respect for our writing about you upon leaving.

At one stage in the project development, we invited the late Professor Edward Soja, Los Angeles, to come to Oslo and Gothenburg to see one of our spaces and to comment on our work. We were grateful and honored that he accepted this invitation. We shall never forget the seminar in the staffroom in the church, filled up with all kinds of researchers and one of the leading space scholars in the middle.

Of course, we do theorize here, but we insist that the theories we use must be developed parallel to the practices we discuss. This in turn also opens all the problems of methodology between the social sciences and theology/philosophy/ethics. The present book does not presume to solve them; we also differ in our approaches as you will see from the different articles. We hope that these methodological challenges can be developed further in the future.

We are also grateful to the Norwegian Research Council (NFR) for the funding we received in the context of the Samkul Program, which allocated resources to initiate the project. This seed money allowed the project to be set up and the book to be planned. Thanks also to NFR for the financing of an important part of the publication costs.

Editor Jörg Persch and editorial assistant Moritz Reissing and their team at V&R has facilitated this book in a very good way, and we are strongly dependent on the competence and friendly professionalism they have exhibited. Joe Smith has been the efficient and generous English proof reader. Many thanks also to his patient way to deal with different manuscripts during the last months of the writing process. MA Helena Schmidt, Oslo facilitated the project during workshops and planning for the future. She has also contributed substantially to finalize the manuscript in the last weeks before submitting. Her assistance has been both competent, generous and very helpful.

Salzburg/Copenhagen/Oslo, April, 2016
Hans-Joachim Sander, Kaspar Villadsen, Trygve Wyller

Contents

Preface 5

Hans-Joachim Sander (Salzburg)/Kaspar Villadsen (Copenhagen)/
Trygve Wyller (Oslo)
Introduction
Discovering spaces of hospitality beyond the religious/secular divide . 9

Topos A: Constructing brotherly love, Copenhagen and beyond 21

Johs. Bertelsen (Copenhagen)
Kristeligt Studenter-Settlement – between Christianity and Socialism . 23

Kaspar Villadsen (Copenhagen)
The Christian Student Settlement:
Between Utopian Ideas and Real Constraints 29

Topos B: The ecclesial clinique or the clinical church 51

Anne Sjøgren (Gothenburg)
Working for undocumented migrants in Gothenburg 53

Trygve Wyller (Oslo)
A spatial Power that dissolves itself
Space, Empathy and Theology – when the Colonized Enter the Empire 59

Topos C: The Hospitality of the Monastic Garden 79

P. Michael Hüttl (Altenburg)
The Garden of Religions at Stift Altenburg in Lower Austria 81

Hans-Joachim Sander (Salzburg)
From Religious Space to Spaces of Religions – the 'Garden of Religions' in Stift Altenburg
A case study in the counter-conduct of a spatial political theology . . . 89

Topos D: The Hospitality of the Urban Space 117

Hilde Kirkebøen (Oslo)
Marginality at Oslo Central Station 119

Kaia Schultz Rønsdal (Oslo)
Murmurs of pastoral care? 121

Bryan S. Turner (New York and Melbourne)/Kaspar Villadsen (Copenhagen)
Counter movements and Space: The Settlement, Occupy Wall Street and the Tea Party 143

Hans-Joachim Sander (Salzburg)/ Kaspar Villadsen (Copenhagen)/ Trygve Wyller (Oslo)
Conclusion
A heterotopian grammar of hospitality 173

List of Contributors 189

Index of Topics 191

Index of Names 195

Hans-Joachim Sander (Salzburg)/Kaspar Villadsen (Copenhagen)/
Trygve Wyller (Oslo)

Introduction

Discovering spaces of hospitality beyond the religious/secular divide

The Intention

In the present situation in the world, values of tolerance, compassion and hospitality appear to be more contested. We have witnessed European nations fencing off their borders in the face of thousands of refugees fleeing the atrocities of war in Syria and elsewhere. The obscene images of death and suffering unfolding at the borders seem to spur only momentary outrage and attention from the mass media. The debates among European leaders have come to center around how to "protect us" from refugees, rather than protecting the precarious lives of the refugees. Recently, ultranationalist and extreme right-wing parties have increasingly gained ground, from Sweden to Greece, promoting a rhetoric of "Sweden for the Swedes!" and "France for the French!"—and perhaps thereby spurring increasing attacks on refugees centers and immigrants in public spaces. Moreover, many welfare states have tightened the criteria for receiving assistance from the national social security systems, the result being that overall poverty levels are on the rise along with increasing numbers of homeless people and children living in poverty.

The reaction to these predicaments from the academic world of social scientists has been rather lenient and sparse. In particular, scholars of a contemporary philosophical and poststructuralist tradition seem to have difficulty finding the normative platforms from which to voice strident critique against the entrenchment of tolerance and care. Against this background, one might think we have sacrificed the traditions of hospitality and generosity. Yet we know there are still thousands and thousands of people out there trying to change, help and provide comfort to those in need.

The authors in this book agree that we should not stop looking for practices of hospitality. At the same time, however, we must not be naive. We need to better understand what hospitality is, where it is practiced and also why it is practiced. This book argues that hospitality and space are inextricably connected. Hospitality is not necessarily something we possess as an inner quality or as something disconnected from others. Rather, this is one of the main ideas in this book, it is practiced in specific ways in particular spaces. The thesis is that we have to look for the characteristics of hospitality in "the other spaces" that Michel Foucault once called *heterotopias.*

In this volume, to improve our understanding, we analyze five heterotopic cases. We have chosen an heterogeneous group—a monastic garden for interreligious dialogue in Austria, a Lutheran congregation that accommodates a project for undocumented migrants in Western Sweden, a busy intersection in downtown Oslo where substance-users stay (and most others pass by), a voluntary organization that works for the creation of alternative life forms in inner city Copenhagen, and, finally, some aspects of the Occupy Wall Street movement in New York City.

The authors are theologians, sociologists and a PhD candidate in diaconia, an illustration of the interdisciplinary composition of the book. This group of researchers has been cooperating in this area for a couple of years now, and we find the interdisciplinary profile, to be both fruitful and necessary for this field of research.

Foucault was fascinated by the significance and critical potential represented by the heterotopic in all societies and throughout history. Heterotopias are much more than just a location or a place; they are the significant other, spaces that can influence and contest the societies they reflect, mirror and invert:

> There are also, probably in every culture, in every civilization, real places— places that do exist and that are formed in the very founding of society—which are something like counter-sites, a kind of effectively enacted utopia in which the real sites, all the other real sites that can be found within the culture, are simultaneously represented, contested, and inverted. Places of this kind are outside of all places, even though it may be possible to indicate their location in reality. Because these places are absolutely different from all the sites that they reflect and speak about, I shall call them, by way of contrast to utopias, heterotopias (Foucault 1984: 46).

Inspired not at least by this famous paragraph, the last decades have seen a significant increase in the amount of research connected to the spatial turn, both in the social sciences and across the humanities—including theology. Scholars like, first, Henri Lefebvre, then Edward Soja and recently Kim Knott are among those who have influenced the field the most. According to Michel de Certeau, urban spaces of this kind belong to the founding elements of a new scientific approach to social realities—cultural science ("Kulturwissenschaft"). This book offers detailed studies on a range of mainly urban spaces. What unites the above-mentioned thinkers (along with Foucault) is their focus on the significant "other" space, to which they applied different names. Foucault called it "heterotopia," Lefebvre "l'espace vecu" (lived space), Soja used the term "third space," and Knott calls them "contested spaces." Whereas Henri Lefebvre particularly focused the urban and political context, Edward Soja moved the growth of urban centers beyond the purely metropolitan dimension. Kim Knott emphasized the contestation emerging in public religious spaces, while Michel de Certeau demonstrated how deeply human beings are influenced by the complexity characteristic of urban contexts. (See e.g. Lefebvre 1996, Soja 1991, Knott, 2005, de Certeau 1984)

We recognize all these important and intriguing insights which inspired our project. Yet we chose to concentrate on the otherness of spaces that display a specific quality, something one may call *hospitality.* The practices of hospitality that we center on are shaped by explicit or implicit religious values. We are interested in exploring how religious (as well as secular) practices and commitments imbue spaces with a kind of hospitality that often contests the legal and institutional structures of secular welfare states. In this way, these spaces become heterotopic, insofar as they expose the deep-seated contradictions and paradoxes of modern societies. We are also concerned with questions of power: Do the practices in the third space affect the power relations outside of the heterotopic in society at large?

We believe that the extent to which heterotopic spaces are always inherently "contested spaces," as Kim Knott (2005) pointed out, still needs to be researched more. One implication of this assertion is that we attempt to analyze and interpret the spatial dimension without hastily defining it as either religious or secular. This analytical openness allows us to operate with a spatial matrix underlying the wide range of counter-conducts possible in the social world. By taking this approach, we may begin to understand how practices of hospitality might develop from unexpected religious trajectories. We may also discover and discuss how these spaces fundamentally highlight welfare problems not adequately addressed by the official service and social security systems.

Pastoral power: An "individualizing tactic" or counter-conducts invoking universality?

Our interpretation of the five practices through the lens of the concept of heterotopia is the key move in this book. In addition, we mobilize two other concepts developed by Foucault in order to approach an interpretation of what kind of practices they really are, namely the notion of pastoral power and of counter-conduct.

For many years now the critical academic public has known that proclaiming hospitality is not the same as practicing hospitality. This is even more true when the practices studied are rooted in religious, more specifically Christian, traditions. Most of the practices analyzed and interpreted in this book indeed stem from such traditions. Hasty claims that this or that practice is a "hospitable" one should be more carefully reconsidered in light of Michel Foucault's concept of pastoral power.

In his genealogy of modern governmentality, presented in a lecture series in 1977–1978, Foucault launched the notion of "pastoral power" or "pastoral technology" for the first time (2007, 1994, 2006). What is probably well-known to most readers of this book is that, by employing the notion of pastoral power, Foucault desired to highlight a modality of power that became a major constitutive element in the formation of the modern welfare state. He suggested that a particular rationality of care and techniques of governing, developed early on in the history of Christianity, were then transformed and subsumed in modern institutions and practices of welfare, cure and caring. Foucault presented pastoral power as a form of power or leadership that cares for the individual subject in a continuous and individualizing manner: "What I mean in fact is the development of power techniques oriented toward individuals and intended to rule them in a continuous and permanent way. If the state is the political form of a centralized and centralizing power, let us call pastorship the individualizing power" (Foucault 1994: 2).

In Foucault's view, then, the secularized welfare state did not do completely away with pastoral power, since this modality of power proliferated and became ingrained in modern welfare institutions (Foucault 1982: 782). The modern welfare state that aimed to secure the secular well-being of citizens did not break completely with religious motives and institutions. Instead, the fundamental imperative of protecting the population implied a re-articulation of the idea of a continuous shepherd ship with the purpose of salvation—only now in terms of ensuring citizens' well-being, happiness and protection against accidents and the misfortunes present in this world. The point is this: Both in the explicit Christian tradition and—in its continued "translation" into secular governmentality—pastoral power constitutes the "technology" of continuous care to which the individual has to submit in order to receive the gift of salvation or, in modern terms, the gift of social welfare.

The influence of Foucault's own, suggestive analysis of pastoral power can hardly be overestimated. Researchers from a range of disciplines, from the humanities and social sciences to medicine and nursing, offer insightful analysis of diverse modern practices of pastoral power.

Foucault thus perceived pastoral power to be one of the constitutive technologies in the formation of the modern welfare state, but he has been ascribed a rather critical emphasis with regard to this inheritance.

One limitation in the typical use of pastoral power, then, is the overwhelming emphasis on technologies and programs that individualize responsibility, prudency and reflexive choice (Dean 1999: 166–168; Valverde 1996: 362; Greco 2009: 357). The continuous guidance of individual consciousness through the unveiling of inner thoughts and renunciation of what is sinful and irrational was a key inheritance passed on to the welfare state from the pastorate. This emphasis on pastoral power as a technology (or as a series of techniques) of subjectification runs the risk, however, of overshadowing "the other side" of pastoral power with its message of unconditional care and grace bestowed upon humanity as such. This book discusses whether there are *modalities* of pastoral power—performed in, or through, heterotopic spaces—that produce something very different from discipline and control. As already mentioned above, the analyses in the following chapters present very diverse cases. Nevertheless, we think that they all present instances of pastoral power that entail more than the simple control of individual conscience through induced self-discipline.

The central thesis in this book is that not all pastoral power can be viewed as a more or less subtle form of social control, or that it can be judged as univocally oppressive. In fact, we wish to emphasize that pastoral power has two sides: one of discipline and one of care. In some (heterotopic) spaces there is a caring dimension of pastoral power which targets individuals in ways that cannot simply be said to oppress them. It is this side of pastoral power that we wish to foreground in this book. The power at stake in pastoral power has been practiced as an authority of guidance and care in contrast to repressive or coercive power. Caring constitutes the fundamental rationality of pastoral power. It involves improving the bodies involved, while at the same time caring itself can be an embodied practice, equipping individuals with additional reflexive and physical capacities. In the last decades, scholars have therefore begun to claim that Foucault himself was aware of this other side of pastoral power.

Counter-conducts and embodied universality

Arnold Davidson (2011) localizes Foucault's own interest in "counter-conducts" within his genealogical exploration of relationships of (political) power and contestation of that power presented in some of the lectures from the 1977–78 lecture series (Foucault 2007).

Foucault suggested that religious practices such as asceticism, mysticism and the pronouncement of eschatology were the counter-conducts of their time, contesting authority and authorized truisms. Notably, these activities were bound to special places where they were performed: deserts, monasteries, the purgatory, book printing houses, etc. Such traditions developed both during the Protestant Reformation and in the process of the Catholic counterreformation: "Spirituality, intense forms of devotion, recourse to Scripture, and the at least partial re-qualification of asceticism and mysticism, are all part of a kind of re-integration of counter-conduct within a religious pastorate" (Foucault 2007: 229).

Davidson notes that the subversive conducts that emerged in the interstices of pastoral power were themselves rooted in Christian traditions:

The fundamental elements of the counter-conduct analyzed by Foucault are not absolutely external to the conduct imposed by Christian pastoral power. Conduct and counter-conduct share a series of elements that can be utilized and reutilized, reimplanted, reinserted, taken up in the direction of reinforcing a certain mode of conduct or of creating and recreating a type of counter-conduct (Davidson 2011: 3).

Davidson quotes Foucault in order to emphasize the point that the resources and tactics mobilized in anti pastoral struggles were not at all exterior to the pastorate. Our interest in the notion of counter-conduct is not first and foremost historical, insofar as we are not concerned with what happened within and around the Christian church in times of reformation. Rather, our use of this notion in the context of this book serves to highlight spatial practices of caring (often religiously founded, though they may also be explicitly secular).

This ambition stems from our thesis that we may find forms of conducts within the Christian tradition and within practices of caregiving inspired by religion which embody concepts like hospitality, compassion, love, etc. We therefore suggest further that these counter-conducts, rooted as they are in the Christian tradition, might contribute to the continual interpretation of what "Christian values" mean. The counter-conducts presented in several of the cases in this book point to a theology that arises from practices and that is not derived from dogmatism "from above."

Common to all analyses presented in the book is an urban focus, and this also appears implicitly in the monastic garden project since according to their own imagery monasteries are spiritual cities. The modern city is an emblematic space of contradiction between different rationalities, some of a religious provenance, others of a more secular nature. Big cities are also the places where urgent and irrefutable problems of *need*, the caring for "different others" and the demand for a tolerance of diversity, are most clearly manifested. That is, in other words, they are a context in which heterotopias emerge and become particularly visible.

Foucault's short paper (1986) on other spaces was initially a sketch or a draft. Hence, we take this initial analysis of heterotopias as a point of departure; several of the authors proceed to engage with other spatial theories developed in different disciplines and areas. Readers will recognize the perspectives of Foucault, Lefebvre, Soja, Knott and others. The aim is not to arrive at the ultimate, "correct" interpretation of these influential authors and their concepts. Though we certainly take advantage of their competence, the main goal of the book is to collect studies that afford an opportunity to discuss the modalities of heterotopia where pastoral power spurs hospitality and compassion.

The organization of the book

The five spaces discussed in this volume are definitely heterogeneous, but they are also paradigmatic in that one can see in them different, but important aspects of hospitality, counter-conduct and transformation.

The presentation of all five spaces starts with an introduction by one of the leaders or someone with specific insight of the practice taking place there We want to underline that the analyses and interpretations of the heterotopic start with the concrete, the actual life and motivations expressed by the people living there themselves.

The first case study illustrates our assumption that we may find (heterotopic) forms of pastoral power which entail both discipline and hospitality. The case focuses on the historical background and current practices of the Settlement movement. The Settlement movement was initiated in London in the late 19th century with the goal of creating urban spaces where the privileged could meet the underprivileged. In this way the Settlement represents a utopia in a context of growing class division and unrest spurred by rapid industrialization, migration and urbanization. Kaspar Villadsen (Copenhagen) demonstrates how, in the Danish context, this Christian-inspired association articulated both universal and particular dimensions of social citizenship. The Settlement workers, many of whom were students of theology, invoked the imperative of "uplifting" the individual conscience of the underprivileged and a nascent modern discourse of equality and universal rights. The chapter argues, on the basis of detailed historical examination, that no strict opposition can be sustained between individualizing care originating in Christian charity and formal rights based on modern and secular notions of universalism.

The second case study takes us to the Protestant context of Sweden. Around 2008, a Lutheran congregation, in cooperation with a voluntary organization, started a project for undocumented immigrants in the church building of the congregation. Trygve Wyller (Oslo) presents and analyzes this variant of the heterotopic. This project establishes itself as an evident heterotopia, using the church building to develop a space for the significant others: the undocumented migrants living in southern Sweden. Wyller finds the most important impact coming from this kind of heterotopic counter-conduct to be a paradoxical manifestation of the power of the powerlessness. The project opens all doors for the undocumented. The result is an almost complete dissolution of traditional church power, whereby the received image of the church becomes less and less visible and a new (church) hospitality emerges.

The attention given to the city as a space for the enactment of care and tolerance is also evident in Kaia Schultz Rønsdal's (Oslo) contribution. Rønsdal describes the surprising practices of embodied care among the police and substance users at an intersection close to Oslo central station. An inner city intersection might not immediately appear to be a proper heterotopic space. Yet, when one looks closer, the intersection can also be analyzed from that perspective. Some people stay for a long time during the day (and at night), while other people experience the specific atmosphere only in passing. Based on fieldwork done at this very busy intersection, Rønsdal localizes practices of embodied caring, which in many occasions also entail an annihilation of power relations. Starting with the spatial theorist Henri Lefebvre, she in this way presents an original interpretation of the internal life unfolding at this "mini heterotopia."

The fourth space, analyzed by Hans-Joachim Sander (Salzburg), is a garden in a Benedictine monastery in northern Austria, which is organized to symbolize a religious hospitality that gives space to the truth claims of other religious traditions. In Foucault's terminology, a monastery is an obvious heterotopia, constituting another space outside normal society, based on the expectation that people live their lives there as a lifelong vocation. Inside the heterotopic, on the monastic ground, but outside of its first wall, the monks have constructed a Garden of Religions. In this heterotopic space, Islam, Buddhism, Judaism and Hinduism are represented in the four different "corners" of the garden. Just outside, on a small hill overlooking the monastery stands the Christian cross. The intention is to create a garden where generosity and respect for different beliefs are spatially revealed. This happens in a country strongly founded on Catholic faith, where negative and ungenerous attitudes to migrants have increasingly become evident. Against this background, Sander analyzes the heterotopic space of the garden as one important invention to reduce ecclesial power and to visually display the relativization of religious doctrines, which at the same time gives symbolic power to people traditionally not supposed to be present in a monasterial garden.

In the last contribution, Bryan Turner (New York) and Kaspar Villadsen analyze different kinds of spatial counter movements that share the fact that they speak up against political authorities. These movements include the American Settlement movement, Occupy Wall Street, and the Tea Party. Even if the contexts of these spaces are very different from many of the others presented in this book, they all share a common feature: the attempt to fundamentally contest the political institutions 'from below'. The US spatial cases also touch on a key issue of this book: Can we, in these other spaces, see traces of a power that empowers instead of dominates? If yes, what are the practices with which it achieve such values?

One striking common characteristic revealed in the analysis of all the five cases is the effect all the projects and practices have on disempowered groups. These five heterotopic spaces, whether they are a monastic garden or an intersection in a European capital, represent practices where established groups of people act in favor of those with little power or those placed at the very margins of society. So, the heterotopic spaces—in Foucault's terms the other spaces—are also the spaces of the others. The five cases are narratives of how monks, volunteers, professionals and more join forces at particular, heterotopic sites to improve the lives of others.

The problem, both historically and theoretically, is that throughout modern history people with good intentions sometimes carry out strongly authoritarian practices toward the non privileged, despite all morally justifiable motivations. The challenge in analyzing such heterotopic spaces is that the practices inside them could very well be ethically negative, even if they took place in the contested heterotopic space. Hence, the analysis and interpretation of the heterotopic quality of practices of hospitality and their social output cannot focus solely on the spatial aspect, but the analysis and the interpretation must also evaluate the practices *inside* the spaces and try to understand how they work, both from the perspective of the people receiving "help" and from the perspective of those acting in favor of the non privileged.

In the five case studies that follow this is done from different perspectives, ethically, sociologically and theologically. However, even if the methodology and the analytical traditions employed differ, all five cases share a common focus: a practice where the hegemony of the powerful is challenged by a new and stronger position afforded to the powerless. From this confrontation of the powerful by the powerless a space emerges where counter conductive practices become visible.

Powerlessness is hard to overlook at those places where it is visible and intensely experienced. One should be careful, however, not to see powerlessness as a stable or inherent quality. The studies of this book reveal, on the contrary, the transformative force that is generated when agents seek to help and speak for the rights and dignity of disempowered people. In these struggles, the organization of space often becomes an active resource in its own right. The spaces can be viewed, then, as a kind of agent operative in the overall social field. Our studies hence demonstrate Henri Lefebvre's insight that a space is never merely a "container" for social activities, but always a factor in these activities. In the spaces we study, powerlessness becomes a resource that can be mobilized in struggles for equality, recognition, compassion or social rights, at times challenging the traditional pastoral authorities. These struggles can be "counter-conducts." They pop up in the midst of experiences of powerlessness and often carry universal messages reaching beyond the specific struggles studies.

In the concluding chapter "A heterotopian grammar of hospitality", the three editors deepen their findings. These are connected to different characteristics that occur when the other space also becomes a space of hospitality. One important aspect is that this heterotopian hospitality seems to develop beyond the secular/religious binary. In the cases where the practices are located in an explicit religious context, the hospitality emerges when the secular moves into the religious. In this way one could claim that the hospitality developing in this book also impacts refigures what a religion of the powerless can seriously mean.

References

Davidson, A. (2011) In praise of counter-conduct, *History of the Human Sciences,* 24(4): 25–41.

Deleuze, G. (1988) *Foucault.* New York: Continuum.

De Certeau, M. (1984) The Practice of Everyday Life. University of California Press.

Ehrkamp, P./Nagel, C. (2014) Under the radar: Undocumented immigrants, Christian faith communities and the precarious spaces of welcome in the U.S. South, *Annals of the Association of American Geographers,* 104 (2): 319–328.

Foucault, M. (1982) The subject and power, *Critical Inquiry,* 8(4): 777–795.

Foucault, M. (1986) Of other spaces, *Diacritics,* 16(1): 22–7.

Foucault, M. (1988) *Technologies of the Self.* Amherst: The University of Massachusetts Press.

Foucault, M. (1994) Omnes et singulatim: Toward a critique of political reason, in M. Foucault: *Power: Essential Works of Foucault 1954–1984,* pp. 298–325. New York: The New Press.

Foucault, M. (2006), Die Geburt der Biopolitik (Geschichte der Gouvernementalität II), Frankfurt: Suhrkamp (= Naissance de la biopolitique, Paris: Gallimard, 2004).

Foucault, M. (2007), *Security, Territory, Population.* New York: Palgrave Macmillan.

Greco, M. (2009) The health society: polemics and problematizations, *Österreiche Zeitschrift für Soziologie,* 34: 2–13.

Hill, L. (2001) The hidden theology of Adam Smith, *European Journal of Economic Thought,* 8(1): 1–29.

Hopkins, P./Kong, L./Olson, E. (2013) *Religion and Place. Landscape, Politics and Piety.* Dordrecht: Springer.

Karlsen, M.P./Villadsen, K. (2008) Who should do the talking: The proliferation of dialogue as governmental technology, *Culture and Organization,* 14, 345–363.

Karlsen, M. P. (2008) *Patoralmagt: Velfærdssamfundets kristne arv.* København: Anis.

King, R. (1999) *Orientalism and Religion. Post-Colonial Theory, India and the "Mystic East."* New York: Routledge.

Knott, K. (2005) *The Location of Religion. A Spatial Analysis.* London: Oakville.

Lefebvre, H. (1991) The Production of Space. Blackwell Publishers Ltd. UK.

Mahmood, S. (2005) *Politics of Piety. The Islamist Revival and the Feminist Subject.* Princeton: Princeton University Press.

Pohl, C. (1999), *Making Room. Recovering Hospitality as a Christian Tradition.* Michigan: Eerdmans.

Rosol, M. (2014) On resistance in the post-political city: conduct and counter-conduct in Vancouver, *Space and Polity,* 18:1: 70–84.

Soja, E. (1996) Thirdspace: Journeys to Los Angeles and Other Real-and-Imagined Places. Wiley-Blackwell.

Valverde, M. (1996) "Despotism" and ethical liberal governance, *Economy and Society*, 25, 357–372.

Villadsen, K. (2012) Paradoxes of Welfare: Universality, Truth, and Power in Modern Welfare Provision. in R. Laratta (ed.), *Social Welfare.* Rijeka: InTech.

Villadsen, K. (2011) Modern welfare and "good old" philanthropy: A forgotten or a troubling trajectory?, *Public Management Review*, 13(8): 1057–1075.

Villadsen, K. (2007) The emergence of "neo-philanthropy: A new discursive space in welfare policy?, *Acta Sociologica* 3(50): 309–323.

Weber, M. (1968) *Economy and Society: An Outline of Interpretive Sociology.* 3 vols. Ed. G. Roth and C. Wittich. New York: Bedminster Press.

Topos A: Constructing brotherly love, Copenhagen and beyond

The Photo displays the social café established by The Settlement and run by volunteers at Vesterbro, Copenhagen. The name of the Café can be translated as "Stir up the Street".

The Christian Student Settlement has been located in an old working class neighborhood in Copenhagen since 1911. The Settlement was established to bring together students from "respectable" families with the working class, hereby creating a space that could bridge the growing class divide. From the beginning, Christian notions of "brotherhood" and human equality spurred social critique and initiatives to combat poverty and misery. During the 20th century, Christian values gradually receded into the background, and the connection to the welfare state became closer. Today, like in most European cities, gentrification and migration have changed the profile of the neighborhood. Still the challenges connected to social change and the aspiration to do radical political advocacy of marginalized groups remain.

Johs. Bertelsen (Copenhagen)

Kristeligt Studenter-Settlement – between Christianity and Socialism

Kristeligt Studenter-Settlement runs a variety of social and educational activities, primarily in the working-class area of Copenhagen, Vesterbro. Today, the organization has around 250 volunteers and 40 employed staff. Among its activities are:

- Extensive work among children and young people (220 children and young people) with an operating agreement with Copenhagen local authority.
- Clubs for elderly and the day college Madam Blå, with support from Copenhagen's public health service.
- Social, legal, psychological and financial counseling provided by both employed staff and volunteers
- The socio-economic employment project 'Vesterbrobyggerne'
- The integration and employment project Sultana
- The employment and environmental project, Sidegadeprojektet, with nine shops in Saxogade street
- The children's holiday camp Lungborgen at Serjøbugten
- SSB (Studenter-Settlement's Ball Club), Vesterbro's biggest sports club with 2,500 members
- Idrætsfabrikken—a foundation that runs many sports facilities.

The foundation

Kristeligt Studenter-Settlement was founded on 1 November 1911 by a group of theology students, clergymen and academics who had been inspired by the English settlement movement. Toynbee Hall Settlement had been founded in 1884 in London's East End, at a time when the city was growing rapidly and poverty was rife. It was different from traditional religious and philanthropic organizations that helped the poor in the city's slum areas. Focus was neither on providing emergency relief in the form of clothing, food or similar, nor on teaching poor people to lead more morally upstanding lives. Instead, Samuel August Barnett, who is regarded as the founder of Toynbee Hall, recruited volunteers from among university students. They were to live at the settlement and organize various social and cultural events for the residents of this poor area. The students thereby gained insight into how people lived in slum areas and the poor residents were given an education.

The idea spread to many European countries and also to the USA, where Hull House settlement in Chicago came to play an important role in the emerging scientific approach to social work, among other things through the nascent development of sociology as an academic discipline.

Kristeligt Studenter-Settlement

"Something is happening out on Saxogade street, something of great importance to society. But it is taking place in such a quiet and unassuming way, with no vociferous publicity, that most people do not know what it is". (*København*, 22 November 1921)

In Denmark, the establishment of the first settlement went almost unnoticed. The founders of Kristeligt Studenter-Settlement (KSS) had little funds at their disposal and faced a challenge in trying to bridge the gap between poor inhabitants of the working-class Vesterbro area and idealistic academics from the well-to-do sections of Danish society. However, this meeting between different social classes was precisely what the founders were most concerned with.

During the first ten years of its existence, KSS had succeeded in gaining a firm foothold in Vesterbro. This was not primarily the result of any great fraternization between academics and the working class, but rather because KSS realized the importance of working with the largest population group in the area, namely, children and young people. In 1920, the population of Vesterbro was about 80,000, while in 2015 it is just over 30,000. These figures tell us something about how densely populated the area was at the time. Predominant in the area were small flats inhabited by large families with many children. Children and young people spent much of their time outside the home, wandering the streets or working in one capacity or another—as messengers, paperboys or doing similar odd jobs.

During this period, day-care centers and youth clubs were still completely unknown and there was a great need for clubs for children and young people organized by KSS. The students engaged in what we now call outreach social work, venturing out into the area and making contact with children and their parents. The children were invited to attend a club a few times a week. The clubs offered help with homework, play, sports, music, theatre and other things, depending on what the students felt competent to offer in the way of entertainment or teaching.

The Christian background

The founders of KSS consisted of a group of socially engaged academics that belonged to the circle around the evangelic Indre Mission (Home Mission) and Kirkefondet (the Church Fund). The group included Pastor Richard Thomsen, deputy head of the Church Fund, Professor Harald Westergaard, and Alfred Th. Jørgensen, leader of De Samvirkende Menighedsplejer (the parish charities cooperative).

The group was part of the religious movements that were active in the densely populated residential areas in Copenhagen surrounding the historical city center. They were concerned with helping to alleviate the catastrophic social conditions under which the areas' large working class populations lived, while at the same time building new churches that would offer room for the many people who had moved to the city from all over the country, and who formed the majority of the areas' population. As previously mentioned, the aim of establishing KSS was not as much to provide physical relief for the needy as it was to kindle an ethical debate about social issues through teaching and talks.

"It is a Christian settlement whose primary aim is to foster a personal relationship between people and God, but it does not stop there. Just as the Reformation led to an ethical reassessment of how marriage was viewed, there are also those who hope that a contemporary religious awakening can result in an ethical revival: a new attitude to social issues. The Settlement is one of the channels through which such a religious-social revival can take place" (P Manniche).

Even though a lot of the social work carried out by KSS came to be centered on the clubs for children, young people and the elderly, the ultimate target group for the work was actually the adult, working population. The intellectual and spiritual meeting between this working class population and the Christian students was at the core of KSS' philosophical foundation. The Settlement thus attempted to run an educational department led by the student P Manniche. He described this as follows in the annual report:

"The workers are very rewarding to work with, many are very knowledgeable and they are all eager to learn more. They are really not the kind of people we originally imagined. They are solid and happy people, most of them originally come from rural districts and are not inferior to many students with respect to their moral and social standards".

He continues:

"Socialism and Christianity are the issues that most engage people and give most food for thought. The workers, nearly all of them socialists, have been able to tell the students about Christians' poor understanding of socialism and their lack of resistance to the attractions of Mammon and the bourgeois life. The students, on their part, have told them about what Christianity has achieved and can still achieve as a driving force for social reform".

Between Christianity and Socialism

KSS' ideological challenge would be to base its humanitarian relief work on a mixture of Christianity and socialism and in the first few years of its existence, there was no doubt about its foundation in Christianity. Together with 15 clergymen from the Danish National Church, KSS invited the workers of Copenhagen to three public debates at Grundtvigs Hus to demonstrate Christianity's democratic and socially engaged philosophy. One of the prime movers, Pastor Birke, began by saying:

"Christianity is therefore democratic, and it demands of its supporters that they fight for equal rights and combat privilege of all kinds. The more democracy wins the day, the greater moral demands are made of people. If you examine what Christianity is and require of your clergymen and your parish leaders that their political views be shaped by the idea of the kingdom of God, then there will be no more war and the barriers between the classes will collapse".

The struggle was therefore about what was the correct and true way to improve society. Should it be based on the Christian faith or should it be based on a socialist struggle for a better society? For good reasons, these debates never resulted in a final conclusion being drawn on the issue. In practice, a division of labor subsequently developed, whereby the Christian charitable organizations concentrated on low-threshold charity work, while the political perspectives were increasingly taken over by the Social Democrats and other left-wing parties.

However, because of KSS' background of using student volunteers as its core staff, the organization continued to develop a more political approach to relief work than other humanitarian organizations. Within KSS, there was constant debate among the student volunteers about what KSS' role in society should be. At the same time, the tradition of educational and lecturing activities in the various family clubs persevered. Both the students' debates and the educational and lecturing activities came to address current social trends and the living conditions of the working class.

The Vesterbro Housing Campaign

For Otto Krabbe, leader of KSS from 1934 to 1963, it was a great source of frustration that the relief work consisted of a mixture of constant tinkering and political debates without ever getting to grips in earnest with the root of the evil. The dire housing conditions and housing shortage were a scandal that was the main cause of the social conditions that people were always trying to patch up. Krabbe writes:

"That crime among children and young people is alarmingly common in such an area, is the area's natural and logical response to a society that tolerates this area for generation after generation. To expect anything else is madness ... While all this can be seen as symptoms of rebellion, it is generally viewed as moral decay and, as far as possible, forcibly repressed. For us who know the conditions, these symptoms are actually a healthy sign. They show that a kind of protest is nonetheless taking place".

In 1950, Krabbe, along with a number of doctors, teachers, architects and police officers, took the initiative to start Vesterbro Housing Campaign, which, through petitions, articles in the media and a big housing conference, aimed to get the city's politicians to take action. The film '*Slum*', directed by Jørgen Roos, was an important part of the campaign, earnestly putting the issue of slums on the political agenda. Despite the size of this campaign, the political results it produced were very limited. The social democratic city council gave priority to inner city clearance at the expense of the underprivileged areas situated outside the old inner city.

A professional NGO

In parallel with the political debates in KSS, its social and educational work became more professionalized and with the development of the welfare society, qualified social counselors and teachers came to play a greater role in the work. Students, who were under increasing pressure to study and find paid work, constituted an increasingly smaller proportion of the volunteer staff as the 1980s and 1990s progressed. Instead, the volunteers increasingly came to be dominated by two groups:

1. Unemployed and pensioners, who sought fellowship and who had time on their hands to do many kinds of tasks.
2. Qualified social counselors, lawyers and psychologists who served as volunteer staff in connection with the social, legal and psychological counseling offered by the Settlement. In recent years, they have been joined

by volunteer financial advisers who help to run the Settlement's debt counseling service.

Student revolt and work in the local community

In the Vesterbro Housing Campaign, KSS adopted a more activist approach. This approach was further intensified during the 1960s and 1970s, when the student revolt at the university also affected the students' social work in Vesterbro. As student matters became increasingly politicized, the students' attitudes to the problems in Vesterbro were shaped more by a political than a religious perspective. At the same time, many workers' political views also became more polarized, forming the basis for a new worker-student alliance that was primarily rooted in socialist attitudes to the left of the Social Democrats and thereby also to the left of the incumbent city council in Copenhagen.

This development gave rise to much debate in KSS, and Villy Nielsen (1963–1972) became leader of the organization in a period where hard battles were fought over KSS' democratic leadership structure. By his own admission, he 'was relieved' to leave KSS and hand over the reins to Arne Skovhus, a left-leaning colleague and theatre figure. Arne Skovhus said in an interview in 1973:

> "While Settlement cannot change the laws, it can become a house where everyone—from different backgrounds and generations—can come together and thereby achieve a sense of security and gain the courage required to formulate concrete political demands and then act collectively to achieve them. That is what the house offers everyone—students, workers, pensioners—and not least the youth".

A community of action was now at the core of KSS, and since the 1970s, it has endeavored to show solidarity with political and social movements in the area. KSS has participated in the work of the local council, in the prolonged urban renewal process in the 1990s and established jobs and environmental projects, such as Sidegadeprojektet (Side Street Project) (1986 onwards) and Kjøbenhavns Genbrugs-Compagni (Copenhagen's Recycling Company) (1992–2008).

The quotes cited in the article are taken from the book *Respekt, historier fra Settlement på Vesterbro* (2011) by author and journalist Pia Fris Laneth.

Kaspar Villadsen (Copenhagen)

The Christian Student Settlement: Between Utopian Ideas and Real Constraints[1]

"Am I a spokesman for the citizens or an inspector serving the administration?" In 2010, Johs Bertelsen, the leader of the voluntary organization in Copenhagen, the Settlement, had to ask himself this thorny question. He was organizing employment projects for the long-term unemployed under the auspices of the Settlement, a voluntary organization that has carried out social projects in the neighborhood of Vesterbro in Copenhagen for over a century. The dilemma Bertelsen faced was between acting as a social critic and acting as a bureaucratic administrator. In the first case, he is a protagonist of civil rights and more tolerance toward different ways of living; in the second case, he is part of an institution that disciplines marginalized individuals to fit the demands of the labor market. In the Settlement, Johs was carrying out experimental social work in a context where the official welfare policy and public authorities had placed employment center stage (Laneth, 2011, 280–282). To be eligible for public funding, voluntary social organizations must pursue this employment agenda by giving emphasis to preparatory training or the "discipline" of individuals at the margin of society. Schematically, we may speak of a contradiction between utopians ideals of unconditional care and fundamental social change versus disciplinary normalization integral to the reproduction of the social order.

The Settlement has organized social projects at Vesterbro since the early 19th century and received quite a lot of attention because of its social projects in the former working-class neighborhood. The organization has Christian roots, reflected in the original name, the *Christian Student Settlement*, and it is perhaps surprising to see such an organization acting as the center for experimental social work. However, the original ideal behind the Settlement movement, of which the Copenhagen-based organization was an off-spring, was indeed to "settle" and work directly with the inhabitants of poor working-class neighborhoods. This idea was adopted from the first "student settlement," Toynbee Hall, founded in 1884 in London, as an attempt to bridge the growing class divide. The Danish Christian Student Settlement (henceforth The Settlement) was established in 1911 by Christian academics

1 A parallel but not identical version of this chapter has been published by Villadsen in *Journal of Civil Society* (2016, vol 12, issue 2) under the title The Settlement Utopia: Brotherly Love, Discipline, and Social Critique.

with the same objective of bridging the enormous divide between the social classes of the rapidly industrializing society.

From the beginning, the project of locating Christian students inside the working-class neighborhood seemed a very difficult one—what Johs Bertelsen described as "an impossible idea" (Bertelsen, 2011, 4). Indeed, there seemed to be something impossible or utopian about the project. From its inception the Settlement was pervaded by a series of contradictions or even paradoxes: The goal was to improve the conditions of the working-class poor, but the means was not conceived as poor relief or charity but as a "friendly encounter" among equals. The founders believed that the culture of the students from a respectable background could "lift up" the working poor, but they emphasized that there was not a hierarchical relationship between a superior giver and a subordinated receiver. The key notions were "meetings" and "friendship" as opposed to "teaching" or "moralizing." The founders were guided by a Christian values including notions of salvation in the after world, but the activities of the Settlement were not oriented toward individual conversion and the proclamation of the Word, but rather had the practical purpose of securing education, childcare and better housing. Hence, the expressed values contained a reference to the transcendent, the divine spirit, but the practical activities tended to eschew transcendent references. Finally, there was a strong emphasis on "meeting" and respecting the working poor "as they were," and yet the Settlement discourse was replete with generalizing ideas about "how the poor were," their depraved morality, irrationality and lack of self-control, all of which should be transformed within the confines of *Student Settlements.*

To sum up, there was a contradiction between the ideal of meeting the poor as undefined and singular, and the impetus to foster certain inherently human capacities in each and every one. This is evident in the prevalent recognition of human and social potential in the working poor. Pointing out these contradictions is not the same as saying that the Settlement project was impossible or self-defeating from the start. On the contrary, one might say that these inherent contradictions spurred great creativity and inventiveness throughout the Settlement's historical development, including a range of pioneering social projects. As we shall see, contradictions and logical paradoxes need not necessarily stifle and paralyze an organization, but may incite an on-going discursive and practical inventiveness.

My interest in the Settlement movement, and in the particular Danish case, is related to the main theme of this book. The experiment at Vesterbro indeed constituted—and continues to do so—a space where social citizenship for the most marginalized groups could be practiced. The Settlement also acted as a center of critique of the social order and official policies. From the beginning of its establishment, the Settlement founders opposed conventional charity, since they wished to establish "respectful friendships," not giver-receiver relationships. Situating themselves inside the poor neighborhood, they wished to create "a different space," paving the way for social change. During the 1970s and 1980s, the Settlement undertook social experiments such as organizing "other spaces" of youth work, community revitalization, alternative employment, local business activity and, more recently, integration of immigrants. In more recent years, the Settlement has been increasingly negotiating the contradictory role of receiving public funding and at the same time criticizing official welfare policies. Again, a "different space" of social citizenship emerged, cut through by divergent and contradictory rationalities. It became, simultaneously, a site of fundamental social critique and connected with the legal and "disciplinary" demands of public welfare services.

Heterotopia as analytical perspective

For the purpose of analyzing the ambiguous space of the Settlement, I will mobilize some of the perspectives offered by Michel Foucault's concept of heterotopia. My selective usage of the concept can be justified by the fact that Foucault was experimenting with the concept, using it loosely as a perspective rather than defining it very precisely. We recall that, when advancing the concept of heterotopia, Foucault suggested that there are sites in our culture which are disturbing and special in their capacity to incite reflection, contestation and critique. They are "other places" in relation to the existent order, not because they stand in opposition to it, but rather because they are places where otherwise unconnected elements of existence co-exist. Foucault said heterotopias are "something like counter-sites … in which the real sites, all the other real sites that can be found within the culture, are simultaneously represented, contested, and inverted" (Foucault 1986: 23). This is the first characteristic that I wish to highlight in the following analysis, which draws upon the concept of the heterotopia: It has a fundamentally hybrid character by bringing together a series of components foreign to each other. Foucault says: "The heterotopia is capable of juxtaposing in a single real place several spaces, several sites that are in themselves incompatible" (1986: 25). In brief, heterotopias reflect the ambiguities of the society in which they exist by juxtaposing several spaces simultaneously. The Settlement displays precisely such ambiguities. It is both a space of charity and "encounters between equals"; it is informed by Christian values and strives for changing secular institutions; it stands in opposition to the state and carries out tasks for the state.

The second characteristic is that familiar sites in our culture are not only represented by the heterotopia, but also "contested" and "inverted." This means that heterotopias display in a particularly intense way fundamental contradictions, arbitrary divisions and paradoxes inherent to our culture. Foucault explained that the spaces he was interested in "have the curious property of being in relation with all the other sites, but in such a way as to suspect, neutralize, or invert the set of relations that they happen to designate, mirror, or reflect. These spaces, as it were, "are linked with all the others, which however contradict all the other sites" (Foucault 1986: 24). The heterotopia displays the impossibility of closure that followed after the advent of a modern notion of an open and infinite space (Dumm 1996: 44). This means that the heterotopia is a purely relational concept, insofar as it articulates, via juxtapositions, the heterogeneous character of the external space.

By putting relations in the foreground, heterotopia is comparable with Foucault's approach to discursive statements in *The Archaeology of Knowledge* (1972) and related writings. A statement stands in relationship with a whole archive of other statements, concepts, assumptions and theories which the statement relies upon and which imbue it with signification. Preference is given to the statement's horizontal relationships with the archive rather than a deep interpretation of the singular statement or the speaker's inner life-world (Foucault 1972: 54–55). In his discourse analysis, Foucault was principally interested in describing the conditions of the possibility of statements, for instance, by way of "historical á priori," underlying assumptions pervading various discourse domains (Foucault 1972: 126–127). However, the heterotopia leads us instead toward recognizing the arbitrariness or "impossibility" of certain conceptions, divisions and conventions of a culture. The selection of and description of such places could become a distinct research strategy: "As a sort of simultaneously mythic and real contestation of the space in which we live, this description could be called heterotopology" (Foucault 1986: 24).

Foucault mentions two kinds of spaces where juxtapositions and contradictions are extensively experienced. The first kind is "the utopia," which is a space of pure imagination, a society in its most perfect and idealized version. Some of the functions of utopias include compensation for the present state of affairs in all its imperfection. Utopias take the shape of fantasies, dreams and critiques of existing conditions, and as such they have the capacity to provoke the desire for social transformation (Johnson 2006: 82). Foucault contrasts utopia with heterotopia, emphasizing that they both relate to other sites by simultaneously representing and inverting them, though, unlike utopias, heterotopias are real sites. They constitute "a kind of effectively enacted utopia" (Foucault 1986: 24). Heterotopias have a potential to spur contestation and undermining of utopias, since this kind of analysis "reveals that heterotopia not only contrasts with utopia, but actually undermines or unsettles it" (Johnson 2006: 82). For example, the Christian-philanthropic utopia of universal Brotherly Love is unsettled or undermined when the philanthropists subject the poor to divisions and disciplinary practices. The Settlement thus displays one key characteristic of the heterotopia, namely, that it serves as an amplifying glass for contradictions and impossibilities, in this case those that inevitably arise when utopian projects are put into practice.

Heterotopias press the limits of language, making it more difficult to use received concepts and thus harbor potentials for transgression of the self-evident. Foucault emphasized this in *The Order of Things:* "Heterotopias are disturbing, probably because they secretly undermine language, because they make it impossible to name this and that, because they shatter and tangle common names" (1971: xviii). Notably, it is not merely language, but the heterotopia's combination of the textual, aural and visual which disturbs our conceptions. It contests boundaries and received distinctions and may thus create moments of transgression. The opening of such transgression is not a matter of reaching for, or invoking, transcendence or some postrevolutionary state. When we look at a heterotopia we see the culture in which we are placed, like one discovers oneself in a distorted mirror. Therefore, the analysis of heterotopia is not a question of transcending the limits of our being; rather, it lucidly displays "the stuff" that our social world is made of, including the structures of ideology and powers that we are caught up in. The concept paves the way for an immanent critique, not any final liberation: "Although Foucault describes heterotopia as 'actually existing utopia,' the conception is not tied to a space that promotes any promise, any hope or any primary form of resistance or liberation" (Johnson 2006: 84). By their unexpected constellation of heterogeneous elements, heterotopias display possibilities of minor transgressions or lines of flight from the existing order.

Finally, we must insist that analyzing heterotopias means adopting a particular lens or perspective, not finding places that would be in and by themselves "inherently" heterotopic. Foucault points toward this when he says that "perhaps no one absolutely universal form of heterotopia would be found" (Foucault 1986: 24). If there is no pure heterotopia, the analysis seems to be as much about applying a particular lens as about indicating definite heterotopic places. It is worth recalling that Foucault does not approach concepts in a conventional representational manner, that is, as descriptors of delineated entities existing "out there", in social reality. Thus, when examining Foucault's rendering of the notion of heterotopia, we realize that his usage displays little effort at conceptual consistency. Rather than pinning the concept down to firm categories, the concept harbors several dimensions that open up for manifold descriptions. Resisting the assumption that the world could be ultimately and truthfully represented, Foucault's concepts are analytical prisms that serve to mark out the coordinates around which categorization and contestation evolve: "It is not a matter of identifying the general principles of reality through them, but of somehow pinpointing the analytical front" (Foucault 2007a: 51). Heterotopic analysis is made possible at a historical juncture where the concern with time gives way to a preoccupation with space and the relationship between spaces: "Our epoch is one in which space takes for us the form of relations among sites" (Foucault 1986: 22). Using heterotopia in a Foucauldian vein means testing out what the concept yields in relationship with particular concerns rather than verifying its ultimate validity. Eschewing the conventional logic of representation would mean, for instance, that the Settlement could be described both as a utopia and as a heterotopia. We return to this issue in the analysis below.

The breeding ground for the Settlement movement

The decades around 1900 in Denmark were marked by growing class division, debates about how to handle "the social evils," and concerns about the relationship between the church and the socialist movement. There was also an increasing questioning of traditional practices of almsgiving and charitable poor relief, which had been under way during the 19th century and which, toward the end of the century, cleared the way for new ideas about how to help the poor. Key to this discussion among representatives of the Church and Christian philanthropy was the theme of what a "Christian spirit" toward the poor and working class should consist of. These are the key components in the particular historical context, from which the Settlement movement emerged.

During the 19th century, the rapid migration to and industrialization of the urban centers, particularly Copenhagen, created unprecedented large working-class neighborhoods. This was a situation in which the passing of the Freedom of Trade Act in 1857 had left the working poor literally without social protection. Another important event was the founding of the Free Constitution in 1849, which paved the way for the establishment of philanthropic organizations and mutual societies in areas like religion, workers' conditions and agricultural production (Henriksen and Bundesen 2004: 608–609).

Yet the very visible urban poverty and the signs of what was taken to constitute moral decay created fear among the more privileged. They feared for the social cohesion of society, the spreading of moral and physical diseases, and political unrest. Bewildered observers from the respectable classes cautioned that a new class of destitute, working poor had emerged in the big cities, people uprooted from the agrarian community, the family and the church, and they were hence "drifting loose" without the moralizing authorities to give them an ethical compass. Some journals published reports from explorations and documentary journalism into "the dark continent of the poor," that is, the dark and decayed neighborhoods where alien norms and strange languages reigned. The readers from the better classes would shudder with a blend of fear and disgust when confronted with these travel reports (Villadsen 2007: 313). This fear created a need for mediation and representation with regard to the new masses of urban poor.

The last decades of the 19th century were also marked by debates on how to practice poor relief. Central to the debates was the critique of the practice of indiscriminate alms-giving and the notion of the giver-receiver relationship, which was raised not only in Denmark but across Western Europe (Donzelot

1979: 66). The practice of simply giving alms was questioned since it did not consider long-term consequences or the motives behind the beneficiary's request. A key element in the push for rationalizing poor relief, then, was the requirement to distinguish more carefully between the different kinds of poor. One needed to differentiate the able-bodied from the sick, men from women, children from adults, the morally depraved from the morally upright, and so on. The attempts at differentiation revolved around one fundamental distinction, that is, the deserving versus the undeserving poor. More detailed examinations of those who asked for poor relief were to ascertain their needs, moral character, capability to work and hence their eligibility. Philanthropists would undertake home visits among the poor families focusing on domestic order, honesty and cleanliness guided by the belief that even in dire conditions of poverty it is possible to uphold order and cleanliness.

Christian philanthropy placed itself somewhere in the middle between the main adversaries at each ends of the political spectrum: On the one hand, the emerging socialist movement, which demanded a state-guaranteed right to work for the poor and collectivization of industries; on the other, liberals and conservatives who maintained that the poverty problem could be solved only via private charity, never through forced taxes. At times the Christian philanthropists criticized the consequences of industrial-capitalist society, but they did not side with the socialists in demanding revolutionary changes to the social order. They emphasized the need for a moral and material uplifting of the poor, which would generate social cohesion. The focus was not so much on state law as the tool for fighting poverty as it was on the moral improvement of the poor and the fostering of responsibilities (Villadsen 2007: 315). Some of the actors within Christian philanthropy saw charity as the means for solving the most urgent problem of the time, namely, a growing class antagonism. It is this central aspect of charity which was given a particular variant by the Settlement founders and their notion of "friendship between the classes."

Cultural spearhead or meeting forum?

Let us look a bit closer at the context and Christian traditions from which *The Christian Student Settlement* emerged (It was one of several associational outcomes of the *Danish Home Mission,* which defended a pietistic and puritan version of Lutheranism. From its inception, the Settlement adhered to a liberal reform theology that inspired its members' aspirations for an interventionist transformation of society. That religion can serve as a medium for political struggle was briefly noted by Foucault in his comments on "counter-conducts" that developed within the Christian tradition (2007b: 208–210). According to Foucault, pastoral power allows for, or even facilitates, different forms of counter-conduct. The power of the pastorate implies a potential for counter-conducts nurtured by the practices, scripture and discipline integral to the pastorate itself. Furthermore, the rationale of pastoral guidance is not simply one of complete obedience or subjection, but rather one of spurring enhanced self-reflection and self-government. This rationale of self-government makes counter-conduct possible, for instance, in the name of equality, hospitality or for contesting received interpretations of the scripture. The agents involved in such forms of counter-conducts may struggle for the total redemption of society or stir revolts to achieve ultimate salvation. However, they may also strive to create better conditions for underprivileged people in a much more mundane and day-to-day fashion. This study of the Settlement displays such mundane forms of counter-conduct that make reference to values of equality and exercise the right to speak against political authorities in the name of equality, rights and universality. The study explores our assumption (discussed in the introductory chapter) that pastoral power has a particular potential for supporting hospitable spaces and for inspiring counter conduct.

Notions of the Divine promise of universal equality would underpin a permanent counter-conduct taking religious or quasireligious forms in contesting authorities and their demand for obedience. That the doctrine of radical equality—whether or not it has determinate religious content—may spur social interventions was exemplified by the Settlement people, who invoked Protestantism as a transformative force in their work for social equality, integration, rights, tolerance, citizenship and plurality. Not unlike the counter-conducts described by Foucault, the Settlement practiced counter-conduct based on revised interpretations of the Scripture that diverged from existing doctrine. Hence, the Settlement's founders practiced counter-conduct toward its own mother organization, the Danish Home Mission, and evangelical Protestantism more broadly. Whereas the latter defined redemption chiefly in terms of the revivalist practice aimed at personal conversion, the Settlement entailed a gradual transfer of redemptive power from religious to secular activities. In this regard, the Settlement reflected the general shift towards *worldly social activity* in late 19th-century Protestant culture, which meant that a redeemed society would not be the work of supernatural forces alone, but of human forces as well (Quandt 1973: 391–392). This shift also implied an increasing belief in the social sciences, social reforms, nascent social work and other secular institutions as agents of progress toward a perfected society. While Foucault's observations on the issue of counter-conduct centered on the Catholic tradition, the present study of the Settlement constitutes a Protestant version of counter-conduct, which provides contextual details hence extending Foucault's very general comments.

In 1911, Richard Heinrich Thomsen, a graduate in theology, established the Settlement in Copenhagen with inspiration from the English predecessor, Toynbee Hall in London. Thomsen had his spiritual roots in the Home Mission movement, while politically he was a social democrat. He served as the leader of the Settlement in Copenhagen for six years (Lindhardt: 1979). At its inception and in its early phase, the organization was tightly connected to the State Church and the theological environment in Denmark. The majority of its members and contributors were students of theology, parish priests or provosts (Bundesen, Henriksen and Jørgensen 2001: 226).

The anxiety caused by urban working-class decay continued to be a key motive during the early phase of the Settlement. Richard Thomsen thus wrote in 1916: "When you walk along Vesterbrogade, the liveliest and most elegant street in our city, you have no idea about what is hidden in the back-streets. But just walk down Saxogade, and at once you're in another world" (Thomsen quoted in Laneth 2011: 14). The descriptions of the decay of the poor neighborhoods often made references to explorers' and missionaries' reports from distant places in the world, the "fields of the heathens," where they witnessed the lower races' ungodliness, lack of morality and need for salvation. Like Stanley Livingstone, one must have both faith and will-power to dare enter the dark wilderness of the urban poor: "The wilderness in Copenhagen is darker and more difficult to penetrate than the wilderness in Africa. But it is possible to overcome it, if one goes to the task in the right spirit" (Vedde 1916). Evident in this quote is an unmistakably missionary tone characteristic of the Danish home mission movement, which seemed to signal aspirations of establishing "missionary stations" that could bring Christian morality, culture or civilization to the dark continent of the poor. However, the Settlement founders placed major emphasis on the idea of a "respectful meeting" with the poor workers, something that was, in fact, distinct to the Settlement compared to other charitable work at that time. The Settlement movement diverged from the Home Mission in emphasizing that the message of Christ applied to society as a whole and was not merely a matter of personal conversion, in striving for the redemption of society here and now through social reforms, and in believing that the churches should take side with the workers, recognizing their material needs.

The Settlement was based on the fundamental idea of students locating themselves in the heart of working class neighborhoods to enable a direct and close exchange with the inhabitants. The words used to describe this meeting were decidedly not "mission" or "conversion," but "meeting" and "mutual exchange." One might say that the missionary goal of individual spiritual rebirth was reconfigured into a notion of the spiritual rebirth of the whole community, or even neighborhood, through the medium of *Settlements.* Nevertheless, it must be noted that this rebirth tended to rely upon a quite specific ideology: The Settlement and its activities could be said to be pervaded by the values of the "respectable" classes: order, useful pursuits, literary studies, enlightened debate, exposure to culture and learning the virtues of marriage. The role envisioned for the poor was neither that of traditional recipient of charity nor that of social client. Instead, they were conceived as "guests invited to share the benefits of 'respectable' home life," and in that sense the Settlement constituted a "middleclass outpost" in a harmful environment (Rousmaniere 1970: 65–66).

Insofar as the Settlement strived to be as orderly, clean and civilized as the surroundings were disorderly, dirty and barbaric, it was a "heterotopia of compensation," to use Foucault's words: "[T]heir role is to create a space that is other, another real space, as perfect, as meticulous, as well arranged as ours is messy, ill constructed, and jumbled. This latter type would be the heterotopia, not of illusion, but of compensation" (Foucault 1986: 27). The challenges of establishing something like a hybrid between a missionary outpost and a center of cultural exchange is indicated by the recurrent complaints about the character of those working poor that the students met. Especially the children were said to have difficulties in adjusting to the norms of behavior promoted in the Settlement's evening clubs—norms much alike the ideal home of respectable families. The working-class children were reported to be unruly, noisy and almost impervious to the educational efforts expended by the well-intended students (Laneth 2011: 50). How to remain gentle, kind, unselfish and helpful in the contact with these children was a permanent challenge to the students. In sum, the Settlement founders' meeting with their neighbors was based on the values of respect, instructive entertainment and the defense of spiritual virtue against primitive class war and consumerist materialism.

Spirit in action: Making Christianity practical and pragmatic

The decades before the establishment of the Settlement had been marked by discussions of how the Christian spirit should best be practiced. Disagreements revolved around whether individual conversion should remain the key strategy, or whether more pragmatic approaches were called for in times of urban mass poverty and moral decay. This debate also took place within the Danish Home Mission. Pastor Vilhelm Beck, the main leader of the movement from 1881 to 1901, stated that the emphasis should be on "the Word and salvation of sinners—the Word in order to make people gather around Jesus. All the rest is minor things, although they may be important minor things" (Beck quoted in Borioni 2014: 135). Opposing this view, Harald Stein, leader of the Copenhagen Home mission in the years 1879–1886, favored more active charitable activity. The disagreement between the two positions was principally one between the priority granted to spiritual conversion or "rebirth" and the "deeds of love" in terms of active care for the parish more akin to social work.

The question whether the mere proclamation of the Word was sufficient in the poverty-ridden neighborhoods was a subject of heated debate. Some questioned whether a spiritual awakening could take place in extreme material poverty, or whether the material conditions needed to be addressed. This issue was made more urgent due to the experience of a growing socialist movement increasingly more appealing to the working class than the church. In fact, a growing number of the working class displayed despise for the Church, seeing priests as parasites on small people whom they made pay for weddings and funerals to sustain a good living. The rising Social Democratic Party largely portrayed priests as footmen of the capitalists. This development spurred Harald Stein to initiate a battle against atheism and socialism by organizing Christian-based care work among the poor at Vesterbro in an attempt to create a bulwark against the alluring "socialist devils" (Laneth 2011: 23). There was a widespread sensation that Christianity was pushed back by the tangible demands of concrete solidarity raised by the socialists.

In the Settlement's newsletter one may find articles that assert the necessity of realizing God's reign on earth by way of concrete actions among the poor and miserable. One contributor makes the distinction between the old Christianity centered on after-worldly salvation versus a new Christianity that brings the message of salvation in this world, the coming of God's Kingdom in this world. In 1928, a contributor to the newsletter writes:

"'Your Kingdom shall come!' We have asked for it—we still ask—but it has not come. It has hesitated so long that many think that it'll never come. This is a crucial point by which what we usually call Christianity distinguishes itself so strongly from the Christianity that conquered the old world … We have got accustomed to believe that the Kingdom of God is not meant for this world—that this in reality is the devil's world, and that the Kingdom of God is placed in another sphere, in which God will admit good people when they die" (Wille 1928: 10).

The assertion is that behind this incomprehensible and cruel world there is an eternal, loving God. This is not a God who calls upon each and every one to work for the good and to combat the forces of evil. Despite our experience of misery, human cruelty and immorality, we must maintain the image, not yet visible, of a world freed from the devil's grip. This is the utopian ideal of realizing the Kingdom of God in this world through concrete intervention:

"But for the one who realizes that it may come for that person who recognizes that he is also called upon to assist in its coming there is, even if he never sees it, enormous reward in the feeling that he … accomplishes something in alliance with the good Force noticeable in the universe, achieves something to wrest this world loose from the devil's claws and turn it into a Kingdom of justice" (Wille 1928: 11).

The developments in Copenhagen seemed to prove that merely preaching the Word was simply not enough in the poor neighborhoods where the working classes displayed an increasing indifference to preaching. Among those involved in charity, still more supported the view that, to effectively compete with the socialist secular approach to social problems, the proclamation of the Word needed to be supplemented with other measures to address the social evils and establish a better rapport with the urban poor (Borioni 2014: 137). This new focus on activity in the poor neighborhoods was paralleled by arguments that directed blame for misery away from the individual and toward more nonpersonal, social conditions.

Such a displacement of emphasis had already been asserted by members of the Settlement movement in England and the United States (Reinders 1982). The same analysis was beginning to be expressed in Copenhagen, for instance, by Richard Thomsen: "In a poor neighborhood many evil forces are at play. Not because the poor are worse than others, but they simply cannot protect themselves against the powers of evil" (Thomsen quoted in Laneth 2011: 16). The Settlement members asserted that Copenhagen was the unhealthiest place of all places to live, both physically and spiritually. The majority of the harmful mores and attitudes were said to originate from a city that had become much too big. In light of this materialist-social analysis, the conventional Christian quest for individual, spiritual rebirth seemed illogical. In practical terms, an explicit emphasis on the holy Word had proved ineffective for establishing contact with the working poor. Accordingly, the Settlement refrained from direct preaching aimed at conversion but rather attempted to establish an atmosphere imbued with Christian convictions and attitudes.

Social critique or individual transformation?

Compared to the famous Settlements in London and Chicago, the Copenhagen Settlement undertook much less activity in terms of social research, which was developed only later on in the shape of descriptions of housing conditions at Vesterbro. When the Danish Settlers voiced demands for social equality, they occasionally did so with reference to Jesus's teaching on the equality between all Christians. This emphasis on securing material equality was an attempt to respond to the advancing socialist movement in Copenhagen, as mentioned above. However, it was a response that found a basis in Lutheran reformed Christianity and the notion of "care for the created world" (Borioni 2014: 144).

The Settlement's commitment to Christian values did not so much emphasize tangible conversion, like the Home Mission, or working for the advent of God's Kingdom, as they conceived this commitment as a source of social critique. This social critique targeted workers' deplorable living conditions and hence converged in some fundamental ways with the socialist party and the labor movement. The latter had achieved an important victory in the 1899 compromise (*Septemberforliget*) between the employers' associations and the labor movement. However, Church officials and proponents of Christian philanthropy felt that they needed to offer an alternative to the violent struggle for better material conditions that lacked a spiritual substance. For their part, the socialists criticized philanthropy for acting as a "lightning rod" for the poor's justified outrage over the misery generated by industrial capitalism. It was in this heated ideological battlefield that the Settlement was established (Laneth 2011: 34).

Notably, like the American and English Settlements, the Copenhagen settlers stressed that their goal was not merely to fulfill material needs. In its emphasis on shaping the content of people's demands, the Settlement's ideology opposed a purely liberal position. Members of the Settlement expressed regret that so many people displayed a completely materialist attitude instead of choosing spiritual development. In contrast to the materialist, they proclaimed, a true Christian believes in the spirit, not in the body! The complaints about the encroachments of materialism in defense of traditional morality made references to the sanctity of the family, spiritual nourishment, duty over pleasure and the need for moderating desire. In the Settlement's newsletter, the emphasis on spiritual nourishment was condensed in the view that, even if the external world was made perfect, nothing would be achieved without a change of faulty human spirits:

"If one asks oneself where misery has its cause, one always returns to the fact that the faults originate from the inside, from the spirit which reigns in people's mind ... For even if all the external things were changed, as if by magic, to become completely fair and good—if the human hearts were not changed as well, we would return to misery in a few years" (Nielsen 1928: 1–2).

Bettering the affairs of this world had to be complemented by efforts at bettering the human heart. By choosing this path, the Settlement echoed the strategy of philanthropists for navigating the heated political terrain of late 19th-century Denmark. Eschewing socialism and laissez-faire liberalism, philanthropy offered a principle for intervention into social problems which revolved around the notion of "the moral cohesion of society." The Settlement displayed the same ideal in its attempt at nurturing a community where a set of collective moral standards and obligations would tie uprooted individuals together (Villadsen 2011: 1069). While demands were raised for material equality and the right of the working poor to decent living conditions—and hence a formal obligation of state toward the poor—the emphasis tended to be toward the moral-spiritual nourishment through exposure to culture, instructive entertainment and meeting with the members from the privileged class. In the report on the first 10 years of activity one can read:

"The recent years of materialism and looseness in moral affairs have proven us right in our principle that it is education and spiritual development which is needed. The turmoil of the time thus only animates us to exert further efforts to develop an efficient religious, moral and cultural work" (Christian Student Settlement 1919: 4).

The idea that the space of the Settlement would exert an "uplifting" influence upon both the students and the working population was fundamental to the project. Hence, the project could be said to rest on the notion of a civilizingeducating-stimulating space; a space of transformation. Later on, in 1936, the Settlement acquired a countryside house for small excursions, and in 1955 a larger property was acquired with economic support from the Ministry of Social Affairs and the Copenhagen municipality for longer stays during the summer. The annual reports described how the removal from the big city, the fresh air, outdoor activities and generous food completely changed the children who reluctantly returned to Copenhagen. The Settlement and its adjacent spaces represented a site of passage, real as well as imaginary, and hence resonate with one of Foucault's definitions of the heterotopias, namely, that they may take the ambiguous form of both "rigorous division and absolute Passage" (Johnson 2006: 80). Foucault defined a heterotopia as a system of openings and closures that define who can enter and under which conditions:

"Heterotopias always presuppose a system of opening and closing that both isolates them and makes them penetrable. In general, the heterotopic site is not freely accessible like a public place. Either the entry is compulsory, as in the case of entering a barracks or a prison, or else the individual has to submit to rites and purifications. To get in one must have a certain permission and make certain gestures" (Foucault 1986: 26).

The point about admission criteria is pertinent since it indicates that heterotopias can only be accessed by undergoing rituals of purification and transformation. Researchers have observed that the Settlement tended to attract the better part of the working class, that is, the people with most resources and cultural capital (Bundesen et al. 2001: 227). On the one hand, the Settlement did not target their efforts at specific groups such as the homeless, the unemployed or drug addicts, arguing that other organizations at Vesterbro were specializing in working with these groups. On the other hand, throughout its lifespan the Settlement has given more emphasis to creating activities for one special group: children. The emphasis on working with children can be explained both from this ideal of transformation and from practical circumstances. In the first explanation, transformation theology leads the Settlement workers toward people they can actually transform, which puts children at center stage. Of course, traditionally, personal transformation was a sign of religious success. Children's clubs matched well the objective of transformation through exposure to healthy cultural and recreational activities, since they replaced the depravity of the street with homely protection and constructive entertainment. Another, more pragmatic, reason for the Settlement's prioritizing of children was that it was the only group that would secure permanent economic funding from public authorities (Bundesen et al. 2001: 238).

Utopian experiment or welfare institution?

We have noted that at its birth the Settlement was a novel, hybrid structure that displayed utopian aspirations. Unlike all preceding charitable institutions, the Settlement was an "outpost" in the middle of the urban wilderness. It was not philanthropy but a meeting forum; it did not offer charitable assistance but bridged an essential class antagonism; it was a home as well as a public space (Rousmaniere 1979: 47). At first glance, it seems an impossibility to merge these divergent characteristics within the same space. In addition, another impossible duality was intensified during the historical development of the Settlement: acting both as a radical, social critic and as a welfare institution. From the 1950s to the 1990s, the Settlement increasingly became a socially critical organization. Their analysis targeted modern society with its chain-gang production that was causing social misery in terms of the lack of housing, loneliness, family problems, stress and unemployment. At the same time, references to Christianity receded, and arguments became more secular. It was increasingly argued that the key problem was a deleterious economic system that could be transformed only through collective action:

"Many of the social problems that we confront on a daily basis are created by a society which places economic interests higher than concerns for humans. We see it as a key pedagogical task to inform the youngsters about these societal failures that they are subjected to, and which cannot be solved at an individual level, but only if a sufficient amount of people decide to act upon the state of affairs" (Christian Student Settlement 1974/75: 9).

The harsh analysis of the harmful effects of market-based society and its production of social problems became more prevalent and frequent. At times socialism would be mentioned sympathetically as a "natural reaction" to a harmful society, but the Settlement never chose an explicit political position (Bundesen et al. 2001: 228). The balancing act of combining utopian ideals with the pursuit of the possible (in terms of minor improvements) continued in a new variant. On the one hand, the Settlement articulated social critique, demanding a fundamental transformation of the industrial-capitalist society. On the other hand, the organization established an increasingly tighter connection to public authorities and their rationales. Its activities for children, the unemployed and, more recently, immigrants became gradually linked up with the rule-governed system of state-regulated assistance and its criteria and divisions.

From 1921 onwards, support from the state and from the municipality begins to appear in the Settlement's budget. This public funding was granted to support "preventive child care." During the period 1919–1931 the proportion of public funding of the organization's expenses gradually increased to reach 38 % in 1931 (Bundesen et al. 2001: 232). However, the collaboration with public authorities became more systematic after the social reform of 1933 (Borioni 2014: 138). The Settlement established a child-care facility in 1939, which received a significant proportion of its children from the public child welfare service, and another group of children was paid for by the Magistrate (Bundesen et al. 2001: 235). Close links were thus established between the Settlement and the public authorities concerning the work with children. But initiatives aimed at other groups were sustained as well. In 1950, the Settlement established a counseling office that offered counseling with a doctor or a social worker once a week. A key function of this service was to assist clients, or 'users' as they were now called, in their interactions with social authorities, have someone accompany them to court or get help with household matters. Doing this work, the Settlement had taken up the role of "mediators" between people on the verge of exclusion and social authorities who can decide to help or not. This role would become still more important in the 1990s and later.

In 2010, the Settlement was asked by the Ministry of Social Affairs if they could organize a preparatory employment project for young long-term unemployed. The leader, Johs Bertelsen, had aspirations to create a "third labor market" where people not easily included in the normal labor market could develop qualifications and self-worth in alternatives activities. The idea was not simply to turn the participants into a labor force, since it was considered just as important to develop their "life-force" (Bertelsen quoted in Laneth 2011: 221). In the time around 1994, Bertelsen had formulated a set of principles in connection with the "Side Street Project" (*Sidegaden*) initiated in 1986 during times of recession and high unemployment. The project was original in that it combined several efforts at the local level in streets marked by years of decay, closed shops and youth crime. *Sidegaden* can be described as a mixture of urban revitalization, outreach community work with the marginalized, crime prevention, and attempts to create spaces of alternative forms of social existence and activity. A key idea behind the project was that full employment is illusionary, and that novel forms of work within areas like social work, ecology, culture and recycling was called for as a response to the economic and social crises. Training the unemployed should not be disciplinary but should allow them to make meaningful contributions to the development of society such as community revitalization. Society should prioritize projects that function like "social laboratories" at the local level where experimentation can take place for integrating the needs of everyday life and worklife (Laneth 2011: 223). In 2010, Bertelsen had to realize that, if the Settlement organized training projects for unemployed persons sponsored by the municipality, they could not remain unaffected by the overriding employment focus. They would have to act like a public authority in relation to the users and could no longer take up a position of straightforward solidarity with them. Inasmuch as the Settlement wished to carry out social work supported by public funding, it would need to subscribe to the employment agenda and then focus on the positive aspects of it.

What we are witnessing is how radical ideas, or utopias, became tempered by legal stipulations and funding criteria inherent to the welfare system. Or in Foucault's terms, once the utopia is enacted it becomes a heterotopia. The Settlement projects became at the same time islands for experimentation and the generation of collective, critical awareness and the moral and disciplinary molding of deviant groups. Schematically speaking, in the early phases of the Settlement's trajectory it was the message of universal, "Brotherly love," found in Christianity that was tempered by the worldly encounters with the working poor. From around the mid-20th century it was increasingly the radical demands of fundamental social change which were criticized as being compromised by the concrete bureaucratic requirements of the modern welfare state. In both cases, we may speak of a heterotopic co-existence of divergent elements that are "simultaneously represented, contested, and inverted" (Foucault 1986: 23).

As a site of juxtaposition, the heterotopia puts language and received notions under pressure. Inasmuch as heterotopias are impossible or unthinkable spaces, they reveal the limits of our language, making it tremble and splinter (Foucault 1971). Perhaps the recurrent difficulties of agreeing on the right name for the Settlement can be understood in this light. First, in 1911, it was the *Christian Student Settlement*, which in 1975 was shortened to the *Student Settlement* and later changed to the *Settlement at Vesterbro.* Throughout its lifespan, the Settlement has challenged and reconstructed entrenched divisions in our culture between the sacred and the profane, between public and private space, between leisure and work, and between the normal and the deviant. This is certainly one of the reasons why the Settlement has inspired, moved, disturbed or provoked its surroundings so much. Consider Foucault's emphasis on the heterotopia's disruption of given oppositions:

> "And perhaps our life is still governed by a certain number of oppositions that remain inviolable, that our institutions and practices have not yet dared to break down. These are oppositions that we regard as simple givens: for example between private space and public space, between family space and social space, between cultural space and useful space, between the space of leisure and that of work. All these are still nurtured by the hidden presence of the sacred." (Foucault 1986: 22).

In situations where language would seem to be pressed to its limits, *Settlement* members sometimes made creative discursive inventions. Terms like "spirit in action," "the third labor market" or "co-vision with the client" offered ways of re-describing what could not be contained within the conventional distinctions. It must also be noted that, from the early 1970s onwards, an increasing part of the workers at the Settlement and its projects consisted of professionals like social workers, nurses and language teachers. Notions of Christian spirit or Brotherly love were clearly not suited as a way to construct collective identity in an organization populated by various secular professional groups.

At a visit I undertook with the other authors of this book at the Settlement's social counseling unit and language classes for immigrant women, one word was repeated as designating the unifying value basis of the work: "hope." When working with severely marginalized persons who tend to be stuck with their psychiatric diseases, drug abuse, collapsed economy, one had to "keep up hope."

This would seem like a very open or vaguely defined notion, but the vagueness might indeed be its very strength. If we borrow for a moment from the discourse theory advanced by Laclau, such open or "empty" signifiers like the ones above play a key role in constructing collectively shared identity or social hegemony. A hegemonic articulation depends upon a representation that can successfully rally diverse actors around a particular social project, for instance, the Settlement. In this process of articulation, one particular signifier assumes the function of unifying representation. Laclau defines "the empty signifier" as a discursive element that achieves its unifying function by canceling out its specific content and hereby allowing diverse actors or groups to identify with it (2000: 70–71). Its function and signification depend not on nondiscursive content, but on its position within a chain of other signifiers. In our case, these could include "respectful meetings," "community revitalization," "working *with* not for the users," and "doing the impossible." We can hypothesize that, in the Settlement's early decades, loosely defined notions of a Christian spirit or "Brotherly love" served as a means for reaching beyond the existing, unhappy world, just as they served to unite members from diverse congregations. Perhaps the need for such "empty signifiers" becomes even more urgent in a time where a shared ontology, a religious cosmology, is no longer available. It is tempting to conclude that, in the absence of a shared transcendent reference ("the Divine providence"), other, more "worldly" signifiers must increasingly do the job of creating unity in the Settlement of the present day. The empty signifier of "hope," one might suggest, makes it possible for different Settlement workers, specializing in social counseling, psychiatry, language training and more, to believe that they are working for a shared goal in their daily practices.

Conclusion: The Settlement utopia in the modern welfare state

Applying the perspective of the heterotopia provides different conclusions than those usually offered by research on civil society and voluntary organizations. Hence, the present analysis does not reveal the contradictions of the Settlement as principally having been created by the growing collaboration with the public sector. It reveals certain contradictions that were inherent to the Settlement right from its inception insofar as it attempted to unite a series of diverse elements: philanthropy and cultural integration, home and public space, religion and social analysis, radical critique and welfare projects. The Settlement became a place in which Christian impulse, social critique and social work converged.

These different elements reflected developments and tensions inherent to the Protestant culture as it developed in the decades surrounding the start of the 20th century. It encompassed religious ideas and scientific knowledge, individual conversion and social reform as well as utopian and pragmatic standpoints. Schematically speaking, the Settlement experienced a movement from the first pole to the second in these sets of dualities. Even in the early years there was a shift in emphasis from the revivalist belief in personal conversion to a vision of a redeemed world through social transformations. The eschatological hopes for the coming Kingdom on Earth were gradually replaced by more pragmatic strategies for influencing and collaborating with secular political actors. Gradual social improvements became the route to achieve a this-worldly utopia. The Settlement became a site of blending of religious, political and scientific ideas in which utopian and pragmatic thinking co-existed in a tense relationship.

The Settlement utopia was one in which people would not interact in the roles of giver and recipient, helper and helped, but develop alternative relationships based on values of mutuality. Later on, it became a space where the universal ideals of caring—without regard to the person—intertwined with certain professional codes and requirements of the public welfare system with which there was contact and routines of referring those in need of professional services. Given these contradictions and our initial conceptual definitions, the Settlement can be viewed as not only a site of counter-conduct, but also as heterotopic. The heterotopic quality of The Settlement arose particularly from the blending of Christian notions and administrative-scientific categories. The message of universal fellowship was mitigated by modern scientific-administrative procedures in the evolving struggle against the social evils of the world.

We have also noticed how radical and utopian ideas were continuously being formulated in different guises throughout the whole period. One way of understanding this is to suggest that the Settlement's ideology has always revolved around empty signifiers. "Friendly encounters," "Brotherly love" and "the Christian spirit" functioned as empty signifiers, just as "hope," "helping each other" and "the third labor market" would much later on. What they shared, however, was a reference to the possibility of achieving a this-worldly utopia that rendered the activities in the Settlement meaningful for its changing members over time.

The Settlement's development displays the unavoidable tempering and compromise that occur when utopian ideals of "universal," "transcendence" or "radical change" are institutionalized and become embodied in concrete social practices and arrangements. While acknowledging that such ideals are compromised or tempered through various political and structural controls of the welfare hegemony, it does not mean that they cannot have transgressive effects. On the one hand, the Settlement contributed to decisive changes of the Danish society during the 20th century such as the establishment of public childcare; as a site of experimentation it still glows and glitters in its incongruous variety, illuminating passages for our imagination. On the other hand, we witness defined needs, regulation and training to fit the requirements of society and the labor market. In fact, debates within the Settlement at times highlighted the paradox that they prepared the users for inclusion in the very society that was the target of fundamental critique.

The principles of unconditional love, "co-vision" and working together with the users stand in opposition to requirements of categorizing users for eligibility, abiding by regulations and normalizing whenever possible, or, in short, welfarist discipline. Clearly, the space of the Settlement did not constitute an enclosure but was pervaded by the heterogeneity of outer space. In concrete terms, it reflected—and continues to reflect—long-standing paradoxes of the welfare state. The most fundamental one is the contradiction between formal universality and the specific needs of particular individuals. The Settlement does not avoid mediating between the legal-political discourse and individualizing pastoral care, the two deep-seated poles of the modern welfare state project. Despite all their radicalism, they eventually had to face the problem of representing the particular group or person in objective and juridical categories. In this regard, this is also a story about the changing conditions for practicing social philanthropy, or "brotherly love," in the Danish context.

The Settlement promised simultaneously the possible and the impossible. It displayed the juxtapositions and contradictions that emerge when the spirit is put into action. We have seen that these incongruences did not freeze up or paralyze the Settlement project, but rather spurred permanent social innovation. Whether we emphasize the utopian dreams or the entangled, contradictory and messy realities is the choice of the observer. The heterotopic perspective offers both possibilities. The Settlement is a place where what can be dreamed intersects with what can be done.

References

Bertelsen, J. (2011) Det umuliges kunst, in P. F. Laneth: *Respekt: Historier fra Settlementet på Vesterbro.* København: Forlaget Settlementet.

Borioni, P. (2014) Danish welfare reform and Lutheran background in the mid-20th century, *Journal of Church & State*, 56(1): 128–150.

Bundesen, P., Henriksen, L. S. and Jørgensen, A. (2001) *Filantropi, selvhjælp og interesseorganisering: Frivillige organisationer i dansk socialpolitik 1840–1990erne.* Odense: Syddansk Universitetsforlag.

Christian Student Settlement (1909) *Annual Rapport 1909.* København.

Christian Student Settlement (1974/1975) *Annual Rapport 1974/75.* København.

Donzelot, J. (1979) *The Policing of Families.* New York: Pantheon Books.

Dumm, T. (1996) *Michel Foucault and the Politics of Freedom.* London: Sage.

Greenstone, J. D. (1979) Dorothea Dix and Jane Addams: From transcendentalism to pragmatism in American social reform, *Social Service Review*, 53(4): 527–559.

Foucault, M. (1971) *The Order of Things: An Archaeology of the Human Sciences.* New York: Pantheon Books.

Foucault, M. (1972) *The Archaeology of Knowledge.* London: Routledge.

Foucault, M. (1986) Of Other Spaces, *Diacritics*, 16(1): 22–7.

Foucault, M. (2007a) What is Critique? In M. Foucault: *The Politics of Truth.* Los Angeles: Semiotext(e), pp. 23–83.

Foucault, M. (2007b) *Security, Territory, Population: Lectures at College de France 1977–1978.* New York: Palgrave Macmillan.

Henriksen, L. S. and Bundesen, P. (2004) The Moving Frontier in Denmark: Voluntary-state relationships since 1850, *Journal of Social Policy*, 33(4): 605–625.

Jespersen, H. (1928) Paaske, *Settlements Bladet*, nr. 3, 10. april, 3. Aargang: 24–25.

Johnson, P. (2006) Unravelling Foucault's "Different Spaces," *History of the Human Sciences*, 19(4): 75–90.

Kahl, S. (2005) The Religious Roots of Modern Poverty Policy: Catholic, Lutheran, and Reformed Protestant Traditions Compared, *European Journal of Sociology*, 46(1): 91–126.

Laclau, E. (2000) Identity and Hegemony, in J. Butler, E. Laclau and S. Žižek (Eds.) *Contingency, Hegemony, Universality.* London: Verso, pp. 44–89.

Laneth, P. F. (2011) *Respekt: Historier fra Settlementet på Vesterbro.* København: Forlaget Settlementet.

Lindhardt P. G. (1979) Richard Thomsen, *Dansk Biografisk Leksikon.* Købehavn: Gyldendal.

Nielsen, C. (1928) Se, jeg gør alle Ting nye, *Kristeligt Studenter-Settlement*, nr. 1, 10. Februar, 3. Aarg.: 1–2.

Quandt, J. B. (1973) Religion and social thought: The secularization of postmillennialism. *American Quarterly*, 25(4): 390–409.

Reinders, R. C. (1982) Toynbee Hall and the American Settlement Movement, *Social Service Review*, 56(1): 39–54.

Rousmaniere, J. P. (1970) Cultural Hybrid in the Slums: The college woman and the settlement house, 1889-1894, *American Quarterly*, 22(1): 45–66.

Van Leeuwen, M. H. D. (2000) *The Logic of Charity*, London: Macmillan.

Villadsen, K. (2007) The Emergence of "Neo-Philanthropy": A New Discursive Space in Welfare Policy, *Acta Sociologica*, 50(3): 309–325.

Villadsen, K. (2011) Modern Welfare and "Good Old" Philanthropy, *Public Management Review*, 13(8): 1057–1075.

Wille, J. (1928) Henry George, *Settlementsbladet*, 10. Marts, no. 2, 3. Aargang: 10–11.

Topos B: The ecclesial clinique or the clinical church

For many years now, a Lutheran congregation outside Gothenburg and a local, idealistic organization of health-workers have cooperated to improve living conditions for undocumented migrants living in all parts of Southern Sweden. Every Wednesday evening the church is open for these hidden people. They receive everything from health advice and psychiatric counseling to legal advice from the members of the Rosengrenska Foundation. At the same time the church and the church people are the obvious context for the project.
Photo: Joakim Magnus Taraaldsen, USIT, University of Oslo

Anne Sjøgren (Gothenburg)

Working for undocumented migrants in Gothenburg

The Rosengrenska Foundation was established in 1998 as a voluntary medical network targeting undocumented migrants. In 2008, Rosengrenska joined forces with the Swedish Red Cross to work on the project 'Health care for undocumented migrants'. Among other things, the Red Cross provides a staff of two nurses who organize the activities. In spring 2015, there are more than 600 volunteer nurses, doctors, psychologists, physical therapists, dentists and others, as well as a voluntary interpreting service. In Sweden, undocumented migrants are defined as people who are staying in the country without a residence permit. We have identified four different paths to becoming an undocumented migrant:

- Denied application for asylum and staying illegally in the country.
- Being smuggled into the country without applying for a residence permit.
- Remaining in Sweden after a temporary visa, work permit or similar has expired.
- Being born in Sweden to undocumented migrant parents, which means that you are not registered or are a citizen of any country.

The undocumented migrants we meet are mostly former asylum seekers whose applications have been denied and who have subsequently gone underground. The majority of the roughly 5,000 patients we have met in the past 17 years have been from the Balkans, Iran, Iraq and Afghanistan.

Rosengrenska was established because Sweden did not offer subsidized health care for undocumented migrants in 1998. By 2013, Sweden passed a new law providing for some subsidized care for undocumented migrants. This law does not entitle such migrants to the same care as Swedish citizens, contrary to Article 25 in the Universal Declaration of Human Rights. It does not provide care based on needs or in accordance with scientific and documented experience, which is a principle that the health care services is required to apply. The text uses the term 'care that cannot be postponed', which continues to give rise to confusion and is an obstacle to care.

Rosengrenska and the Red Cross are part of the 'Right to Care' initiative together with 63 other organizations that continue to raise the issue of care on equal terms in Sweden.

Voluntary health services are at the center of the work on the right to health care. Undocumented migrants and others who are outside the welfare system seek our help to obtain health care or advice about how they can gain access to it.

In Sweden, there have been seven non-profit networks in six different locations to meet this need. Reports from voluntary organizations are still very important in terms of following up the law and informing about the needs of vulnerable people.

What is required for Rosengrenska to continue its work?

The answer is divided into four categories: the premises, the 'staff', the visitors and the study visits.

1. We borrow premises for one evening a week

It is a church with hospitality deeply ingrained in its walls—from the basement to the upper floor. The various rooms in the church are the parsons and the deacons' offices, large and small cubbyholes, the kitchen and assembly room. The church premises are at our disposal, together with NGOs of all kinds, working with a common target group.

2. We are many who work together

We are approximately 40 volunteers every evening, half of whom are qualified in one healthcare profession or another—doctors, nurses, dentists, psychologists. Legal volunteers offer consultations in some rooms. Experienced lawyers and committed students have started a separate organization based around this meeting place, which is recognized as a practical training placement for law students.

Parts of the church function as a health center that specializes in referring people to ordinary health services and as a support center for people experiencing psychological crises, or who are damaged by war and traumas. The basement is where the children play, bake, draw and sing safely under adult supervision. The church has a second-hand store where clothes, donated personal hygiene items, sanitary pads, nappies, shampoo and toothbrushes are handed out for free—if they are available. There is a free hairdresser's in one of the staff rooms, an optician comes once a month to fit free glasses that have been donated and interpreters circulate in the premises, sit in long conversations or help people with quick questions. Theirs is often one of the most difficult jobs—interpreting for their fellow countrymen in acute crises, people who are threatened, homeless and suicidal. At the center of all the varied activities is the church hall, which is transformed into a café for refugees, while at the same time serving as a waiting room for the different services.

The church is like one big marketplace. Over the years, more and more organizations have joined us on the premises and we have to adapt to each other and get along. One of our strengths is that each organization does what it is good at.

3. People in need who come on these evenings

During one evening, several hundred people can pass through our doors, although only about 60 of them come for health care reasons. We get to know them as individuals with names and worries, diagnoses, a recognizable handshake and voice, hopes and fears. We have known some of them for more than ten years. In all, our health care service deals with around 850 patients a year.

About half of them only come once during the course of a year. At the opposite end of the scale, there are about fifty who come between 15 and 30 times a year.

These visits often concern common primary health care problems such as infections, minor injuries and psychosomatic complaints, stomach pains and headaches caused by anxiety and worries.

A lot has improved since the new law was introduced on 1 July 2013, when undocumented migrants were given the right to a certain level of health care. Since then, we have increasingly gone from having many doctors to—with the help of nurses—referring people to the ordinary health service.

We do see, however, that counseling is necessary for those to whom we are unable to obtain help in the ordinary health service, for those who are most wretched and those who are afraid to seek help from the regular health service. Counseling and finding ways into the dental health system are the areas where our help is still most needed.

4. Study visits

Word has spread about our activities, our evenings and our meeting place. We receive study visits nearly every week. Students, researchers, politicians, decision-makers, and the media—it is useful to be able to come to a place where undocumented migrants feel safe and can speak without fear about the shadow world they inhabit.

There have been many discussions about this. Is it unethical to expose our patients and everyone else on the premises to all these study visits? Do the patients end up in a moral blackmail situation where, in order not to seem ungrateful, they feel they cannot say 'no' to interviews or to being observed?

Status

We have struggled with the issue of health care for undocumented migrants for almost 17 years. In parallel, research and public discourse have progressed with regards to dealing with people in crisis and suffering from post-traumatic stress disorders (PTSD). We need all the knowledge we can get, and we are learning every day.

The question that often arises in our work is what we really can do, and how we can work. We can be there for the undocumented migrants, organize meetings between people, gain the trust of people who have lost faith in everything and keep trying to get them into the public health care system. Gaining the trust of people who do not even trust themselves any more takes time and requires flexibility. For those who have lost faith in their own human dignity, in their very identity as people, it is important that we meet them with deep respect. And those who feel completely inadequate and harbor feelings of guilt as parents for having put their children in this situation—how can we support them?

Perhaps one such desperate person needs a capable psychologist who can follow her rambling thoughts. She has come to us in a state of dissolution, she believes she is going mad because of everything she has experienced and needs to speak to someone right away. Another one only needed to come and be reassured that we were there. He would not be able to speak for another two years, but he came every week and liked to hear that we remembered his name. We give him a smile and put an arm around his shoulder, ask him how he is doing and whether he has had a cup of coffee. Some people need 50 kroner to buy medicine at the chemist's. Another one wants to end his life and at least four people swiftly form a team to try to find ways of reaching him and saving his life.

We have been in the same place once a week for eleven years, or around 550 times.People are found by the police and sent back and then come back to us and tell us about their flight and persecution, torture and rape.People get word of their parents dying in their home country and they cannot be there for them. A beloved daughter gets married and her father cannot be with her. Armed men come looking for a man in a faraway country. When they do not find him at home, they shoot his brother. He is told the news by phone and comes to us. Some young men say 'mum' to one of our grey-haired volunteers in the waiting room. They have not called anyone 'mum' for years, and they play around with the word and repeat it often.

A man in his fifties comes to us with a big smile on his face and tells us he has become a grandfather. A lonely young woman from his home country is sitting in the waiting room. She has two small children and he decides to support her and the children as best he can, even though he is an undocumented migrant himself.

Large groups of people sit around the tables in the waiting room. They speak in Persian, Arabic, Balkan languages, English, Romany, but the mood is calm.

During all the consultations I have attended, there have almost never been any conflicts that seriously disturbed the peace on the premises. So many unbearably poor people, so many stressed, anxious, powerless people in one place, yet so few conflicts.

Trygve Wyller (Oslo)

A spatial Power that dissolves itself

Space, Empathy and Theology – when the Colonized Enter the Empire

To Theorize Spatial Practice

When is pastoral power more than discipline and control? The correct answer is that, when pastoral power contributes to the recognition of others, it is hospitality, counter-conduct and not control only. The real question, however, is how to know why, and when, this hospitality occurs.

In one recent article (Calvo: 2014) Ana Maria Manzanos Calvo claims that hospitality can be located both in the hospital and in the home. Her critical analysis of current literature on the theory of hospitality concludes that when hospitality occurs in a hospital space it will first of all be control-, and not other-oriented. In other words, more pastoral power than counter-conduct, to relate to the terminology in this book.

The thesis in the following is that there still might be a connection between an other-oriented (counter-conduct) hospitality and a heterotopic space. This becomes especially crucial when the actual space is a church. Churches can be interpreted as heterotopias, contesting the surrounding world, but perhaps a heterotopic requirement for the church is more than just "being there", it involves what activities and people that fill the church.

In this article the focus lies on what a heterotopic church might look like and how such a heterotopia could be decisive when we discuss what hospitality is. Calvo claims that the hospital space becomes the space of control just because of its specific spatiality. The patient needs to act according to the rules in that space. One could suspect that a church would come even closer to such a controlling hospitality. In the following the intention is to argue that a church could be real other-oriented hospitality when it reduces its own traditional (controlling) space and lets the spaces of the others become visible and evident. On this background Calvo should be corrected. To theorize a church heterotopia might still open for a counter-conduct hospitality in church spaces. But to achieve this, the spatiality of the church itself needs to be reconstructed.

It is against this background that the following article discusses and interprets the Rosengrenska project for undocumented migrants in Sweden, presented above. The project was started by Rosengrenska, but has, for many years now, been situated in a specific Lutheran church near Gothenburg, Sweden. The intention is not to analyze the project sociologically, but rather to theorize, spatially and theologically, what it means that there is something called hospitality there.[1]

The article tries to investigate a pastoral power that lets the subaltern speak by leaving space to them.[2] This might be one way we can think theologically relevant thoughts about Foucault's reflections on pastoral power and the heterotopic.[3]

The Rosengrenska Project for the Undocumented

The case under discussion is the project presented by previous leader Anne Sjøgren in the first pages of this section. The project invites undocumented migrants to receive counseling, health/social care and some glimpses of everyday life.

The project/space is located in a Lutheran church situated some 20 minutes' drive outside Gothenburg, Sweden. The modest church building, designed not to stand out in any way from its surroundings in an immigrant-dominated commuter town, makes up part of the central square of the community, whose school, public offices, restaurants and a supermarket are located around the church.

This is the area in which most (documented) immigrants in Gothenburg

1 There are an increasing number of books and articles on the theology of migration and the undocumented. In recent years important contributions come from by Daniel Groody (Groody: 2007, 2009) at the University of Notre Dame and Susanna Snyder (Snyder 2012) from Roehampton University, UK. Groody works within the Catholic Vatican II tradition and tries to combine the doctrines of Social Teaching with dogmatic theology, very often under the influence from Christological thinkers, both from the Protestant and Catholic vantage points. Snyder's book, on the other hand, is more practical and concrete. In her concluding chapter, Snyder writes; "Groody has begun to develop a systematic theology arising from migration, seeing migration as "a way of thinking about God and what it means to be human in the world," (Snyder: 2012, 211). Even if my case study works with other kinds of theory and also dogmatic, I think these general words from Snyder cover most theologians' approach to migration. The present article, however, has a more Lutheran than a Catholic trajectory, well formulated by Leopoldo A. Sanchez, who writes: "I argue that an ethic inspired by the Lutheran theological tradition allows for a spectrum of positions in immigration law and reform, which are arrived at on the basis of the competing claims of various advocates on behalf of different neighbors. These claims are in turn informed by different themes found in Lutheran theology to approach ethical issues, Christ's self-identification with vulnerable neighbors, God's work in the two kingdoms or governments, and the Christian's calling to vocation in society." (Sanchez: 2015, 42)

2 Here, I follow Snyder, who writes: "The pervasive reality of migration points towards a recognition that local, liberation, postcolonial and subaltern theologies can no longer be seen as theologies of the majority world—as optional extra add ons—but rather as intrinsic to *any* theology wishing to be considered as meaningful. While some reflections are available from the perspective of relatively privileged migrants…, the experience of being a *forced* migrant may present new and challenging insights." (Snyder: 2012, 212)

3 I have published earlier on the same project, see Wyller: 2014, 2016

have lived and the congregation has had high immigrant attendance for many years. Consequently, the Sunday services are multicultural and multi religious. Some members still belong to the classical Swedish Lutheran tradition, but many participants also come from Christian traditions that are definitely neither Lutheran nor even necessarily Protestant, and my impression is that not only Christians attend. Many people participating in the services are dressed according to typical Muslim traditions.

According to the minister, there is currently strong support in the congregation for opening the doors to undocumented migrants and for cooperating with the philanthropic movement Rosengrenska Stiftelsen and the Red Cross. The initiative started when the Rosengrenska project for undocumented migrants needed more space. The head of Rosengrenska, who worked as a nurse in the community near the church, asked the minister if he would let Rosengrenska use the church premises one evening a week.

Rosengrenska is a network of professional health workers, lawyers, social workers and dentists, etc. Established more than 10 years ago, this network has organized a very efficient body of workers. Every Wednesday at 6 p.m., this little army of volunteering professionals moves into the parish church and runs a very strong, ambitious center for meeting most of the needs of the *sanspapiers.*

On their professionally designed website, Rosengrenska presents itself as follows: "Rosengrenska is a nonprofit, independent network consisting of medical staff that helps undocumented migrants. Individuals are assisted through our telephone hotline where they can get in contact with nursing staff within or outside of the normal healthcare system. Several times a year we send out invitations to our lectures. We collaborate with other nonprofit organizations, and since 2008 we have cooperated with the Red Cross in Gothenburg."

Its vision is to establish a degree of human dignity for the undocumented. Humanity-based reflection and practice are the foundations of its work.

The Heterotopic Inside

A couple of years ago the research group behind this book arranged a workshop in the church building where the Rosengrenska project takes place. A group of international scholars discussed the profile and the interpretation of the project with the leaders, volunteers and undocumented persons themselves. At a crucial moment during the discussion the group discussed what was the driving force; Christian compassion, ethical involvement, something else? One of the ministers said: "I think it is human rights, which is the core of the project." Then the project leader spontaneously replied: "It is something more."

The content of that "something more" did not become more concrete in the following discussions in the workshop, but everyone present still remembers that dialogue. The minister referred to human rights, but the nurse/project leader meant something that human rights did not cover. She obviously did not want to skip human rights, nor did she want to reintroduce classical Christian concepts, like compassion or charity.

One obvious theoretical perspective to catch that "more" is to interpret the Rosengrenska/congregation project as part of the practices Foucault calls heterotopic. It is "another space," outside the evident normality in Sweden. At the same time it is a space that mirrors the normal spaces in society—and it does so in a strongly critical way. "These spaces do not offer enough for the undocumented people in Sweden, but we do." This is obviously one message emerging from the Rosengrenska heterotopia.

But still the more demanding question is what kind of heterotopia this is and how such a heterotopia could be interpreted. By asking this question one immediate reminder is urgent: Foucault, in his famous article on the heterotopia (Foucault: 1986) was primarily occupied with the other space, not with the spaces of the other.

But one cannot determine the relationship to the outside without also looking at the inside. There are qualities there that influence what the impact and significance of the other space is. Even if I do not think that the question of hospitality can be determined only by empirical research, one must acknowledge the experiences and interpretations from the people inside.

A sociological approach would, of course, monitor how the participants respond and act. But a more modest ambition would be to look for traces: Are there specific practices that point toward hospitality?

One man says that he arrived in Sweden with his wife and children more than 5 years before the interview took place. After a couple of years their application for asylum was rejected. But instead of leaving Sweden, he and the family started their lives as *sanspapiers.*

First he went to another congregation, to a denomination he belonged to in his home country. But the local minister said: "I cannot help you. You can sleep on one of the benches outside the church." Later on, the family was invited by a stranger into her house for a period of time. They have probably been moving on ever since until the time of the interview, moving from one place to another and then somewhere else again. This man expresses the paradox very concisely: "There are people who want to help, but everything is closed to me. You do not have a name; you do not have a number." For him, Rosengrenska was something different. It gave him a name and offered him counseling and networking to survive the difficult life without a passport and the legal acceptance of a permanent place to stay.

The same kind of experience is articulated by a woman from the Middle East. She refuses to tell the story of how she was able to travel from her home country to Sweden, but she will narrate what it is like to be hidden from view.

One very concrete part is a narrative in which anxiety plays an essential role. The tram regulations in this specific Swedish town are unbearable. She needs to use the tram to move around, but to do that one needs a monthly pass, which can only be issued on showing a valid ID card. And this is the card an undocumented person obviously does not possess. So instead she travels without a ticket, and every time controls are carried out, she lives with the very real possibility of being sent to the police, with no ticket and no ID card. She says: "I am so tired! How can a person live like this! You are fleeing from the police all the time. I feel that my life has stopped. I cannot do anything. I am nothing." And, like the man above, she finally points to Rosengrenska as one of the few places that represent something else, a place for fleeting safety and care.

These narratives present a more precise picture of one of the basic criteria for pastoral power as counter-conduct: The other needs to experience a space that is open to their legal otherness. The pastoral power must be a power that respects the embodied other as other. And, finally, this kind of pastoral power becomes a counter-conduct when the practice has a societal impact. Offering assistance to hidden people on such an obvious and large scale may be presumed to have societal impact. Over the years the Swedish government changed the law in a more liberal direction so that, today, undocumented people have access to the health services they did not have before.

The experience of recognizing legal (and social) otherness might also be reflected on in a more theoretical context. In several meetings with the Rosengrenska people, the issue of this central core value came up repeatedly, both among the leaders, the volunteers, and the undocumented and their families. One feeling, almost from the very beginning, was that the experience of being recognized is something special and important. But what does it mean and how can we conceptualize it?

Empathy and the Other

The undocumented people report that Rosengrenska offers something specific, something important not experienced in other spaces. With this we already have one clear criterion of what a space for the other is: It is somewhere the other has a recognized space. The question is still what this means. It is the same as Foucault, who in several books taught us not to trust anyone who claims they are doing things for your sake. In most cases they are doing it for their own interest, ending with discipline and control. So how can we trust that the other is really being recognized as *an other?* Can we know more about what a hospitable pastoral power might be? And does the space in itself impact the kind of pastoral power we are dealing with? This last question is the most crucial one; the last part of this article tries to address and answer the challenges that arise from this question. But before that, some theoretical observations regarding the experience of being recognized:

If you ask the Danish phenomenologist Dan Zahavi, empathy is a necessary part of the other-experience. In recent years Zahavi (Zahavi: 2014) focused on whether something called empathy even exists and how such a phenomenon may be characterized. The decisive point is that empathy presupposes otherness, and that this empathy cannot but be embodied. Zahavi's context is the critique that empathy is not, like the phenomenologists claim, a phenomenon outside the consciousness of the subject. This is why many (analytical and postmodern) researchers do not recognize empathy as anything else but pure subjectivity. Zahavi argues convincingly against this.

For Zahavi empathy is much more than just an internal emotion. Rather, empathy implies that there are other bodies outside my own self. Empathy has to do with the way I react in my body to other fellow human beings' embodied situation. When we express empathy it presupposes that there are some real others outside me. The existence and embodied presence of the other is sensibly experienced by me. Through my senses I become aware of the other's presence and embodied situation before I communicate my experiences in language or react to the other practically. Empathy comes from this first original meeting where my sensibility is shaped through the awareness of the other's body.

Zahavi's position is therefore that empathy is not a subjective emotion; rather, empathy comes from embodied experiences, which presupposes others.

In Zahavi's phenomenology this is important; to dig deeper into the reasons for the "more than human rights experience." It might mean that one part of the "more" is the experience of a truly felt empathy, a phenomenon. Zahavi (Zahavi: 2014), presupposes that the other is experiencing and recognizing themselves as other, not only as a part of one's own consciousness. The emotion one experiences is immediately absolutely embodied: wounds, diseases, breakdowns, torture, money, accommodation, but also food, games and dancing. It is no wonder that one of the project leaders in Rosengrenska summarized the experience of being exposed to all this in this way: "You feel rather nude." One is emotionally exposed to the embodied presence of the others. Empathy, for Zahavi, presupposes the existence of others, because it is exactly the awareness that something outside of me requires my presence and challenges me to a response, which is decisive. According to Zahavi, therefore, empathy and otherness are closely connected.

Empathy is the emotion that occurs when we are confronted with embodied difference. Zahavi calls this relationship between otherness and emotionality the "we-experience." (Zahavi: 2015) By insisting on the relationship between empathy and otherness, Zahavi rejects the "only consciousness" critique. The conclusion is that instead of phenomenology being "only" a theory of consciousness, it is primarily a philosophy of the "we-experience". We experience other persons as embodied, and therefore, and in the same way, we live our lives deeply connected to embodied others.

The "we-experience" and the empathy emerging from it implies that one should be aware of all kinds of connectivity that takes place in Rosengrenska. Empathy and the implicit connectivity are decisive when one researches what it means to experience pastoral power as hospitality. In Rosengrenska there are many practical exposures of such kinds of connectivity:

- *The outside/inside.* Being inside the church building connects everyone because of the fear of being imprisoned or hunted down. This is confirmed when volunteers meet an hour before consultations open and the minister urges everyone to gather in the church nave if there is any violence or if neo-Nazis enter the church.
- *Activities for children:* A sort of children's club has been established in the basement of the church building. Chaired by a group of young volunteers, it offers an alternative "normal" life for children.
- *The informal gathering in the cafeteria:* The cafeteria is where the families stay throughout the evening. One of the family members may have come for a consultation, but many other family members may join them. They can sit in the cafeteria and talk to other people, often people from the same country as themselves. These informal gatherings therefore seem to function as both an informal meeting place and at the same time a very important place to share and obtain information.
- *The informal gathering just outside the main entrance:* Some of the young men who come to Rosengrenska spend a lot of the time just outside the main entrance. It appears that they do not come for any form of consultation, but primarily just to talk. I don't know what they talk about, but they step aside when I get too close to them, as if they do not want anyone to listen to what they are talking about.
- *The consultations:* These are the main activities of Rosengrenska, and they appear to be like any other professional consultations. They resemble a parallel welfare state activity and connect the undocumented with the Swedish society that does not accept them on a legal basis.
- *The connectedness to the community and its activities:* Many non-ethnic Swedes participate in the congregational practices. It is not easy to determine whether they all have legal residence in Sweden or not. But some of the undocumented persons also connect to the congregational practices.

Traces of empathy are also heard in different meetings with volunteers and project leaders[4]. They all underline how they are moved and motivated by the

4 A more sociologically oriented research should, of course, look at more qualitative interviews with the participants to study how far this possible empathy could be addressed and articulated or whether there are (of course there are) lacunae of non-empathy in the Rosengrenska context.

context, by their own participation and by the strong emotions that come from being with the undocumented. With respect to Zahavi's reflection, the comments from the volunteers and leaders become significant, also on the theoretical level. Empathy and the recognition of an embodied other seem to belong together.

During some of the interviews with volunteers and project leaders, they all emphasize the unambiguous and strong dedication they have toward the project. This strong dedication might be a small sign of the three criteria of the hospitable pastoral power so far registered: recognition, empathy and a we-experience. When asked about her motivation, one of the volunteering nurses said: "This is the best evening in the whole week. I love being here." Later on she admitted that she personally did not belong to any church, but being in the project made everything different for her: "I would really consider joining the church to have the possibility of participating in all the good things this church does."

On another occasion the topic was whether she—as a woman—considered it a challenge to be in a context with so many Muslim men, many of whom may foster a possible hostility toward relating directly with a non-Muslim female nurse. The question surprised the interviewee; she said that, up to that point, she had never even considered the issue. But upon reflection she claimed that such problems had never occurred in the project. She had experienced such problems in other public wards where she had her regular job during the week. She found it strange, but then she suddenly said: "Here (in the project) one is rather nude."

The same kind of experience of being exposed, even if this experience belongs to another context, also came from another volunteer, a male nurse. He first underlined his rather classical Hippocratic motivation: "Nurses are taught to help even enemy soldiers." But he also was interested in the impact on his own professional education. He was volunteering in the project every Wednesday and mentioned how he could be better trained for volunteering in Rosengrenska.

When asked whether the location in a church represented a problem for him, he responded that it did not, even if he belonged to a non-Christian confession. The nurse denied that it was a problem, because, as he said, "The church has a spirituality. God is important, not the confessions. There are not such big differences among the confessions on this issue."

Still, there was one kind of anxiety, also for this volunteer: the fear of whether the police would enter the church or not. "Remember they once went into a monastery to pick up some undocumented persons," he said and added, "You really have to hope they fear God." In all these interviews we hear a strong

But the present article is not primarily sociological; rather, it uses spatial theory to discuss what a heterotopic space that includes hospitality *might be.*

tendency toward focusing on being on the edge and being in a kind of exposed situation.

In yet another setting, the same attitude of radical exposure was also expressed by one of the ministers affiliated with the project. Even if Rosengrenska is a specific organization that runs the weekly "clinic," all staff of the hosting congregation also are present during the Wednesday meeting. They clearly identify with the project and reflect on it in a specifically Christian way. With strong emotions the minister told the story about how he had tried to sort out a radically complicated situation for an undocumented family, together with two doctors, one Muslim, the other Jewish. He still remembers this as a paradigmatic experience: "It was a very important evening, indeed." They all felt that caring for the other went deeper than their confessional differences. One could say this narrative illustrates all three criteria of a hospitable pastoral power: the other as other, empathy and the we-experience.

One can sum up what these three criteria might mean with yet another narrative: One day the minister in the congregation cooperating with Rosengrenska reflected on the complicated question of what it means to help. He presented the story where another minister in another project for marginalized people insists on interviewing the volunteers themselves. The crucial question is whether the volunteer *in spe* wants to help the clients or not. If they say yes, they are really motivated to help, so the minister rejects them as volunteers. His position is that most of his clients are in such a bad shape that if you have expectations of helping, you will not be able to act as a volunteer. You just have to "be there," he said.

This situation was presented to the minister at the Rosengrenska project church. He immediately concurred; he could identify with the position of the other minister: If you want to volunteer primarily in order to help, you will not do the job right. "It would not be right for yourself and especially not for the other person," he said. In other words, respecting the other as other is paradoxically a more basic task than caring and helping.

The narrative above, then, and the three criteria developed through them, might be summed up as follows: Recognizing the other as other, empathy and the we-experience can be seen as important aspects of the kind of hospitality which one could experience in the Rosengrenska/church project.

A Heterotopia of Compensation

The indications of the pastoral power hospitality as other-oriented empathy are important in themselves. But this hospitality happens inside the heterotopic space of the local, Lutheran church. The question now is the space itself. We move from the space for others to the other space. What kind of heterotopia is the Rosengrenska/local church space?

One important way of responding to this question is to start with Foucault's claim that all heterotopias are counter-sites (Foucault: 1986, 24). The Rosengrenska/local church project is a heterotopic space because other real sites definitely are contested and inverted. The Swedish welfare state does not offer enough acceptable welfare to the undocumented. The heterotopic Rosengrenska/local church thus contests the Swedish welfare system.

The undocumented are hidden people. The name employed for being hidden differs depending on the perspectives—from "informal migrants" to "undocumented migrants" and "sanspapiers" to the more prerogative term "illegal immigrant." Whatever name is used, the legal situation for most of these people is that they are not legally accepted in Sweden, either because their request for asylum has been denied or because they never actually applied to stay and just live outside the Swedish welfare state.

There are, of course, also other persons participating in the project: friends of the undocumented, people who still have preliminary permission to stay and people who have received permanent permission to stay in Sweden but continue to come out of sympathy or any number of other reasons. So far the total number of participants and the participant's motivation have not been sufficiently investigated. Without more empirical support the basic issue remains: This is a project that includes and supports people who the public authorities definitely call "illegal." These are the "illegals" present in the church building every Wednesday.

Recently (2013) the authorities modified the Swedish law on Health and Social Care. Up to 2013, an undocumented migrant was entitled to receive health care from the welfare state only in explicitly life-threatening situations. This motivated the foundation of the Rosengrenska/Church project, where the undocumented can obtain normal and necessary (but non-emergency) health care, and where they also receive assistance for entering the welfare state if a life-threatening situation does occur. In addition to this, much legal assistance is given to the undocumented by professional lawyers and other legal experts. Most of the undocumented want to achieve permanent permission to stay in Sweden.

This 2013 modification to the legal system has reduced the overall rigidity. Now it is also possible for an undocumented person to receive normal health assistance and still not risk being jailed. Some of the people connected to the project expected a decrease in the number of people coming after the new legal development. But to date (late 2015) this does not seems to be the case. The need for assistance and every kind of support has not been reduced, even if normal health care is not open to more people.

This new development, however, is not decisive for the perspective of this article. With or without more liberal health care legislation, the brute fact remains that the majority of all people participating in the project can be jailed immediately and then returned to their home countries. This is the political and personal radicalism of this project. This project gives people risking jail both full access to the church building and to all kinds of other health/legal/ social assistance.

Against this background one can easily say that one obvious criterion for being a heterotopia is fulfilled by the Rosengrenska. The mirroring of society belongs to Foucault's general definition of the heterotopic. But the specific practice in the Rosengrenska indicates that such mirroring occurs through the very presence of the undocumented.

Still, the really spatial impact has not been addressed in this analysis. The three characteristics, the recognition of the real other, empathy and we-experience are practices that take place *inside* the space, and have so far not been commented on from the spatial perspective itself.

To do so, we need to look at the heterotopia as a religious, indeed, Lutheran church space. The Rosengrenska project is located in a local Lutheran Church of Sweden church building. But only a very small minority of the undocumented people actually belong to this Lutheran church by denomination or by confession. A good guess is that the majority is Muslim, and that there are also many Orthodox Christians among them in addition to people many other denominations and confessions. The Lutherans are more or less absent, except for the volunteers from the congregation itself. This means that the religious perspective must be addressed on the level of the space itself. It is the Lutheran church space that is impacted by the presence of the undocumented. People, who for religious reasons do not frequent this space, are given a prominent place in it. The others are not only political/ social others, they are definitely religious others as well. This provides a good opportunity to discuss what kind of heterotopic space the Rosengrenska really is.

In his heterotopia article Foucault mentioned six subcategories of heterotopias (Foucault: 1986, 24). The last one, number six, is presented like this:

"Finally, the last characteristic of heterotopias is that they have, in relation to the rest of space, a function that takes place between two opposite poles. On the one hand they perform the task of creating a space of illusion that reveals how all of real space is more illusory, all the locations within which life is fragmented. On the other, they have the function of forming another space, another real space, as perfect, meticulous, and well arranged as ours is disordered, ill conceived, and in a sketchy state. This heterotopia is not one of illusion but of compensation, and I wonder if it is not somewhat in this manner that certain colonies have functioned". (Foucault: 1986, 27)

At first sight the Rosengrenska does not at all seem like what a heterotopia of compensation might be. In Foucault's own text the Jesuit colonies in Latin America of the 17th and 18th centuries function as illustrations of what a heterotopia of compensation is supposed to be. They are real and at the same time "meticulously ordered"—the heterotopia of compensation is the perfect other space.

Now, not much is "meticulously ordered" when one enters the Rosengrenska for the first time. People walk around, many rooms are totally overcrowded, there is too little space in the corridors, and people sit, waiting, sometimes looking desperate. Still, from the perspective of the radicalism of the project, one could look at the religious generosity as an unexpected way of being perfect.

The other space of the undocumented is not the perfect life of the colonies, though; yet, it is still perfect because of the implicit theology of this paradoxical upside-down church. It is perfect because the non-persons from the outside are given a prominent spatial position on the inside. One could say, in this case we are confronted with the classical, hierarchical church power that (almost) dissolves itself. There is, of course, no doubt that the project still takes place at the local Lutheran church. But this church space is filled with other people, both politically and religiously other, than what one might expect from all traditions. The church (almost) dissolves itself as a traditional church by developing a space where the subjectivity and the agency of the other counts more than usual.

In this way this heterotopic space is a space of compensation because the traditional space (almost) dissolves itself and instead we are in a space where the agency of the other is evident and strongly felt. This does not, of course, dissolve the church itself. On the contrary, the heterotopia of compensation happens precisely *because* this Lutheran church possesses a hospitality that gives agency to the undocumented and still remains the church practicing this kind of hospitality. But to see what heterotopia of compensation could mean in the field of theology, one needs only radicalize the interpretation of what a church might be—in its good moments: this kind of heterotopia of compensation.

A spatial theology of heterotopic compensation?

The impact of heterotopias is increasingly discussed in contemporary theology (Westhelle: 2004, van den Wyk: 2014). The interpretations above obviously provides the opportunity to continue that discussion. How can one develop a spatial theology from the practice of this specific and paradoxical heterotopia of compensation?

A generation ago Virgilio Elizondo published his still very influential *Galilean Journey: The Mexican-American Promise* (Elizondo: 1983). This is a book about refugees, especially the undocumented, and their way of being part of the biblical trajectory. Shaped by first-generation Latin-American liberation theology, Elizondo frames the parallels between Jesus from Galilee and contemporary (undocumented) travelers to the North across the long US-

Mexican border. They were both (victorious) victims in a story of sacred significance.

A parallel, philosophically based position is developed in the thoughts of the Italian philosopher Giorgio Agamben. He is one of the most influential in contemporary interpretations of the undocumented. Agamben and Elizondo are in many ways very different, both by age and discipline. Still, they share the same trajectory: The undocumented are the victims (Elizondo), the "Jews" (Agamben: 1995), of our time. Agamben even presents the undocumented as non-citizens, living in a non-place, the camp.

Following Agamben, in the non-places, except for some exceptional witness, there is hardly any agency or possibility for the subaltern to speak. But the analysis of Rosengrenska shows a different perspective. Rosengrenska could have been interpreted as a camp in the agambian sense; a place where there is such s dominating embodied control and no one might speak at all. Agamben thinks that the contemporary refugee camps are the current representation of what he called the non-camps of the Second World War concentration camps. But the analysis above means that the Rosengrenska project cannot be named a camp or a non-place in this sense. It is definitely not a non-place; it is clearly a living heterotopic space where people share embodied hospitality. The symbolic sign that there is a heterotopic space and not an agambian non-place is that the subalterns "speak" (Spivak: 1988) by participating and sharing in the paradoxical heterotopia of compensation.

If we follow the theology developed in the tradition of Elizondo, the decisive part is that the undocumented, the migrants, are the victims, crucified Jesus-icons. They move toward their Golgotha and they suffer just like Jesus did. But the analysis above questions this kind of a victim interpretation. The connectivity, the empathy and the life world among the undocumented and between the undocumented and the volunteers in Rosengrenska point at some other way of interpreting than by using the victim discourse like Elizondo, Groody and their followers. It seems like they are too quick developing a theology "from above" by applying a biblical or biblical/traditional terminology into the life experience of migrants without really starting from "below" and constructing a possible theology of migration coming out of the life world experiences of the undocumented themselves. That might open for a theology where God as a difference that at the same time builds life is more adequate than the victimized God, just to start this discussion, which has to be developed more substantially elsewhere.

Frank Boedeltje (Boedeltje: 2012) analyzed some theological aspects connected to the new wave of persons crossing the EU border. Boedeltje uses Foucault's distinction between the utopic and the heterotopic, utopia being the unreal, the non-existent place, heterotopia the real place.

According to Boedeltje, one could see the EU border policy as the utopian vision of peace and harmony both inside the EU as well as with respect to its neighborhood. On the other hand, the heterotopias exist in opposition to this utopia: "In this context heterotopias are considered places that disturb the utopian image by means of complexity, contradiction and diversity" (Boedeltje: 2012, 1). These heterotopias are the formal and informal camps that develop more and more these days outside the European borderland. Boedeltje focuses on Algeria and Cyprus, but since the publication of his article, these camps have become numerous and one of the most dominant heterotopias today, due to what the colonial discourse calls the European refugee crisis.

Following Boedeltje one could say that the Rosengrenska—and all the heterotopic spaces following the same kind of trajectory—disturb the utopian (European) image *inside the Empire.* One thing is the heterotopic disturbance coming from Algeria and Cyprus (Boedeltje cases), but the heterotopia in the middle of the utopian disturbs in another way: It is a different and unexpected kind of resistance that disturbs the utopian space from the inside.

Looking at the Rosengrenska from this perspective provides us with an awareness more similar to the postcolonial claim for a new subjectivity than to the trajectory of victimization from Agamben/Elizondo. The postcolonial position ("the subaltern can speak") is about claiming a voice and a place. The heterotopic experience learned from spaces like Rosengrenska makes it relevant to look for *spaces* that could claim to be of postcolonial significance inside the Empire. These are the spaces that I in the following name "spaces that dissolve themselves"

The power that dissolves itself

By opening the discussion whether the dissolving of the controlling space and the emerging of another space could be seen as important aspects of what hospitality is, analyzing and interpreting the heterotopias seem to lead to fruitful comments to the ongoing discussion of hospitality.

One influential contribution to the postcolonial era outside of Europe came from Saba Mahmood (Mahmood: 2005) on the veiling of Egyptian women. Mahmood claims that instead of seeing oppression one should see the veiling as embodied proclamation of a new subjectivity. The same approach is taken by Richard King (King: 1999), who empirically studies specific Indian (Dalit) communities. These communities are often represented as strongly marginalized and victimized in all sorts of ways. In opposition to such trajectories, King claims that the potential for a subjectivity development inside these communities, has been both neglected and under-researched. Both authors claim that an awareness of different kinds of embodied practices leads to the discovery of previously not reckoned subjectivity, both among the veiled Egyptian women and inside a specific community in India.

It is, of course, a relatively long road from Egypt and the Dalit/Indian communities to the western coast of a still very Protestant Sweden. Nevertheless, a theoretical challenge can be transferred from these two studies. From Mahmood and King we learn not to restart a second chapter of orientalism. In the context of this article the crucial point to learn from the two postcolonial researchers is that one can at the same time be marginalized and still in the process of subjectivity and resistance.

Ruben Andersson (Andersson: 2014, 6) presents a narrative from what Freerk Boedeltje calls Europe's heterotopic disturbance:

"Alpha was 23 years old and had left his family home in Dakar behind the previous night, he explained on a tea stop in western Mali; his mum had made him a sandwich for the transcontinental journey ahead. His plan was to cross the desert, reaching Egypt and eventually Israel—a new route now that the European ones had closed, owing to tough controls. 'I'm not afraid,' he said coolly, a cigarette dangling out of his mouth, yet his resolve faltered briefly as I warned him of the rebels, bandits, and deadly stretches of desert on the road ahead" (conversation with the author (Andersson: 2014, 6).

"We reached Bamako before sunrise. 'Everyone says this is *the* crossroads in Africa,' Alpha whispered as we rolled into Sogoniko *gare* (bus station). As the day began, we entered a ticket office, asking for trips toward Niger. 'We have a bus to Agadez but no further, after that you use other means of transport,' we were told with a wink, but Alpha wanted none of the deadly Libyan desert. He scrolled over a rasta-colored map of Africa on his smartphone, tracing alternative routes via Niger and Benin, ready to decide on a whim on his next destination—the road lay open ahead."

There is agency in this narrative; the traveler, the person, who Europeans call "migrants", "foreigners", strangers", etc. are here persons constructing their own future. Their competence in travelling routes, technologies and general coping is something very different from being a foreign victim. This is why what Boedeltje calls "heterotopic disturbance" this agency is all about. The analysis of the Rosengrenska project above has, however, added one important characteristic of how this disturbance is happening. The pastoral power constructing Rosengrenska is a power that partly dissolves itself, and the Rosengrenska heterotopia of compensation is a spatial-ecclesiological power that also partly dissolves itself. Both the pastoral power and the spatial-ecclesiological power end with the insurgence of both other persons and other spaces as influential and sometimes leading subjects.

Spivak's famous question was whether the subaltern was able to speak at all; when Derrida and Levinas postulated the impossibility of reaching the "real" other, they left us with only traces or hardly nothing at all (Spivak 1988, 199). But Spivak and her interpreters also left us with the paradox that, if the subaltern did say something that mattered to us, then it would not be subaltern (Beverly: 2004).

In other words: We should not look for the magnificent and very prominent discourse. The "small" and minor things like the ones located in the Rosengrenska/church project are more important when the subaltern speaks and acts. The otherness located and respected in the Rosengrenska tells a story of undocumented people emerging and gradually constructing own life worlds, on the inside and on the outside of the established Lutheran church in the area.. Foucault found the model for his heterotopia of compensation in the "perfect" Jesuit societies in Latin America. Rosengrenska is everything else than a perfect Jesuit society. But it might be that its spatial practice is perfect and a heterotopia of compensation in the opposite way. The "perfect" and the compensation is that here is a space that seems to dissolve itself and thereby opening for a new space of other.

The contextual argument is helpful. The emphatic inclusion of the religious and social others is hosted by the local Lutheran congregation and its church building. To host the heterotopic in this way is therefore much more than to be a container. The host him-/herself becomes formatted and reformatted by this embodied act of hospitality. This is also confirmed in the referred interviews. All leaders in the congregation, from the ministers to other leaders and the volunteers, agree: The way of being church is never the same after these experiences. It is "something more," something new.

The melancholy and almost mournful feelings that became visible when the local Red Cross, which was financially behind Rosengrenska, discussed and, in 2015, decided to withdraw from the church building and continue the project in a "neutral" building also indicate how many of the project leaders thought about the significance of the Rosengrenska project. As stated above, because of the decision of the Swedish government in 2013 to be open for an expansion of legal health care services to the undocumented, the Red Cross leadership decided to move from the local church building to a more "open" building downtown. The church leaders, people from the congregation and also the original leading persons in the autonomous organization Rosengrenska and their volunteers protested against that decision. It was as if the quest for "more" indicated by one of the leaders in the workshop narrated above was about to be lost. Their decision was to go on with the Rosengrenska/church project even if the Red Cross itself withdrew and established a neutral, and very legal, center for refugees in downtown Gothenburg.

Vitor Westhelle (Westhelle: 2004) discusses what it means to interpret the sacred and the church from a spatial perspective. Westhelle frames what he calls "epiphanic spaces" and distinguishes them from the more common "sacred spaces." The argument is that calling something sacred often originates in an essentializing trajectory and marks a difference between the sacred and the profane that is no longer meaningful. It is important not to set this specific space apart from the rest of creation, so that Westhelle chooses to call it the "epiphanic": "Epiphany marks a differential space, but not for any presumed ontological quality. That which is proper to it is an event, the event in which the divine is made manifest in a given space" (Westhelle: 2004, 374).

The interesting aspect of this is that the possible epiphanic significance in Rosengrenska is not what happens in the church proper (altar, pulpit, organ, hymns, sermons, etc.). The church naves open during the project hours, candles burn there, and the local choirs might be rehearsing during project time. But the project for the undocumented itself is never an active part of a church service during the project hours. On the other hand, the congregation always gathers for a short service one hour before the doors open for the project. The service starts at 5 p.m., the doors open at 6 p.m.

This is obviously in order to signal and to celebrate that—from the point of view of the congregation—the project for the undocumented is included and contextualized in the self-interpretation of the congregation through prayers, psalms and a short sermon. Still, during the rest of the evening there are no other formal signs of explicit Christian activities.

From the perspective of a more classical and traditional ecclesiology one could claim that the Rosengrenska project is a challenge for a Lutheran congregation. Charity and Christian social practice (diaconia) are, of course, vital parts of most Christian ecclesiologies. But charity and diaconia very seldom lead to giving the "others" the position they have during the Rosengrenska's Wednesdays. Instead of letting the doors open to the outsiders, it seems very difficult to know who is other and who is non-other in the hectic Wednesdays hours. This is more than normally accepted in traditional charity work.

From the analyses and interpretations above it seems obvious that such an ecclesiology has to be discarded. It seems more appropriate to start from the perspective of Westhelle when he writes: "Unlike office buildings, houses, gyms, streets, hotels and cars, a holy space belongs to a different economy. Its end is not a return to investment; it divests" (2004, 376). This is a position that could be embodied with the spatial practices found in the Rosengrenska.

What does it mean theologically that a heterotopic space communicates because it "divests" (in this article even stronger: "dissolves") itself? To start the discussion, one should look for criteria like the ones presented above: recognizing the other, empathy, the we-experience, giving the other an implicit political significance and not the least an agency inside the religious church space—a significance and subjectivity. The presence of all, or at least some, of these practices embodies what it means to divest or dissolve oneself. One could say that the presence of embodied others is one of the most evident signs of a divested and dissolved ecclesia.

Against this background it becomes clear that the spatial turn needs to be radically criticized and reformulated when applied to theology. The spatial turn in theology, if formulated uncritically, could lead to a new essentialization of a specific body or a specific place and could thereby also imply a re-sacralization. The massive presence of the others in the Rosengrenska congregation is first of all a significant reduction of the traditional church subjects and a corresponding, massive, embodied presence of traditional objects, almost becoming new subjects.

This, then, is the heterotopia of compensation as ecclesiology. The compensation, the perfect, is that the church itself is "othered." In the conclusion to her article "Church as Heterotopia" (van Wyk: 2014), Tanya van Wyk cites Emmanuel Levinas: "Instead of seizing the Other through comprehension and thereby assuming all the wars that this comprehension presupposes, prolongs, and concludes, the I loses its hold before the human Other (autrui), and, unjustified, can no longer be powerful" (van Wyk: 2014, 6) This article argues that the "I loses its hold" when the subaltern speak. A heterotopic church is the event in which it dissolves itself to let the subaltern remain.

In his book *Cities of God* from 2000 Graham Ward writes: "The Christian community always waits to receive its understanding, waits to discern its form. It is a community that produces and occupies a space transcending place, walls and boundaries, a liturgical, doxological space opening in the world onto the world" (Ward: 2000, 258). (Later on he follows the same trajectory: "The eschatological personhood that issues from following Christ situates Christians in a place beyond the times and spaces of a particular environment" (Ward: 2000, 279).

This article has followed a path contrary to the one presented by Ward. Foucault's basic premise is the difference between the heterotopia and the utopia. The heterotopia is the real place, the utopia is the un-real place (the place to come, one day). The power that dissolves itself, the core concept in this article, happens in a real place, the Rosengrenska project inside a local Lutheran church building in Southwestern Sweden. This might be the "more" of the Rosengrenska. Hospitality comes from the power that dissolves itself. This is a pastoral power that can become an important counter-conduct of our time.

The introduction to this article took its point of departure with Calvo's claim that the hospital space first of all will be dominated by control. The reason for this, according to Calvo, is that the hospital tends to work with binary like outside/inside, stranger/native etc. Based on Derrida's (Derrida: 2000) linguistic construction "hostipitality", a construction that combines the two Latin words that signify both host and master. This ambiguity is then reconstructed by Derrida's "hostipitality", meant to keep the ambiguity of the hospitality within the word. The interpretation of the Rosengrenska project and the tendency to discover a church space that (almost) dissolves itself connects to the discussion of the ambiguity of hospitality. The conclusion is that hospitality as counter-conduct can occur in church spaces when the space of the others becomes the most significant and when the question who is guest and who is host becomes more open and difficult to respond to.

References

Agamben, G. (1998), *Homo Sacer: Sovereign Power and Bare Life*, Stanford: Stanford University Press.

Andersson, R. (2014), "Time and the Migrant Other: European Border Controls and the Temporal Economics of Illegality", *American Anthropologist*, 2014, Vol.116(4), pp. 795–809.

Beverley, John (2004), Subalternity and Representation. Arguments in Cultural Theory, London/Durham: Duke University Press.

Boedeltje, F. (2012). "The Other Spaces of Europe: Seeing European Geopolitics Through the Disturbing Eye of Foucault's Heterotopias", Geopolitics, 2012, Vol.17(1), p. 1–24.

Calvo, A.M.M. (2014) "Janot Díaz' "Otravida, Otravez" and Hospitalia: The Workings of hostile Hospitality", *Journal of Modern Literature* (2014), Vol.37 (1), p. 107–123.

Caroll, M.D./Sanchez, L.A. (Ed.) (2015) *Immigrant Neighbors among Us. Immigration across Theological Traditions.* Oregon: Wipf and Stock Publishers.

Derrida, J. (2000) "Hostipitality", *Angelaki: Journal of the Theoretical Humanities*, 5.3, p. 3–18

Ehrenkamp, P./Nagel, C. (2014) "Under the Radar": Undocumented Immigrants, Christian Faith Communities and the Precarious Spaces of Welcome in the U.S. South, *Annals of the Association of American Geographers*, 104 (2): 319–328.

Elizondo, V.V. (1983) *Galliean Journey: the Mexican-American Promise*, Maryknoll: Orbis.

Foucault, M. (1986) Of other spaces. *Diacritics. A Review of Contemporary Criticism* Vol. 16 (1), 22–27.

Groody, D./Campese, C. (Ed.) (2008) *A Promised Land, A Perilous Journey. Theological Persepctives on Migration.* Notre Dame: University of Notre Dame Press.

King, R. (1999) *Orientalism and Religion. Postcolonial. Theory, India and "the Mystic East,"* New York: Routledge.

Mahmood, S. (2005) *Politics of Piety. The Islamic Revival and the Feminist Subject*, Princeton: Princeton University Press.

Sanchez, L. (2015) "Who Is My Neighbor? Immigration through Lutheran Eyes," in: M. Daniell Caroll R./Leopoldo A. Sanchez M. (Eds.) *Immigrant Neighbors among Us. Immigration across Theological Traditions*, Oregon: Wipf and Stock Publ.

Snyder, S. (2012) *Asylum-seeking, migration and church*, Vermont: Ashgate.

Spivak, G. (1988) "Can the Subaltern speak?, in: Nelson,C / Grossberg,L (ed.) *Marxism and the interpretation of culture*, Urbana: University of Illinois

Van Wyk, T. (2014) "Church as heterotopia", *HTS Teologiese Studies/Theological Studies*, Vol. 70(1), pp. 1–7.

Ward, G. (2000), *Cities of God*, London: Routledge.

Westhelle, V. (2004), "Wrappings of the divine: location and vocation in theological perspective", *Currents in Theology and Mission*, Vol. 31(5), p. 368(13).

Wingren, G. (1957) *Luther on Vocation*, Philadelphia, Muhlenberg Press.

Wyller, T. (2014) "The Undocumented Embodied: Shaping the Space where the Sacred and the Secular Intertwine" in: v.d. Breemer, R. / Casanova, J. / Wyller, T. *Secular and Sacred? The Scandinavian Case of Religion in Human Rights, Law and Public Space*. Göttingen: Vandenhoeck & Ruprecht, 221–236.

Wyller, T. (2016) "Heterotopic Ecclesiology. Critical Reflections on what the Church on the Margins Might Mean" in: *Diaconia. Journal for the Study of Christian Social Practice* (2016), Volum 7.(I) 43–57.

Zahawi, D. (2015) "Self and other: from pure ego to co-constituted we", Cont Philos Rev (2015) 48:143–160.

Zahawi, D. (2014) *Self & Other. Exploring Subjectivity, Empathy and Shame*, Oxford: Oxford University Press.

Topos C: The Hospitality of the Monastic Garden

Europe, and especially Central and Southern Europe, still has hundreds of living and practicing monastic institutions. Most of them are Catholic, some of these are in the midst of big cities, but some are outside. The Benedictine monastery in Altenburg, Northern Austria, seems to be deeply rooted in tradition, in architecture and the black clothing of the monks. But these monks have constructed a Garden of Religions in their own context.

P. Michael Hüttl (Altenburg)

The Garden of Religions at Stift Altenburg in Lower Austria

The scientific project "UMIS" (Living with creation) was initiated by the University for *Bodenkultur* in Vienna (BOKU) and was run by the institute for ecological agriculture, the institute for marketing and innovation, the Sustainability Research Consulting in Munich, the Institute for Austrian history (University of Vienna), the Committee of the Friends of Pilgrim-Schools, and six Benedictine monasteries in Austria and Bavaria. The project was to research the basic activities of monasteries, how they develop their lived spaces and how they deal with their resources. The preparation for the project started in 1999, the same year as politics in Austria changed completely. The first government of Chancellor Schüssel led to complete international isolation of Austria and to sanctions against Austria by the European Union due to the government coalition with the rightwing party (FPÖ). In August 2002 an enormous flood caused catastrophic and expensive damage and this "Jahrtausendhochwasser" changed the landscape in the eastern Austrian area. Old environmental sins reemerged and the need to reconsider ecological relations on a broad scale became obvious. The consequences for the environment and nature were easier to acknowledge than the consequences for the social, cultural and political habits in society.

Especially in "Waldviertel" (the north western part of Lower Austria) the situation was so dramatic that the provincial government initiated an extraordinary investment project in the region. The agricultural sector, which was heavily hit and which gained national attention all of a sudden, should be changed to a blossoming garden land within a period of four years. A project "Natur im Garten" (nature in garden) had already been initiated in Lower Austria in 1999 by the provincial minister for finances Mag. Wolfgang Sobotka. The project was now used for improving the ecology of private and republic spaces. Within this project and initiated by the provincial government of Lower Austria a garden festival was organized in Kamptal, the region where the monastery of Altenburg is located. Using close contacts to the monastery, Mag. Wolfgang Sobotka invited the monastery to participate in this project. The only structural guidelines given from the provincial government was that the monastery had to contribute "something with religion".

The beginning

Within the monastery two monks worked on the subject and after a relatively short discussion they agreed to implement the declaration of Vatican II *Nostra Aetate.* This declaration deals with non-Christian religions and the kind of relationship the church wants to establish with them. For these two monks the document seemed to provide the appropriate actuality and intellectual intensity for the monastery's contribution to the regional garden project.

Preliminary experiences

The year before the flood a garden in the internal part of the monastery had been rebuilt as "a garden of creation". In this garden a member of the community had created a theological concept through seven aspects of the theology of creation. Together with a regional landscape gardener this concept was translated into a sort of a "language of garden". Visitors of the monastery welcomed the unusual garden design and subsequently the administration of the monastery, working on cultural and touristic aspects, realized the significance of the subject "garden". "Nature in garden" of Lower Austria, and the committee of "the gardens in the valley of Kamp" sought a close cooperation with the monastery at a time when there was a high sensibility for ecology. For that reason, another traditional focus of monastic activities became important: sustainability, a concept that originates from forestry. This concept is an attempt to establish a sort of contract between generations in timber economy. One is obliged to use only reusable resources. Today, UNESCO applies the concept of sustainability in four different areas: ecology, economy, social responsibility and culture. These are also the essential areas of monastic activities: the responsible use of the environment, a long-term vision of managing capital, creating fair living conditions for the people who are connected with the monastery, and the democratic nature of human expressiveness in religion, politics and art.

In the end these were the shaping conditions for the planning of the new concept of garden. They promoted the project "nature in garden" and the long-standing convictions of the monastic community and for the monastic economy at the same time.

The planning

After the definitive decision to apply the document *Nostra Aetate* (NA) from the Second Vatican Council for the garden, different groups discussed its propositions. At first, there was a broad range of ideas regarding landscaping, and although the initial intention was to invite all religious communities that are mentioned in Nosta Aetate to be part of this planning process, the essential subjects were discussed with friends from Buddhist monasteries and with Muslim friends. The basic topics of Nostra Aetate are presented in the garden by walk sides and symbols of water. The four communities that are named in Nosta Aetate are Hinduism, Buddhism, Judaism and Islam. All four were allocated a quarter of a field in front of a pavilion built during the baroque era. Another goal was that all of these fields should be accessible also for wheelchair visitors. Audio guides in German and English should be provided for individual visitors and guided tours for groups.

The implementation

Hundreds of alternative plans were considered, discussed and finally discarded, and after three years of planning and landscaping work the garden was finished. Two members of the convent were the representatives of the monastery in this process. They were responsible for the detailed implementation of the theological program and for its realization on the ground. In the chapter, which is the highest committee for decision making in a monastic community, the project was discussed and finally agreed upon. This was the requirement for providing financial support by the monastery itself. In all those years of planning and construction a lot of other institutions were discussing that matter as well, such as guests, representatives of the sponsors and a couple of members of the Lower Austrian government visiting the construction-site – all of their comments were being considered in the principal discussions of the steering committee and their suggestions were very helpful.

The opening

On June 5, 2006, the Monday of Pentecost, the garden was opened. A year earlier the monks had elected a new abbot, Christian Haidinger OSB. Haidinger was very much in favor of the garden of religions and had made it one of the main objectives for his time as abbot.

So the garden of religions was not only geographically located in the monastery but it has deep roots in the spiritual leadership within the community. The actual edification of the garden and the related discourses had an impact on how life and economic activities were organized in the community. When the ethnological institute of the University of Göttingen wanted to do research in the monastery it was welcomed. The community had the researchers, as well as five leading bön-monks from Tibet as guests. The garden was formally opened by Landesrat Mag. Wolfgang Sobotka, and among the 2500 guests who were welcomed to the monastery was special honorary guest Prof. Anas Shakfeh, the president of the "Islamische Glaubensgemeinschaft von Österreich".

The effects of the garden

During the first year a high turnout of visitors could be observed. Nowadays Stift Altenburg and its garden count approximately 30.000 visitors per year. The entrance fee includes visits to both the monastery and the garden. This means that since 2006, the year of the opening, about 270.000 people came in contact with this spatial dialog of religions. In the monastery we have guest books for visitors who want to note their impressions. What they write about the garden is very positive. Many people are willing to be confronted with their own religiosity and they are open for a dialog and mutual understanding of different communities of faith. People frequently ask for more honest engagement by the religious hierarchy. But of course, we cannot measure to what extent an individual is willing to overcome stereotypes and prejudices. For that reason a guided tour given by members of the convent is very helpful and instructive. At these tours spontaneous, often controversial, discussions about faith take place. Reoccurring subjects of discussions are those on Judaism and Islam. Ignorance and deficits in knowledge and information seem to be some of the most frequent obstacles to overcoming prejudice.

The garden as a place of dialogue

After nine years of experiences with the garden we consider it to be an important place for dialogue. Members of the convent take regular walks through the garden, where they have the opportunity to talk with individual visitors.

St. Benedict's rule offers a variety of ways to meet people. The beginning of chapter 53 of the Rule says: "All people coming from the outside should be welcomed like Christ..." An additional sentence specifies that brothers in faith and pilgrims should be warmly welcomed and that we shall not ask for their religious conviction. This is the basic habit of Benedictine hospitality. This kind of hospitality accepts others without asking where they come from and where they want to go.

Consequences

The garden as a monastic locus affects the habits of all people visiting it. This applies to members of the convent, to the employees of the monastery and visitors. They all take a stand in relation to the garden and are challenges to react. This ranges from open acceptance to defensive resistance.

Besides being a place of dialogue the garden in Altenburg has been planned as an ecological project, which meets the intention of the department "Kultur. Tourismus" bringing Stift Altenburg to the attention of the general public by organizing exhibitions and cultural events. Ecological responsibility goes hand in hand with a spirituality closely linked to our "responsibility for creation". We are trying to restore the balance to the classical division between fundamentalist approaches and realistic propositions within the ecological movement. In this respect some significant meetings through the Garden of Religions were possible, demonstrating that it is a place that has importance for society. For instance the city of Vienna organized a "Bildungsfahrt" where 50 employees participated. There were significant encounters with the monastery; discussions on ecology, spirituality, social diversity and the cooperation of different world-views as well as debates about religion and faith.

Becoming local

For us in the monastery all the activities connected with the Garden of Religions come together in organizing the VICISU (The Vienna International Christian Islamic Summer University). Since the end of 2006 we have been in contact with P. Andreas Bsteh, one of the pioneers for interreligious dialogue in Austria. He is a member of the "Societas Verbi Divini", a Catholic missionary order. P. Bsteh has dedicated his whole monastic life to the service of dialogue. He has significant diplomatic skills, and has among others organized a round table for the foreign minister of Austria, Dr. Alois Mock, with Islam, with the intention to start a dialogue with the Islamic Republic of Iran. When P. Bsteh heard of Stift Altenburg and the Garden of Religion, he contacted our Abbot, Christian Haidinger, with the idea to establish a summer university. In 2008 the first conference VICISU took place with 47 participants. The leadership was provided by Ao. Univ.-Prof. Dr. Irmgard Marboe (Department for International Law) and Univ.-Prof. Dr. Ingeborg Gabriel (Institute for Social Ethics of the University of Vienna), two very competent and internationally connected scholars. The participants have studied for at least two years at university level and some of them are involved in post-graduate academic work. Especially invited are students of law, economics, communication-sciences and politics.

For three weeks the participants of VICISU spend the whole time in Stift Altenburg, attending lectures by international scholars. The daily program combines discussions, excursions and commonly shared leisure time. Without real intention the area of the monastery is transformed into an international campus in these weeks of VICISU, at the same time attracting its daily visitors. Young women with headscarf, sometimes wearing a burka, young people sitting on the lawn smoking shisha, Arab students in traditional garments—all of this creates a breathtaking, to some extent unreal picture giving authenticity to a completely changed space. This space cannot be organized, it is a gift and opens a window to what a monastery is essentially about.

Monastery as "other space"

I would like to refer to Michel Foucault's lecture on other spaces. I can only mention the idea that there is a mutual relation between utopia and heterotopia by the mirror. It seems relevant to me that this mutual relation opens a window to come to terms with the lived space of a monastery like Altenburg. The Rule of St. Benedict tries to create a reality of life that needs constant reflection towards oneself and towards the immediate environment. But the utopia this rule gives to our daily life probably becomes very unrealistic. If the ideal is the true reality, then there are utopian expectations of people and the world as a whole. Pope Francis mentions this danger in his exhortation "Evangelii gaudium" (No. 231, 232, 233). Mirrored by Holy Scripture, guided by the Rule and its traditional understanding it is possible to explore a new space. The land that God gives us day by day is transformed into a meeting place and a promised land where human life finds its true goals.

In 2011 Stift Altenburg was awarded with the Mies-van-der-Rohe award. That ranks it under the 40 most impressive modern architectural projects in Europe. This includes all gardens, their ecology, the spatial approach to interreligious dialogue and the promotion of national and international humanitarian aid projects. All these are only instances for realizing other spaces. We try to become aware of them and to create spaces of true life on a daily basis.

Being in a different beginning

In January 2014 the monks of the convent elected a new Abbot, Thomas Renner OSB, who is skeptical of the Garden of Religions. The election is probably caused by a debate within the community about which spiritual topics the Altenburg Monastery should stand for. The election will influence its internal discourse for the next years. The Garden of Religions in Stift

Altenburg is a place full of chances. It has its history. It opens for the present. And one has to struggle for its future. This proves the Garden to be really a lived space.

Hans-Joachim Sander (Salzburg)

From Religious Space to Spaces of Religions – the 'Garden of Religions' in Stift Altenburg

A case study in the counter-conduct of a spatial political theology

The common modern expectations that religious modes of power will be put aside in public affairs have been proven wrong. There is an enchantment of the world, but this does not mean that there is no publicly present religion. Enchantment and religiosity go hand in hand in the public space. They are not building opposing camps. In the contrary, for the globalized civilization religion is one of the major public factors within migration, political unrest, cultural differences, and habits in economy. It rises where modern utopian expectations are enchanted.[1] Utopian expectations belong to modernity and nobody with a modern life style can live without them. At the same time modern people have learned to be sceptical about their ability to change the world for the better or our lives in a productive way. In earlier times people being critical towards religious truth claims were sceptical. Nowadays it is a religious advantage that people are sceptical about their own utopias. Due to the presence of this scepticism religion is an increasing important factor in the globalized world in relation to power mechanisms and for bringing in powerlessness to public discourses. It seems that secularity and religiosity are no contradiction but mutually encouraging factors.[2] Another form of public religion seems to rise. It follows a different form of grammar than the former mixture between religious and state powers. This grammar is not focussed on public affairs and it is not simply generalizing human problems towards an

1 This leads to a continuously increasing number of people being religious which is not a result of demoscopic developments, cf. Barrett/Kurian/Todd M. Johnson (2001). This survey of pure demographical data worldwide shows that all great religions are growing. The most growing religious community is Christianity. Within Christianity the charismatic sector is much more growing that the others. The fastest growing religious communities within this sector are the Pentecostal Churches and Neo-Pentecostal Churches. They very much fit to mega-cities where they constantly increase the numbers of people attending their services although they are continuously are losing heavy amount of members—but yet much less than new members their missions and missionaries bring in for joining their local communities.

2 Cf. Vanhoozer/Warner (2007). For a history of a discipline confronted with this problem cf. Blasi (2014). The current continental European situation is no exception from this combination of secularity and religion, cf. Nassehi (2008).—As *pars pro toto* for researchers still holding the opposite position that religion is decreasing in processes of individualization cf. Pollack (2014), Pollack (2012), and with a modest doubt on the thesis now: Pollack/Rosta (2015). For the debate within religious sociology cf. Gabriel/Gärtner/Pollack (2014).

acceptable political level. It finds orientation by being in touch with human affairs intensifying public problems on a precarious political ground.

In the first grammar human problems are elevated up to a sort of universal arena. In the second grammar the public meaning of political affairs is a kind of local arena for human confrontations. Here, human needs define that what is necessary for a convincing religious approach. Through the first grammar religion has to transcend the local level in order to find the right debate to open the political arena. Within the second grammar religion has to find the right space for transcending political affairs towards a local human focus.

To find this new, second sort of public religion one has to look for spaces where religiously based communities provide a space for dealing with pressing human, political, cultural and religious questions. This space may be an unspectacular place but the discourses involved here are transcending its locality towards a much larger scale which cannot exist independently from the local level. In this context even very traditional, main-stream Churches and/or religious communities which are constantly loosing influence can belong to the hot spots of public attention. This may have relations to political, cultural and religious fundamentalism, but it may also be otherwise. This is not the decisive issue. The real problem is the combination of space, society and human needs. This is an old subject because human beings in need of help have to be *somewhere* and one has to go *somewhere* to provide them with help. But this old subject can have a completely new face. One has to start with the space in order to get an idea of this new face.

My question here is if this only applies to spaces where actually suffering people are present like in the case studies of the clandestine clinic in Gothenburg or the settlement house in Copenhagen. Do these spaces of resisting hospitality depend on suffering on the ground or on a discourse coming out of suffering? I will look to this question from a Garden in a monastery. Normally a garden is not a space where people are suffering. It is a place not for urgent needs but for leisure, not a place of political confrontation but of culture, not a field of social confrontation but of spiritual empowerment. The Garden of Religions of the Benedictine monastery of Altenburg in Lower Austria located just in front of the monastery itself and open to all visitors I will refer to is filled with all these expectations and it can keep them on its ground. It provides with places for leisure, with informative introduction to truth claims of other cultures, with spiritual perspectives on Christian and non-Christian religions. Yet there is something else present in it and this is part of its special spatial character. In order to get a hold on this otherness and its productive formations I use a threefold tool as provided by theories of spatial turn. In the theory provided by Henri Lefebvre the analysis follows a triad of firstspace. secondspace and thirdspace whose logical continuation cannot be changed. In realizing what is actually there at the place one is connected with ideas, expectation, observations, concepts which are intertwined with this place and in the mutuality between these two dimensions a third factor comes in which is opening the space for the actual living world. In this analysis space itself is offered as a liquid factor for interactions etc. Space is not a container which simply holds together what happens at a place. It is a threefold factor for that what happens there.[3] We start first with observation on what is really there at this Garden.

The Garden of Religions at Stift Altenburg in Lower Austria—a firstspace exploration

In dealing with a religious space one may look to the religious community which build, owns and runs it. Such a community has to accept that its religious motivated space has an impact which cannot be stopped by the relevant actors in the field. They run it but it belongs to a much broader, even universal claim. It is built for reasons to transcend everyday life and its problems. So, a space of Religion is traditionally capable to challenge the identities of those bound to it, especially the utopian aspects in them. At the same time religious spaces are closely linked to utopian expectations by contradicting them and they are challenging them by using them to go beyond their range. Religious spaces do not encourage identities already existing but giving hints towards other, to some extent "higher" worlds. They can do that by simply introducing this otherness as having a right to be present. They simply bring that in. The Garden of Religions in the Benedictine Monastery of Altenburg does so.

It is located within an area relatively conservative religious catholic setting, Lower Austria. Altenburg is a Benedictine monastery close to the village of Horn, a small community in Lower Austria in the so called "Waldviertel", i. e. the region around Vienna towards north-west which traditionally is dominated by catholic religion.[4] The Waldviertel is in a rural area north of river Danube towards the border to Czech Republic. In the past it was a very rural, marginal territory which has been changed in the last decades into a sort

3 See Lefebvre (2010). Lefebvre's dialectics discusses three productive forms of spaces, especially of urban space—the perceived space (*'le perçu'*) of everyday social life, the conceived space (*'le conçu'*) of cartographers, urban planners, property speculators which all follow their own professional and theoretical perspectives on spaces, and finally the lived space (*'le vécu'*), which is full of surprises which are often only demonstrated by art and literature. The plot of his idea seems to me is the dialectical manner of this taxonomy which enforces a double negation of space. One has always to go through all three modes in the same logic so that the conceived space is the negation of the perceived space and the lived space is the negation of this negation. This means that the lived space has to provide access to both other spaces in a negative manner which brings in relativity to all three phases of spatial production.—Lefebvre is widely discussed in this book, especially by Kaia Schultz Rønsdal and Trygve Wyller.

4 For the monastery's history and legal status cf. Andraschek-Holzer (1994).

of business district for small but pretty successful high-tech companies. For centuries the area lived from an economy based on agricultural and vineyards. Now the Monastery introduces in its public Garden space just in front of the traditional monastic buildings four religions—Judaism, Buddhism, Hinduism and Christianity—by means of landscaping. Symbols and signs in each religion are used for landscaping. Christianity holds a place lifted higher up than the others because its site was a Calvary in the former baroque Garden at this place. By intention the monks created a space of hospitality to other religions and to people linked with those other religions and for people interested in interreligious dialogue.

The spatial production of this Garden of Religions is transforming a religiously motivated property of land within a relatively conservative religious catholic setting and it is creating a space of hospitality to other religions and to people linked with those other religions which do not belong to location and this religious move invents another form of secular presence of people on the margins of the predominant religious setting. The monastery was founded in 1144 as a donation of a local countess which created it as a cultural place for worldly and spiritual improvement of her family. In the religious war between Catholics and Protestants in the first half of the 17th century Swedish troops attacked the monastery. Turkish troops did the same in the war between the Austrian and the Osman Empire in the second half of the 17th century. After all those wars, the monastery's church was devastated.

As done in other big Benedictine monasteries in the Habsburg Empire like Melk, Göttweig, Seittenstetten, Kremsmünster of that time, Abbot Placidus Munch took the chance and completely rebuild the Church between 1730 and 1733, followed by a total reconstruction of the monastery. Since that time the monastic site has preserved its pure baroque ensemble. After World War II Russian troops used it for military purpose. Several renovations lead to a complete restauration of the original baroque stile financed by the regional government on the basis of means from the European Union. For the integral baroque stile the Stift is referred to as 'the jewel of baroque in the Waldviertel'.

Stift Altenburg is one of those few monasteries which had to provide space for the Habsburgian Emperor at any time. For that reason the monastery owns an Emperor's chamber which is, besides the Church of course, its most representative room. So, Altenburg is a 'Stift' in the strict sense of the term which means that its land is considered to be "imperial land". This gave the monastery an independent status, especially in economic matters. The local bishop had no jurisdiction above the monastery besides sacramental jurisdiction in relation to ordination of priests and other internal spiritual matters. On the other hand the Emperor in Vienna had a direct access to everything within the monastic community.

Since Austria has entered the European Union in 1995, means for rebuilding and renovation became pretty affluent. For that reason the monastery holds close ties to the regional Government of Lower Austria in St. Pölten. When a big flood ended in late August 2002 in the area which was a national disaster, the regional government in St. Pölten financed innovative reconstruction activities. This had to be done quickly in order to prevent people from resettling elsewhere. On the other hand they needed projects representing a different but hopeful future. So for getting the aid, one had to create something innovative. The younger monks of the monastery took the chance and brought forward their project to commemorate Vatican II's different approach towards religions. This was offered as the project of the Stift for reconstructing after the flood. So, the political agenda to regain ground in a heavily damaged area and the religious agenda to create space for other religions within a region once completely dominated by Catholicism made an innovative joint venture. All of a sudden, the new habit of the Church towards other religions could be presented as a profane agenda to encourage a different economic and cultural future of a damaged region.

In a Stift the political and the religious have always found a special form of melange and it is no exception if the political has the major gravitation on matters of the monastery. This is an important tradition which applies to the Garden of Religions. It may even be the very reason that is was built. Even for a monastery such a Garden is still a pretty unusual ecclesial spatial activity. If they wish, the Benedictines of the monastery could claim a copyright for the idea. There are all sorts of gardens within representative compounds of the Catholic Church, but their Garden of Religion is unique in the Catholic world. Slowly, but continuously they find followers.[5]

The secular need and the religious option fit almost perfectly together in this Garden. In the new doctrine of the Catholic Church towards other religions is stated that the Church would nothing negate which is true and holy in other religions.[6] That what is true and holy within religions was considered in the reconstructing project as a secular help for healing a heavily damaged area. A doctrine meant to be a purely internal religious affair created innovative space for a truly secular approach. Now in Altenburg this doctrine made space in a mode which demonstrates the new agenda between secularity and religiosity in the epoch of Public Religion. By providing space for a *topos* which is meant to create an innovative place for an important secular turnaround this Garden of Religions has a heterotopic grammar on a basic level. It confronts with a meaning of religious doctrine which is not seen before and it offers a space for secular reasoning which was not thought of before. This Garden is a sort of 'place of fullness' the secular age is longing for as experiencing authenticity. It is not realized by people as a specific place of a

5 For details, cf. the presentation of the Garden by Pater Hüttl in this book. Meanwhile there are some other Gardens of Religion, e.g. the Garden of Religion by "In Via" in the City of Cologne (cf. www.garten-der-religionen-koeln.de).

6 This is the position of Vatican II in its "Declaration on the Relation of the Church to Non-Christian Religions *Nostra Aetate* ", article no. 2.

church.[7] I would prefer to speak of a 'heterotopic grammar' in this combination of religiosity and secularity since in the beginning of the project this Garden still had to proof that it is a heterotopia.

The Garden of Religions was created in the first place as a religious space for a monastery which itself is already a religious place. At the same time it brings forward new discourses within the Convent and the Catholic Church as a whole and it opens the region for different aspects of a new, globalized civilisation which fit to their economic hopes for the future. So, in the firstspace it is a religious place representing a religious space and a secular space representing a secular perspective on the ground. At the same time the Garden creates a space of religion, for religious ideas and by religious activities and a secular space, making visible different aspects of modern, globalized life relevant in a global economy the region wants to expand into. So, this spatial innovation has a political impact on the spiritual side of Garden and it has a theological impact on the social awareness of the region. What is it what we see here: A contested space created by religion in society?[8] Or is it a forum for late modern pastoral power, or an urban hospitality in the middle of a rural landscape?

A triangle of religion, faith and spirituality—the Garden of Religions' secondspace

The Stift Altenburg is an impressive religious building with a political design. It is a monastery demonstrating the close ties between Church and State, Convent and Emperor, Christian Faith and the catholic ruler directly chosen by God. Nowadays these are *tempi passati.* Yet in Austria, old imperial places still have a common authority. The close and friendly relations of the Benedictine convent with the regional government are transforming the old Habsburgian coalition between State and Church into the current democratic context.

As imperial landmark, the Stift is a place for the combination of power and truth. It has to present catholic faith claiming to be the backbone of a Christian society. At the same time it is a monastery, i.e. it is a place providing spirituality. People living there, i.e. the monks, are willing to be constantly confronted with transcendence and fundamental questions of life and death by liturgy, prayer, personal worshipping. This spirituality is not in tension with the power claims of the buildings or the truth claims of the faith. In the contrary, this spirituality is celebrated by the buildings and they are demonstrating its truth. It is a spirituality ruled by religious power claims

7 See Taylor (2007). See also Taylor/Casanova/McLean (2012).

8 Knott (2013), Knott (2009), Vásquez/Knott (2014). See also Post (2014).

and faithful truth claims. Political influence is within the range of the goals of the claims.

But by their Garden the monks of the monastery provide a place for a different mode of spirituality and in consequence they aim at another mode of political power. This mode is not part of their traditional spirituality holding space for an Emperor and it is not reaching out for their Church's advantage in politics. It is a spirituality which invites other religious spiritualities in tension to the traditional one. Other religions and other spiritualities have a space provided by the religious hospitality of the Monastery. The monks caring for hospitality are not looking for power mechanism in favour of their own spirituality and they do not dispute the truth claims being different from those of their Christian faith. They simply give way to different views about God, the Spirit, the World, Nothingness, sacrifice. In this sense the spirituality of their Garden is opting for a mutual relationship between the freedom of religion and truth claims of faith.

One may even say that their faith shaped by Vatican II provides the freedom for other spiritualities and they hope that these other spiritual traditions can take ground in the place they provide for them. In any case they relativize the power claims of their own religion. Their Garden is a spiritual counterpart of the traditional combination of power and truth, faith and religion for which this monastery once was built. In this respect it provides a space with an alternative order of things for the monastery and for the Benediction order. For the traditional combination of religion and faith this Garden is a heterotopos within the Church in relation to its religious power claims and faithful truth claims.

Here, one can see how religiously based activities are factors for alternative social productions of space.[9] Only activities being close and being distant to utopias at the same time are capable to produce such spaces. It is necessary for the topology of these spaces that they are linked to expectations within a utopian range. But at the same time it is also necessary to be very close to realities which cause deep scepticism about the truth claims of utopias. For that reason there are several possibilities to what sort of space these activities can be related to. Some of them are related to utopias, some to heterotopias and sometimes utopian activities are turning into heterotopias if a precarious reality comes up. This means that it is not sufficient to look into the activity in order to decide what sort of alternative is created here. It depends on the space in combination with the activity. Utopias tend to lure hospitality into activities leaving the reality on the ground behind. Heterotopias can be detected if activities are at the same time willing to challenge the overall situation but they cannot leave the space although it is challenging the activity itself. The

9 Spaces are not simply a presence of localities. They do result from formal and informal social activities and they are internal factors within these activities. In this sense they are productive by themselves. See Lefebvre (2010).

empowerment of the challenge and the powerlessness of a possible false perspective go hand in hand. At heterotopias the religious motivation cannot allow that activities are turning counter-productive but that they are counter-conductive. Here, being powerless is turned into a source of energy for empowerment of others and those running this place.

How can one realize this shift? Is there a sort of breaking point of utopias into heterotopias based on religious convictions? What happens if a religious motivated hospitality is confronted with a space pushing them beyond their own borders? This problem leads to a complicated grammar in religiously based spatial activities. It is not enough to simply see them as simple religious phenomena. It is more complicated. For analysing this grammar I propose a triangle active in such religious realities—a triangle out of religion, faith and spirituality. This triangle provides a contested space.

To some extent these three realities are more or less the same. All three are linked to religion as social phenomenon. So, for religious sociology it doesn't matter if it is religion, faith or spirituality as long as it produces socially embedded communication, social relations, habits of distinction etc. But at the same time these three concepts are related to different aspects of activity. *Religion* is dealing with society—at least in modern times -, *faith* i. e. believe-systems producing and reproducing transcendental issues, is related to a community and issues values and truth claims and *spirituality* is linked to individual human beings personally involved into spiritual activities. So, to some extent religion, faith and spirituality are different and different factors for a social production of space. In relation to space one should be able to identify these differences if religion, faith or spirituality is involved in this space. And then, one can see why such a space becomes contested. The reason for that is the inner tension within this triangle.

It is relatively easy to combine two of the three angles. Yet the third one will oppose, contradict or resist this combination. This becomes even obvious if one relates to each angle specific claims and tactics. One can say that religion is usually inclined to claims of power, faith to claims of truth and spirituality to claims of freedom. The combination of power and truth is pretty common within religious communities, as the combination of freedom and truth and as the combination of freedom with power. One may even link that to big religious communities within Christianity. Catholicism is traditionally tuned to powerful religion imposing faith with a lot of truth claims. Protestantism prefers faith in Scripture with a spirituality opting for the free subject in front of God. And the Pentecostal Churches which are very successful nowadays in big cities all over the world, love to bring spirituality free of conventions in contact with a strict disciplinary religious regime, i. e. powerful religion strengthening spiritual freedom.

This becomes even more obvious if one relates to religion as some kind of power-quest, to faith truth-claim, and to spirituality freedom-claim. The combination of power and truth is pretty common within religious communities. More or less all big religious communities are active in political, economic and cultural matters and they try to shape morality, laws or at least habits to their advantage by claiming that they stand for truth in all these matters. A highly secular organized society is more open to this combination. Here, such claims are accepted on the basis of religious freedom as a human right. Especially Catholicism has always been very eager to combine power and truth for its activities in society. And through all ecclesial history, mysticism had a critical stand towards the Church. People claiming their right of an original spirituality like Meister Eckhart, Mechthild from Magdeburg, Theresa d'Avila, John of the Cross, Thomas Merton or Ernesto Cardenal run into trouble with the official Church.[10] But a religion claiming power and influence has to create impressive places where this agenda can easily been seen and even felt. Church buildings, places of pilgrimage, art of high quality, liturgies with all sort of symbolic capital can create such places.

Like most of institutionalized religion the official Church tried since late Antiquity to build places demonstrating their claim for power and authority like Constantin's cathedrals in Rom, Jerusalem and Bethlehem, the Hagia Sophia in Constantinople, St. Peter in Renaissance Rome, the Prussian Dom in Berlin and the big Churches in Scandinavia with a self-definition of being a Cathedral. They all have the same powerful implications. Buildings representing power can very well be combined with truths one is claiming for or within a society. For impressive religious buildings this is a *condition sine qua non.* They demonstrate the one and true God, the Almighty, and his presence within a Church. They demonstrate who is sovereign in a territory. They can even demonstrate who is capable to rule directly in the line of God's will. The most prominent example for that is St. Peter. Its construction triggers the Reformation because the popes couldn't finance it without selling indulgences.

Religion and politics, Church and State, spirituality and secularity are in a relation which obviously cannot be broken and which is unavoidable in the space of such buildings. So, the space brings them together and keeps them apart at the same time. For that reason, space is a sort of third agent in their mutuality. In it, a special political theology comes up—a political theology of a space representing spirituality which is not holding together religion and society, faith and community, Church and state but being a critical factor against their utopias. In this case, this spiritually creates a heterotopos. Spirituality does not always create a heterotopos but in this constellation it does.

The normal political theology of a monastery like Stift Altenburg is bound to a space which empowers the relationship of religion and faith. But spaces can also be activated in this third, heterotopian matter. Then another political theology enters the scene—a critical political theology towards politics and

10 Cf. Keul (2004) for the female mystic of the Middle Ages.

religion at the same time. But this spatial dimension is hidden behind the political and the religious utopias. It must be activated as soon as the space for the alternative spirituality is endangered.

The struggle about the Stupa of Gföhl—a thirdspace experience with the Garden of Religions

In 2011 a Vienna based organisation working with ideas close to Buddhism proposed to build a Stupa near a small village in Lower Austria called Gföhl. The stupa should be a landmark, symbolizing peace and a Buddhist centre should be built nearby the Stupa. The area near Gföhl and the village itself is a traditional catholic place. The organisation couldn't bring forward a clear argument why this Stupa should have been built at the vicinity of this village. Yet, the village's mayor was in favour of the plan. He wanted to have it in the village because he was hoping for major amounts of people coming for visiting the landmark. He was looking to improve the job opportunities in relation to the planned centre. To some extent, this Stupa would have fit into the new economy of the region looking to come in touch with global markets. It would have been a religious symbol for that.

Yet in the region, a lot of people, organisations and groups located at the right side of the political spectrum were opposing the project. Especially Ewald Stadler, a former politician from the FPÖ (Freiheitliche Partei Österreichs), which is the rightwing party in Austria, was standing at the front.[11] He said publicly that as a catholic he would not be willing to accept that in Lower Austria idolatry and blasphemy would be allowed to find ground. At that time Stadler was member of the European Parliament and at the same time he was facing a bunch of corruption challenges. In several campaigns within the last years the FPÖ had some very visible slogans using Christian faith-claims in order to attack people migrating to Austria as people not belonging here. In the last campaign at the national level they had a slogan: "Love your neighbour as yourself—and for us these are first and foremost our fellow Austrians". The party got more than 20 % of the vote in the last election.

11 Until 2014 Ewald Stadler was member of the European Party. In 2006, he was the opponent of the now leading figure of this right-wing party, Heinz-Christian Strache, and he lost the fight. Since that time he changed parties several time. In June 2014 he was indicted for a serious case of coercion to 14 month in prison. The verdict was reduced to 12 month in October 2015. In August 2014 Stadler joined a pro-russian group of self-declared observers for the referendum by which the Crimea-Peninsula voted to become part of the Russian Federation. In Octobre 2014, he became the agent in law matters for the Vienna part of the so called 'PEGIDA'-Movement ('Patriotische Europäer gegen die Islamisierung des Abendlandes'—Patriots of Europe against the growing influence of Islam in Occident), which has been organizing demonstrations every Monday in Dresden on the basis of a nationalistic German ideology.

At that point the abbot of Stift Altenburg gave an interview and held townhall meetings arguing that the Buddhist community had a right to propose such a project and that Christian faith and Catholic doctrine are in favour of the visibility of other religions in modern societies. He argued that beyond the question if this Stupa would fit to Gföhl, religious freedom and interreligious dialogue are major achievements for the internal peace of a modern society and that catholic Christians should be on the side of this dialogue and that freedom. One of the arguments Abbot Haidinger brought forward was Vatican II's doctrine on other religions, i. e. the ecclesial basis for the Garden of Religions in his monastery. This interview had a broad public attention and it made its impact in the heated debate. Finally, the 'Gemeinderat' (local parliament) decided to hold an election in the village about the Stupa. At the end about a third voted in favour of the Stupa which was of course not enough. So, it was not built.

Beyond this religious-political issue the spatial dimensions of this debate are interesting. It makes a big difference if plurality simply is a historical option, present in the time-line but existing somewhere else, or if this plurality actually takes place in an area of pretty homogeneous religious identity. A Buddhist Stupa being three storeys tall is not only a landmark, not only a confrontation with a different culture but firstly a visible symbol of the fact that times significantly have changed. The people in Lower Austria know for long that other cultures are present in Austrian but their actual presence, even if it is only a proposal for a religious building, destroys the ruling utopia that the others might be present in Vienna but not on this area. This becomes an even more urgent matter if a representative of a Monastery like Abbot Haidinger openly takes a stand in favour of this other religion and its right to look for a space. Then the question of hospitality is confronting with the relativity of one's own social order, political options and religious convictions. This relativity is a hot issue. It gives a feeling of powerlessness. Then one has to decide between two habits: to accept hospitality towards these others because powerlessness is a common ground, or to react with resentment because the visible presence of others confronts with one's own weakness.

In the context of the contested religious space in Gföhl the Garden of Religions was transformed from a visible presence of a doctrinal shift within the Catholic Church towards a heterotopos for deciding if one follows spiritual hospitality or sticks to political resentment. The convent didn't build it to create this sort of other space and certainly not to turn it into a contested space. But the monastery couldn't remain silent in the heated debate over the Stupa of Gföhl. They had to take a stand or their own religious place even if it would turn their place into a contested space in order to remain faithful to their own spiritual hospitality. So, their own Garden is not only a religious sign for them but at the same time a political confrontation. The Garden gives way to spiritual challenges they cannot avoid to be in touch with as a religious community.

Abbot Haidinger's argumentation is a decision for solidarity with those being attacked by unjust activities. There is not only spatial justice involved here but a sort of "spatial solidarity". One can sum up that spatial justice combined with religious perspectives is a social production of spatial solidarity. This is the social impact of religiously based hospitality. The Garden was transformed into a public space being relevant within a public debate on political and religious matters. It provided with a locus for arguments claiming truth towards a religious plurality which is a fact in a globalized society even in a still mostly rural area like Lower Austria. This approach has in itself a political perspective. It provides other religions a space of hospitality where they can live and flourish if they wish to do so. This reveals elements of a political theology which is of another sort than the usual ones.

Creating a spatial political theology beyond universal claims

People being at the margins of society have to live with a social hardship of places considered to be a-normal. They cannot avoid being bound to them since they have no alternative. The normal places look to them as unpleasant persons, dangerous figures and an economic burden and they are kept out of such places. The a-normality of spaces which remain for them is a political problem which is not resolved in late-modern capitalist societies and very often the political will is lacking to search for the best option to solve it. Usually one tries to avoid making a hot issue out of such spaces. One tries to control them but not to solve them. Yet, the problems of human dignity are present there and this creates space for other activities to look after them. Religious activities very often start at this point and one expects that religiously bound people are willing to act there with such intentions. One may even say that religious communities have traditionally placed themselves to such spaces. In modern societies this leads to a semi-political nature of their religious activities, and/or it leads to the semi-religious nature of the problem of social marginality present there.[12]

The spatial dimension of this Garden is part of that but at the same time it is different to usual religious-political constellations in two respects. It is neither a declaration for a political alternative to religious normality nor a spiritual intensification beyond political normality. I begin with the first difference. Normally in a modern open society religions and representatives of religious

12 For instance Johann Hinrich Wichern (1808–1881) and his "Rauhe Haus" in the city of Hamburg, or Adolf Kolping (1813–1865) and his movement, which started in Cologne, for running houses for apprentices having no family place, or Friedrich von Bodelschwingh (1831–1910) and his foundation in Bethel for disabled persons. They represent the social wing of powerful religious communities and all three had to resolve the problem how politically powerful they interact with society on behalf of powerless persons.

communities belong to the ruling order of society. Sometimes they are even the stronghold for it. They do not become 'a-normal' people or religions by having close contact to marginalized people in need of help for keeping a human decency.

When such religious groups belong to the fundamentalist branch of the religious business or when they belong to violent subcultures of religious communities they are not belonging to the territory of social normality. In such cases the spaces created by religious activities do not belong to others but they belong to their own a-normality. At these spaces completely different rules are in place which have to be contradicted by the normal order and which are to some extent created to stand in opposition to society. For such communities this contradiction is a major advantage to create a political tension for proving that they themselves are in possession of a higher calling of whatever sort und this calling is the backbone for what they want to achieve in political terms by their own religious activities. So, their political theology has a universal claim of power overruling the law of an open society. Their spaces are special cases of religious territory which do not belong to the focus of this book. Here, the normality of religious presence in society is the starting point. The religious motivation of a Monastery to build a Garden of Religion is part of normal religious activities although it is above the normality. This position can be challenged by a fundamentalist calling which wants to trigger an alternative political order on the basis of a higher calling. The debates around the Stupa of Gföhl brought that forward. Then, all of a sudden, the normal religious activities which created this Garden reveal themselves as a place where alternative visions of the public order enter the scene. They do not fit into the ruling order of things.

At the same time this revelation lives from a second difference to a universal vision how public things should be, this time a spiritual one. Due to religious freedom a modern society cannot deny 'normal' religious communities to get in contact to people living at the margins of society and to provide them with help for a decent human living. In the contrary, in times of trouble and of vagueness for the traditional social welfare state the relation between a-normal people and normal religious activities are very welcomed. It is considered to be an advantage for both sides—a social advantage for the people living on the margins and a spiritual advantage for the religious people providing hospital care for them. This sort of secular political spirituality is not the focus of the Altenburg Garden. It is not a place linked to human a-normality out of a vision of universal human claims. It brings forward a political universality of a spiritual tradition which is not coming from above and claiming to be important for people living at the margins. The Garden's political spirituality is coming from below, from the ground so to speak, because it provides space for others who are anormal people but who are not claiming to get this space. They are invited because of their tradition, i. e. because they have something to offer which is missing in the usual ordering of things. It is their political marginality which gives them a special authority in spiritual matters. The Garden gives way to that. And this changes its own picture of universality completely. It loses its authoritarian character which is unavoidable in the monastery which is a Stift, i. e. having extraordinary close ties to the ruling mode of things.

Looking into both differences one may raise these issues: What if an anormality becomes an anti-universal clue to the spatial character of normal religious activities? What if the place's a-normal spirituality points towards the anormality of a society which is in need of such places but which is neither willing nor capable to organize them? What if the political anormality of such places can only be pushed by staying away from universal claims? What if these places have to get rid of universal claims in order to create anormal religious activities?

These questions deal with three realities which are present in the usual secular and the usual religiously motivated political theology: society and its deficits, religious motivations and their political impact and marginalized people bound to spaces they cannot avoid to deal with. But here, this triangle of society, marginalized people and religious motivations is creating a different arena. It creates a space which has to speak for itself.

As soon as a mutual relation between two angles of society, religious motivation and marginalized people is set up empowering the same two angles the third angle creates a denial, a contradiction or at least a tension relativizing the mutual acceptance of the other two. So, this triangle is similar to that of religion, faith and spirituality mentioned above. It combines experiences of powerlessness (marginalized people and marginalized spiritualities), fragile truth claims (the religious motivation of a monastery in favour of alternative ecclesial order) and the fragile reality of social order (its social deficits and vagueness towards social and religious plurality). It is possible to enter the problem at all three angles.

The project of the Garden of Religions starts with the religious angle and it combines it with society. The territory owned by an old and very traditional monastery of Benedictines is used in an a-normal habit. It is dedicated to religious plurality present in a society in the context of a globalized civilisation although the Monastery has to stand traditionally for a homogeneous religious character.

At first hand the Garden looks like a pure internal religious affair without political implications or secular intentions. A convent of a monastery has decided to open its spirituality to the question how to deal with religious plurality and how to pay respect to other faiths and religious values. It looks as if no social and no political confrontation is involved. This picture changes if one looks to which combination is left behind. And then, one can understand why the Monastery had to take a stand in the local debate about the Stupa in Gföhl.

This Garden is leaving behind a local religious utopia, which is the catholic homogeneity of the region. To some extent it is even destroying a broader political utopia, the cultural homogeneity of a region. In this Monastery one can no longer believe that there is only one true religion and this religion is the monks' faith. And it doesn't stop there. In the area where the monastery is located, Lower Austria, one can no longer believe that this region is a homogeneous social environment where more or less all people are catholic and that this homogeneity is the best of all possible worlds. A deep cultural transformation has taken place and the monastic locus of the Garden is a mirror of it.

This reveals a common character of places related to marginalized people run by religious belief-systems or at least by religiously motivated convictions. They go beyond an order which once was ruling in the area and which had a power to define normality. At the same time these places are still to some extent part of that order and very often they are even a result of it. As soon as these places are made capable to reach beyond borders which were once very fixed, a new type of public religion within secular contexts comes forward. It is a spatial public religion providing places which represent alternative political and religious ordering *by themselves*. It is not the marginalized people which represent this alternative and it is not the different political or religious vision representing that, it is the place which is bringing in the alternative. Realities of marginalized people, their urgent problems, their open questions, and their unresolved confrontations become a discourse here and nobody involved in these places can avoid to be related to them. Any idea of homogeneity of social life is shaken which usually is the case where this combination of religion and politics enters the field. Something different comes in and it has a grave impact. It is the real space in question.[13]

Spaces, especially those representing a contested space like the Altenburg Garden, are socially produced independently of those who live within it and this production cannot be contained to this specific place. It is Henri Lefebvre's major achievement, that the production of space he discovered, is taken place at first by the space and only secondly by those using this space. For that reason, one can open the space up to Lefebvre's already mentioned threefold analysis of firstspace, secondspace and thirdspace.[14] In all three dimensions the relation between the political and the spiritual has to find its balance, as I tried to show above in the case of the Altenburg Garden.

A contested space like that has its own power-range which can be activated in special circumstances as in the debate around the Stupa of Gföhl. Something which one does not see or can easily speak of enters the field if a person, a community or a society becomes aware that such a place does not fit to the normal order since but can provide an arena to get connected to alternative

13 This is starting already in earlier times in modernity as could be seen in the affair Calas in Toulouse in 1762. Cf. Hunt (2007), 70–112.

14 See footnote 7.

visions of political, religious, cultural order. This is possible because such a place is related to ideas which confront with realities contradicting this order or even overruling its normality. This does not apply to all spaces but to spaces where utopian expectations have been proven to be wrong and where they are relativized on a large scale. For that reason one can apply Michel Foucault's discourse on heterotopias to a space like the Altenburg Garden.[15]

One can look to heterotopias as a narrative about alternative visions of normality. Then they mark longings for a different world. This longing is close to utopias which are more outspoken and intellectual alternatives than other places. Then, utopias are a sort of intensified intellectual longing for a better world whereas other places look for the same more down to earth but they still are shaped by people longing for utopias like in the cases of ships full of migrants, first-night-bedrooms for couples just married or graveyard as story-telling for a *memento mori.* Then heterotopias can grow into utopias and utopias can be downsized to heterotopias. Then, the Garden of Religion would be a sort of Gulliver's World for interreligious dialogue.

But one can also look to heterotopias as a category about the vast difference of longings for a better world and confrontations with harsh social, political, cultural, economic and religious realities. One can discover at heterotopias like the one just mentioned where utopias break when people have to realize that they cannot get out of realities as they exist now and here. Then, analytical strength of the category comes forward where utopias are confronted with realities demonstrating that their disciplinary power cannot solve any problem. For that reason non-utopian, heterotopian spaces, always combined to surprising and confronting experiences can be present in all sorts of spaces where utopias are contradicted and where discourses on other orders of things are enforced. One can assume that in contested spaces usually heterotopias make the difference. Their otherness in socially produced spaces contrast the disciplinary regimes, bringing forward its borders and open the eyes for surprises enforce to those which are confronted with the otherness of these spaces.

I prefer this second approach to Foucault's idea of heterotopias. In looking to the power quest one can see what this idea as an analytical category brings to light. Utopian social spaces are almost by necessity bound to some sort of homogeneity which means that they encourage already existing ideas to go beyond places which are full of a precarious plurality. As soon as this homogeneity is challenged the relevant utopia bound to it is challenged as well and it has to create a disciplinary power in favour of homogeneity. For that reason, other spaces are not only challenging utopias because such other spaces demonstrate that there is another order of things behind the relevant place but they are challenging the disciplinary power as well. The challenging aspect lies in the spatial nature of other places. Without this spatialisation of

15 Michel Foucault (2003) and Foucault (1994).

time other places would simply be longings for dreams not yet fulfilled. But at other places one is confronted with spatial realities which bring forward that nightmares are dreams as well but ones which contradict expectations for a better form of life.

This means that it is important to look into the reality of the place in heterotopias whereas in utopias it is much easier—and even necessary—to ignore the spatial dimension. It is no argument against utopias if there is no chance to find its spatial reality. But it is always possible to argue against the importance of heterotopias if one ignores their spatial realities.

One can see that in a triangle out of: society and its deficits, religious motivations and their political impact, marginalized people and the disciplinary places they are bound to. One can easily find utopian expectations being present in all three angles. As soon as one combines two angles, these expectations can even grow. They can even beyond the utopias linked to one of the two angles. Then, e. g. marginalized people can even be more disciplined by places they are bound to if one wants to solve the deficits of a society. The discipline grows into a regime full of biopower. But then, the last angle stands in contrast to that and it brings a heavy tension to that utopian duopoly. But the condition for this resisting power is that it is linked to a real place. Without that there will be no resistance but simply an alternative idea taken for granted.

For that reason I want to argue that Religious motivation can foster and express strict opposition to disciplinary biopower coming out of a combination of social deficits and awareness of marginalized people as soon as this religious motivation can present a real place where marginalized people are linked to the social deficits. In these spatial cases where the duopoly combines religious motivation and marginalized people the deficits in social life relativize all efforts in it. And for a coalition of social deficits and religious motivation marginalized people resist the heavy disciplinary power which comes out of it. In this book we have examples for such constellations.

The Altenburg Garden is a combination of religious motivation and marginalized people. Its importance lies in the spatial nature of its spirituality linked to events in present times. The religious motivation is not simply ideally present in it—it is put into the ground and this gives a social gravitation one cannot ignore easily. They are not marginalized within the social welfare state but they are marginalized in cultural terms as the dispute about the Stupa demonstrated. As soon as the spaces of marginalized people are combined with society or with religious motivation another grammar applies to them. It becomes a counter-power demonstrating that there are social deficits which ought to be overcome. They do not allow escaping into a social, political or religious nowhere. Another approach has to be found.

The Garden as impossible space for Christian pastorate

At this point the problem of pastoral power comes into the picture.[16] This is an almost inevitable if social, religious, cultural, political deficits become obvious and religiously motivated people create a contested space to overcome them. The Altenburg Garden's involvement in the Stupa-debate demonstrates that. It is a form of pastorate to take care of other's people spiritual projects in the political sphere. One cannot restrict such an involvement. Pastoral power is a principle affair which starts in local constellations. It has a disciplinary aspect on the one side, but it can evolve into a resisting power, or to be precise: into a counter-conduct.[17]

16 For the notion of pastoral power cf. Foucault (2009), lectures five until nine.—For Foucault's interpretations of traditional power struggles in politics and society cf. Hoffman (2013).

17 For that concept cf. Foucault (2007), lecture eight. Foucault brings forward five forms of such resisting practices (ascetic practices, egalitarian religious communities, mystic, adoring a Holy Scripture, eschatology) which are neither a revolt nor a revolution but a practice to improve the dominating order of things in terms of a higher goal. Counter-conductive practices want to improve a situation in relation to a higher goal. For that reason pastoral power is always explicitly or implicitly involved to such practices: "The fundamental elements of the counter-conduct analyzed by Foucault are not absolutely external to the conduct imposed by Christian pastoral power." (Davidson, 2011: 3) In the German edition of that lecture series (Foucault 2004) a pretty important part of the idea is mentioned which Foucault didn't present at the ninth lecture on 8 March, 1978 but which was obviously part of the prepared manuscript. There Foucault reflects on the improvement dimension of counter-conductive practices: "Auf der Tatsache bestehen, daß diese Gegen-Verhaltensformen nicht zum Ziel hatten: wie man sich allgemein des Pastorats, jeglichen Pastorats entledigt, sondern eher: wie man von einem besseren Pastorat profitiert, wie man besser geführt wird, sicherer erlöst, den Gehorsam besser aufrechterhält, der Wahrheit näher kommt." (Foucault 2004, p. 337, footnote *) Such a practice is not imposing a difference to what it resists but another series of developments which is necessary and urgent but not present. It is not dissenting but reforming. A major aspect of this reforming attitude is the modern subject: "Der abendländische Mensch ist in dem Maße durch das Pastoral hindurch individualisiert, wie das Pastorat ihn zu seinem Heil leitet, das seine Identität für die Ewigkeit fixiert, wie das Pastorat ihn einem Geflecht uneingeschränkter Gehorsamsleistungen unterwirft, wie es ihm die Wahrheit eines Dogmas in eben dem Moment einschärft, in dem es ihm das Geheimnis seiner inneren Wahrheit abnötigt. Identität, Unterwerferung, Inferiorität: die Individualisierung des abendländischen Menschen hat sich während des langen Jahrtausends des christlichen Pastorats um den Preis der Subjektivität vollzogen. Durch Subjektivierung. Man muß Subjekt werden, um Individuum zu werden (alle Bedeutungen des Wortes 'Subjekt'). Nun, in eben dem Maße, wie das Pastorat Faktor und Agens von Individualisierung war, setzte es ein ungeheures Zeichen, eine Pastoratsbegehrlichkeit [*einige unlesbare Worte*]: wie Subjekt werden, ohne unterworfen zu werden? Überwältigendes Verlangen nach Individualität, lange vor dem bürgerlichen Bewußtsein, das zudem das Christentum dem Buddhismus (Fehlen des Pastorats/der Mystik [*ein unlesbares Wort*], Entindividualisierung) radikal entgegensetzt. Die große Krise des Pastorats und die Angriffe der Gegen-Verhaltensformen, die diese Krise beschleunigt haben, führen nicht zu einer pauschalen Verwerfung jeglicher Verhaltensführung, sondern zu einem übertragenen Verlangen nach Führung, wie es sich und wo es sich gehört." (ibid.) In the next lecture series in 1978–1979 Foucault could even refer to neoliberal economics as such a sort of counter-conduct which wants

In such cases as the internal relation of the Altenburg-Garden and the Stupa-Affair it is inevitable that the people backing the Garden cannot avoid accepting giving hospitality of any kind for people bound to such contested places like the Stupa without having a mandate to speak for the people bound to it. The fact that they take care looks like dissolution of subjects in favour of other interests of power. They are suspected to create this sort of implicit power by providing help for marginalized people. Then, their *pastorate* looks like a disciplinary mechanism in favour of Christian churches which create a power generator for their political and economic interest within larger communities and they use such an affair like the Stupa-debate.[18]

But in bringing the picture into a broader scale it changes completely. The pastorat is not simply about control but of being responsible for others one is in control of. One has to explain oneself towards a higher power, i. e. God in the Christian way of pastoral power. So, there are three parts of it—the people one is in pastoral charge of, oneself and God. And the pastors are not simply the prolonged arm of God, they have to find what is best for them and for God at the same time—and they do not know it in both cases. That is, why the simple solution of controlling people by stricter discipline does not work in this constellation. The people which control pastoral power—which 'are in pastoral power' so to speak—cannot do that simply by controlling people. They have to take care not only for all but for anyone they are in charge of. Foucault called that "omnes et singulatim".[19] People actively involved into a pastorat have to find a solution for a contradiction, at least if one looks to the problem only from the people involved. As soon as somebody in charge of pastoral power is looking to a single person he or she loses the others, and vice versa. You cannot do it right without doing something wrong at the other side. For that reason the sort of power one gets in touch with by pastoral power is powerlessness. One can find it in Jesus's narrative about the lost sheep (Lk 15,3–7). There is no way for the good shepherd not to go after the lost sheep, although then, he leaves the other sheep completely on their own. But the one which is lost is more important than the 99 which stand to normality. To get the problem right one should look to the place mentioned here. The project to

to improve a given situation by a subjecting all ruling practices under the higher goal of the free economic subject: "Mit anderen Worten, im klassischen Liberalismus verlangte man von der Regierung, die Form des Marktes zu achten und die Marktteilnehmer handeln zu lassen. Hier kehrt man nun das Laissez-faire in eine Beschränkung des Regierungshandelns um, und zwar im Namen eines Marktgesetzes, das ermöglicht, jede Regierungshandlung einzuschätzen und zu bewerten. Das Laissez-faire wird somit umgekehrt und der Markt ist nichtmehr ein Prinzip der Selbstbeschränkung der Regierung, sondern ein Prinzip, das man nun gegen sie wendet. Er ist eine Art von ständigem ökonomischen Tribunal gegenüber der Regierung." (Foucault 2006, 342) Neoliberal counter-conduct does not create a free space for economical enterprises against the State but an improvement of governementality by creating an overarching space through economic rationality. It is a sort of secularized pastoral power.

18 For this interpretation cf. Steinkamp (2005). No places of this power are discussed.

19 Foucault (1981).

combine 'omnes et singulatim' is situated in the wilderness, which is a dangerous place for sheep and their shepherd. This wilderness is a heterotopos which implies that one has to go over the normal rule for solving the problem: the one lost sheep is for now more important than the other. The shepherd leaves the ninety-nine behind to go for the one. So, he dismisses the danger for the majority in favour for the wellbeing of the one. And then, if the one is found, the joy is greater than about the normality to keep the majority together.

This applies to all pastoral power. It cannot rule by normality, it is bound to realities which need the extraordinary action. One has to go beyond the ordinary to find a solution for pastoral power. If such a place becomes a factor in ruling with pastoral power, the 'ruling' changes into something which seems to be impossible. It is not simply to imply 'ordinary' discipline but to find a sort of extraordinary practice which fits for the special place where the contestation is present. Under normal control, the pastorate will always fall apart.

The Altenburg Garden is such an extraordinary place since it had to be combined with a contested Stupa. This Garden implies to take care for other religions which have no place in a traditional monastery. In giving them a place the monks have to change their normal ordering within the public sphere and this change implies a different sort of discipline for themselves. First and foremost they have to find a disciplinary regime for themselves which suits to the place where they cannot succeed with their pastoral power as in the case of the Stupa-dispute. Pastoral power linked to other places is breaking unavoidably the universality of a normal order. For that reason the places where one finds pastoral power turn out to be a counter-power towards the ruling normality. They are first and foremost precarious for those in control of them. Implicitly the marginalized people which are given a place in a context of pastoral power have more control over the people in charge of it than those controlling the pastorate. This precarious rule can be observed in spaces where religiously motivated people are dealing with problems a society has left undone and with people depending on solving them. Such spaces are socially produced and they are filled with all sorts of surprises—bad ones and good ones—which shake the ruling order of a society. And it is the place implying this alternative to the people running it because it forces them to go beyond normality. This going 'beyond' is not pointing towards an utopos. It is connecting to a negative insight: The place the monks control, i.e. their Garden, is not implying where to go but it is demonstrating where they should not go. Their Garden of Religion does not say how to create a harmonious order between the major religious communities on Earth. It is simply a Garden in a monastery. But it demonstrates where there will be no solution for the interreligious problem if they do reject to stand for plurality in the social and political world around them.

This turns their Garden into another place than a usual monastic garden.

This turn adds social creativity to the powerlessness of a contested religious space and for that reason the pastoral power of such a place is resisting ruling power mechanisms in the social field. By their Garden the monks are pushed into a counter-conduct in the social field which raises their spiritual agenda in public.

This goes beyond a typical modern theological perspective which has been developed to deal with the contradiction of religiosity and secularity. This is political theology. The Altenburg case reshapes it by the heterotopian dimension of this Garden. This dimension has an impact on the persons active in the monastery beyond their actual functions. It is in place beyond the question who is Abbot, Prior etc. because it belongs to the spiritual identity of the monastery. This overturns a classical blind spot in political theology.

Political theologies and their blind spot in space

A political theology is at the same time a political enterprise and a theological experiment to describe the contradiction between (secular or religious) beliefs and official power structures. Yet, political theology was not invented for arguing with spaces, neither the original one which is located at the right of the political spectrum nor the new one which is located at the left of the religious spectrum.[20] The goal of political theologies has been to create new chances for subjects by dealing with contradictions in political and religious affairs.

In modernity, different sorts of political theologies were developed—from the right wing of the political spectrum as in the case of Carl Schmitt or from the left wing of the ecclesial spectrum as in the case of the new political theologies after the Shoa.[21] There is a mixture in between, an earlier one by Erik Peterson and a current one by Giorgio Agamben. Both are challenging the authoritarian goals of Schmitt and both are not going along the emancipatory goal of the left-wing modern theology. We concentrate here on the original right- and left-wing approach.[22] Both political theologies are directly

20 For the first one cf. Carl Schmitt, Political theology. Four chapters on the concept of sovereignty, Chicago: Univ. of Chicago Press, 2005. For the second one, which calls itself New Political theology, cf. the theological works of Jürgen Moltmann, Dorothee Sölle and Johann B. Metz (cf. Schüssler Fiorenza (2011), Tremel (2004) and Metz (2016). For a sort of keeping the legacy cf. Manemann (2008). For an introduction to their mutual relationship cf. Rissing/Rissing (2009). For a claim of critical distance from the New Political Theology to the Schmittian version see Manemann (2002).

21 Schmitt (2005), cf. also Mehring (2009).—A parallax between the longing for sovereignty and the despair about God's weakness, i. e. the left and the right in political theologies, is discussed by Crockett (2011).

22 For a contemporary analysis cf. Losonczi (2011). Losonczi also argues that there is a precarious nexus between the left and the right approach to political theology in terms of eschatology, cf. Losonczi (2015).

challenging ruling utopias either in politics as Schmitt did with his pledge for a legitimate authoritarian state beyond the failing national state, or in religion as Moltmann, Sölle and Metz did with their option for a dangerous memory to the victims of history, beginning with Jesus of Nazareth, which is forcing religious communities to oppose leading structures within their churches which collaborate with the authoritarianism of the State.

Within political theology spaces are not relevant, only subjects and powers do count—the power of a state of emergency (the original political theology of Carl Schmitt) or the power of a Final Judgement (the new political theology of progressive modern theologians), the one different ruler above all other powers or the many forgotten victims below all historical events. Powers and subjects serve as starting point for very broad, even universal utopias. But on the other hand these powers and those subjects are bound to spaces which have to be disciplined for the sake of those utopias: the state and the church.

In all cases of political theologies the human person is locked into a sovereign position in contrast to normal social structures—either as a Schmittian authoritarian 'Führer' standing beyond the normal order or as a victim of violent politics and religion representing a crucified God as in a Moltmann's, Metz's and Söll's political theology. Traditionally these political theologies are bound to the relevant subjects in specific historical situations—the authoritarian despot ("Der Führer schützt das Recht"—Carl Schmitt) as well as all the victims of history ("Der gekreuzigte Gott"—Jürgen Moltmann, "Das politische Nachtgebet gegen den Vietnam-Krieg"—Dorothee Sölle, Auschwitz in relation to "memoria passionis et resurrectionis Jesu Christi"—Johann Baptist Metz). All these historical situations are not bound to spaces where powerlessness enters power-structures although all their major figures are fixed to real places and are dealt in this respect. It is Auschwitz as reference point for history in the case of the leftist political theology. And in the case of the rightist political theology it is the 'greater area' ("Großraum") beyond national borders where the 'nomos of the Earth' has to rule.[23]

In this respect, both lines failed. In Schmitt's case it is obvious. He failed because of his support for the Nazi-Regime and everybody using emphatically Schmittian insights is attacked for reason of supporting authoritarian thinking and acting.[24] And the left political theologies failed in respect to their churches which are not willing to give up the traditional coalition with the state for the sake of their own interests. With these failures the basic agenda for political identity failed as well. Both claimed a different 'who we are' on the basis of the need for radical fight against liberalism or authoritarianism. This question who are we when our civilisation has caused Auschwitz—the left

23 So Schmitt (2011).

24 Even if one is keeping a big distance to Schmitt's political ideas, suspicion of promoting authoritarian regime even in democracies are raised. This can be observed in the case of Münkler (2002).

approach—leads to a restricted time which cannot get away with its guilt. And the question who we are when we need a ruler like Hitler—the right-wing approach—leads to a restricted freedom in order to keep up with sovereignty in history. But both new identities claim the long historical vision.

For the same reason both modes of political theologies are contradicting each other in terms of history; they claim opposite forms of revolution. The Schmittian political theology was formulated before the Shoa. It was not intended to contradict political decisions leading towards mass murder. In the contrary it still tried to create legitimacy for authoritarian ruling going beyond legality even if this leads towards an utmost violent regime. For that reason, after the downfall of the Nazis, Carl Schmitt never got away from being personally involved in the regime of the perpetrators. Moltmann's, Sölle's and Metz's political theologies were formulated after the Shoa because of Auschwitz and were not able to change the Churches' normal position that finally the religious communities were not responsible for this apocalyptic event—and, of course, in a way innocent of it. Their challenge of the Churches tried to turn the hierarchy which has been a traditional stronghold for the ruling elite away from its political and religious authoritarian goals towards a politically emancipatory side for the individual subject. This was not successful and in this respect it has the same intellectual fate as the Schmittian authoritarian legalism. Yet both forms of political theology were pretty successful in demonstrating that the contrast of politics and religion, of faith and human needs, of social developments and divine narratives is creating an alternate power to deal with social problems. Claiming authority with a stricter power or claiming for breaking the power of claims of authority, both are relying on a mutual relationship between religion and politics which seems to be necessary because normality has proven to be a disaster. Both lines read out of the relevant disasters a need for a universally different history. This culminates in a religious or a secular eschatology whose time has not yet come.

For that reason, spaces where religious or secular deficits provide an arena for proving universal claims of political theologies to be right or wrong are not that important. They are crystallizing realities for historical visions, not the very field to make a distinction by its alternative. This aspect of political theologies is even implicitly present at those places where religiously motivated people work hard to counterbalance the deficits of society, welfare state, religious institutions like the places in Gothenburg and Oslo, Copenhagen and Altenburg we discuss in this book. Usually, the people running these places see their own work as a small part of a much bigger task. In this respect they are in the line of the new political theology.

Yet, there is a major difference. People working at such places cannot give eschatology the last word. They do not have room for that because they have to work with a real place. The spaces they work with urges them to find a relevant position here and now. This is demanded from them by the very place they work with. They are focussing of human needs of people living at the margins of society, i.e. where a universal vision for history has proven to be not successful. Here it is neither the sovereignty of an authoritarian ruler but the broken sovereignty of people in need and neither the sovereignty of a decisive victim in mankind's history but the victimisation of suffering people to the margins of history which pushes towards an alternative where there seems to be no alternative. The locus of the need for an alternate order of things cannot be a virtual one. This counterbalance inevitably needs a real place to become obvious.

This has a final consequence. They are not up for revolution or revolt or universal turn arounds. Their tactics and practices are smaller but at the same time they built up a more intense resisting force. Spaces where religiously motivated people start a different sort of caring for marginalized people different modes of memories, of narratives, of broken sovereignty are bound to the relevant places where this activity is located. For that reason one may raise the question to the usual political theology: But what if it is not the subjects creating the opposing narrative about history but the spaces these subjects are bound to are pushing to find such a narrative? And what is the range of this pushing if the spaces are a sort of subject in the history of people?

As long as one cannot find such a solution these places keep on pushing. That even belongs to the original ideas of political theologies. In the case of the state of emergency—the right-wing political theology—it is turmoil or natural catastrophe where the normal order breaks down and chaos takes over. In the case of a dangerous memory—the leftist political theology—it is the history of victims which is changing the already fixed status of narrations. In both lines, something else enters the relevant field of arguments: the breaking down of utopias which is contrasting history radically.

If political theology can be developed based on such relevant spaces as dealt with in this book which are representing a different order of caring, of sovereignty and of unspoken memory then a different form of practice comes up. It is lesser powerful but much more effective to bring in a completely different discipline needed on the ground of such spaces: a precarious knowledge about failed utopias. But then, space and discipline have to fit to one another in respect to the place. The marginality of hospital spaces and the normal discipline not capable to be enforced at such spaces but only to be proposed belong to each other. This different form of discipline comes out of surprises of urgent human needs one cannot avoid to be confronted with, since they are nothing less than personal states of emergency. There are not a bunch of other places where these people can go to. Very often it is the last place they can go to in their need of caring hospitality. For both reasons the alternate discipline calls for another sort of spatial activity than utopias.

Any combination of politics and religion which is needed at such places stands beyond a secular state of emergency or a religious state of dangerous memory. The point is not to change society and state on a universal level but to change the fate of marginal people on a local level. Such places can only hint to the deficits of society, state and religion. They cannot solve them completely. Their universal claims towards a society have only authority for local solutions not being in line with the ruling order of things. This is a humble universality but at the same time a breakthrough where it is needed. These claims create by themselves a heterotopos towards normality. This heterotopian dimension of such places is not coming from their universal meaning. It is coming out of local details found there. Their heterotopos is in the details of a space. It is not in the context of its universal consequences but in the realm of its local grammar. The result of this is a form of counter-conduct which Foucault analysed only in respect to crisis of pastoral power.

This space-based counter-conduct creates a sort of extraordinary experience of the relevant spaces: The hospitality for people at the margins is more important than the pure religious nature of the place. The secular confrontation with human needs becomes an exceptional form of religious caring for marginalized realities. This is the religious capital in places where religiously motivated people work for a different sort of life respecting people on the margins there. It is a secular awareness to human needs being so exceptional that one is immediately forced to pay attention to them. This implies to rethink the religious nature of a religious space. It implies a secular counter-conduct in favour of the people involved in the space. One can see that in one of the major religious narratives for caring hospitality.

The Good Samaritan—an example of spatial counter-conduct

The narrative of the Good Samaritan deals with a secular problem—a human being is fallen prey to robbery. But it reveals the deficits of those bound to a purely religious place like the temple. The Good Samaritan has no religious reason to care for the unconscious person lying at the street. He has only human reasons. The Levitt and the Priest have no secular reason to pass by. They have only religious reasons for not-taking care. Yet, the Samaritan is doing the best religious practice one can imagine. He cares for somebody who needs care to survive right on the place where it is needed. And the Levitt and the Priest are doing the worst secular practice in such a situation. They do not care for life and death of anybody else then themselves. The place where the victim is lying, the street, becomes a revealing place for good and bad in religion and for bad and good in secularity. This revealing factor is used in the narrative as religious capital. The one who cares is climbing up the religious ladder. The two others who do not care are fallen down in authority. This capital is not found in the normal order but in the a-normal state of emergency. This has a breath-taking consequence in the narrative: Caring of a marginal person between life and death is all what the Law and the Prophets are about. This caring literally takes place where this 'between' can be localized and it is linked to the final religious outcome of history which is salvation.

The Levitt and the priest are only representing the normal order which is dividing secular needs and religious tasks and this order has to be overcome. A different form of religious activity is brought into the picture: Secular caring of marginal people is a religious activity at places where one cannot pass by such people. This is the dual role of the Good Samaritan. He is the representative of a spatial political theology without universal claims but with a spatial counter-conduct of universal political and religious perspective. His example has an eschatological representation without claiming that time will end definitely. In this respect, the Good Samaritan is an example of a counter-conduct without the pressing disciplinary dimension of a pastoral power. It is not eschatology which creates this counter-conduct but the urgent present time. He is the elementary figure of pastoral authority being a present counter-conduct in history. The rule 'thou shall love your neighbour' depends on the neighbour on the ground and not on universal love beyond all space and time.

For such reasons religion is not one factor of all sorts of other factors present at such marginal spaces of caring. It is an eminent factor for creating an alternative state of emergency in daily life and an alternative opposing memory to victims on the ground. Such an abnormal place like the street where the victim of this narrative is fallen prey to robbery is itself a religious capital, i. e. a place for another social production of religion and of politics, of the relation between religiosity and secularity, of spiritual and social activities. This capital is a result of spatial activities. Then, one can change the focus towards such a space of marginal hospitality due to religious motivation: A religious place is transformed into a space of religion and in this transformation the place is filled with a counter-conductive sort of secular power.

References

Andraschek-Holzer, R. (1994) Benediktinerstift Altenburg 1144—1994. 850 Jahre Benediktinerstift Altenburg. St. Ottilien: EOS.

Barrett, D. B./Kurian, G.T. /Todd M. Johnson, T.M. (Ed.) (2001) World Christian Encyclopedia. A comparative survey of churches and religions in the modern world. Oxford: Oxford Univ. Press, 2. edition.

Blasi, A. (2014) Sociology of religion in America. A history of a secular fascination with religion. Leiden: Brill.

Crockett, C. (2011) Radical political theology. Religion and politics after liberalism. New York, NY: Columbia.

Davidson, A. (2011) "In praise of counter-conduct", History of the Human Sciences, 24(4): 25–41

Foucault, M. (1981) "Omnes et singulatim. Towards a Criticism of Political Reason", in : McMurrin, S. (Ed.), The Tanner Lectures on Human Values, vol. II. Salt Lake City: University of Utah Press, 223–254.

Foucault, M. (1994) «Des espaces autres», in: Dits et écrits 1954–1988, vol. IV (1980–1988). Paris: Gallimard, 752–762.

Foucault, M. (2003) "Of Other Spaces", in: Preziosi, D./Farago, C. (Ed.) Grasping the world, 371–379

Foucault, M. (2004) Sicherheit, Territorium, Bevölkerung. Geschichte der Gouvernementalität I. Vorlesungen am Collège de France 1977–1978. Ed. by Michel Sennelart. Aus dem Französischen von Claudia Brede-Konersmann und Jürgen Schröder. Frankfurt: Suhrkamp.

Foucault, M. (2006) Die Geburt der Biopolitik. Geschichte der Gouvernementalität II. Vorlesung am Collège de France 1978–1979. Ed. by Michel Sennelart. Aus dem Französischen Jürgen Schröder. Frankfurt: Suhrkamp.

Foucault, M. (2009) Security, Territory, Population. Lectures at the Collège de France, 1977–1978. Ed. by Michel Senellart and Graham Burchell. New York: Picador.

Gabriel, K./Gärtner, C,/Pollack, D. (Ed.) (2014) Umstrittene Säkularisierung. Soziologische und historische Analysen zur Differenzierung von Religion und Politik. Berlin: University Press, 2nd edition.

Hoffman, M. (ed.) (2013) Foucault and power. The influence of political engagement on theories of power. New York, NY: Bloomsbury.

Hunt, L. (2007) Inventing Human Rights. A History. New York: Norton.

Keul, H. (2004) Verschwiegene Gottesrede. Die Mystik der Begine Mechthild von Magdeburg. Innsbruck: Tyrolia.

Knott, K. (2013) The location of religion. A spatial analysis. Durham: Acumen.

Knott, K. (2009) "From locality to location and back again. A spatial journey in the study of religion", Religion 39 (2009), 154–160

Lefebvre, H. (2010) The production of space. Transl. by Donald Nicholson-Smith. Malden, Mass.: Blackwell, 29th print.

Losonczi, P. (Ed.) (2011) The future of political theology. Religious and theological perspectives. Farnham: Ashgate.

Losonczi, P. (2015) "Humanization, eschatology, theodicy. Metz, Schmitt, and the 'hidden nexus'", in: Political theology. The journal of Christian socialism 16/2 (2015), 116–129

Manemann, J. (2002) Carl Schmitt und die Politische Theologie. Politischer Anti-Monotheismus. Münster: Aschendorff.

Manemann, J.(Ed.) (2008) Politische Theologie—gegengelesen. Berlin: Lit.

Mehring, R. (2009) Carl Schmitt. Aufstieg und Fall—eine Biographie. München: Beck.

Metz, J.B. (2016) Neue Politische Theologie—Versuch eines Korrektivs der Theologie. Gesammelte Schriften 3/2. Ed. by Johann Reikkerstorfer. Freiburg: Herder.

Münkler, H. (2002) Über den Krieg. Stationen der Kriegsgeschichte im Spiegel ihrer theoretischen Reflexion. Weilerswist: Velbrück.

Nassehi, A. (2008) "Erstaunliche religiöse Kompetenz. Qualitative Ergebnisse des Religionsmonitors", in: Bertelsmann-Stiftung (ed.) Religionsmonitor, Gütersloh: Bertelsmann, 113–132

Pollack, D. et. al. (Ed.) (2014)Grenzen der Toleranz: Wahrnehmung und Akzeptanz religiöser Vielfalt in Europa. Wiesbaden: Springer.

Pollack, D. (2012) Säkularisierung—ein moderner Mythos? Studien zum religiösen Wandel in Deutschland. Tübingen: Mohr Siebeck.

Pollack.D./ Gergely Rosta, G. (2015) Religion in der Moderne. Ein internationaler Vergleich. Frankfurt: Campus.

Post, P. (Ed.), (2014) Sacred spaces and contested identities. Space and ritual dynamics in Europe and Africa. Trenton: Africa World Press.

Rissing, M./Rissing, T. (2009) Politische Theologie: Schmitt, Derrida, Metz. Eine Einführung. München: Fink.

Schmitt, C. (2005) Political theology. Four chapters on the concept of sovereignty. Chicago: Univ. of Chicago Press.

Schmitt,C. (2011) Der Nomos der Erde im Völkerrecht des Jus Publicum Europeaeum. Berlin: Duncker & Humblot, 5th edition.

Schüssler Fiorenza, F. (Ed.) (2011). Politische Theologie: neuere Geschichte und Potenziale. Neukirchen-Vluyn: Neukirchener.

Steinkamp, H. (2005) Seelsorge als Anstiftung zur Selbstsorge. Münster: Lit.

Taylor, C. (2007) A Secular Age. Cambridge, Mass: Belknap Press of Harvard University Press.

Taylor, C./Casanova, J./McLean, G.F. (Ed.) (2012) Church and people. Disjunctions in a secular age. Washington, D.C.: Council for Research in Values and Philosophy.

Tremel, M. (2004) Politik und Theologie bei Dorothee Sölle. Die Herausforderung der Frauenbewegung durch Carl Schmitt. Frankfurt: Lang.

Vanhoozer, K.J./ Warner, M.(Ed.) (2007) Transcending boundaries in philosophy and theology. Reason, meaning and experience. Aldershot: Ashgate.

Vásquez, M.A./ Kim Knott,K. (2014) "Three dimensions of religious place making in diaspora", in: Global Networks 14/3 (2014), 326–347.

Topos D: The Hospitality of the Urban Space

Two blocks from the central railway station in the Norwegian capital Oslo, there is a small intersection that many people pass by every day. Most of these people are on their way to somewhere else, but not all. The area around the station, including the intersection is also part of Oslo's drug scene. The substance users deal, meet and stay in the area, and so do the police and all other kinds of surveillance and security agents.

Hilde Kirkebøen (Oslo)

Marginality at Oslo Central Station

The area and space surrounding Oslo Central Station (Oslo S) is the meeting point for nearly all public transportation to and from—and within Oslo. Every day 150 000 people pass through Oslo S, which has become a center for tourism, trade and industry. There are three large department stores located within or nearby the station, in addition to Oslo's main shopping street, Karl Johan. The new Opera house lies adjacent to the station, by the seaside.

In addition to being an established trade and communication center, Oslo S has been characterized as one of the main sites for Oslo's drug scene. Since the 2007 EEA regulation on Free movement of Persons, increasing groups of migrants from South- and Eastern Europe have arrived in Norway, many of whom are affecting the street scene and business activity in this area. EEA migrants subsist through activities such as: begging, recycling bottles, entertainment (human statues, music), shoplifting, as well as illegal trade of drugs/narcotics, cigarettes, spirits and stolen goods, on a smaller scale.

For some, Oslo S is an important social arena, meeting point, work place, for others a heated shelter and even an alternative home for a limited period of time. This applies to homeless Norwegians as well as poor migrants. Different interests in and intentions for this relatively small area lead to conflicts and battles over the various places and spaces.

In the summer of 2013 a sleeping ban was introduced in central Oslo. For people who sleep outside this implies a continuous risk of being awoken and chased several times during the night. Many of them use the central station as a heated shelter when it opens around 5 am. Large groups accumulating in spaces otherwise meant for consumers, commuters and travellers are nevertheless undesirable and those who use the facilities for resting and finding heat, are often chased and expelled from the premises, on more or less factual grounds.

For example, prior to a religious street service (gategudstjeneste) outside of Oslo S, where a woman begs for money on a daily basis, she was chased from the area while quietly waiting for the service to begin. Or how certain people who buy a coffee or something to eat, are not allowed to finish their food or drink before they are asked to leave the premises while others are not. Occasionally, rather rough conflicts arise between, and within, the varied groups of poor migrants and people from the drug environment and there are often struggles over the right to stay in the best locations. Meanwhile, there are also stories of cooperation between these diverse groups.

Lately, various youth and youth groups have also begun to utilize the area surrounding Oslo S, particularly as a location for conflicts and riots. Loners, those who have lost their footing or people with mental disorders also tend to hang around in the area for shorter or longer periods of time.

Thus, Oslo S is an intersecting point for more than traffic to and from Oslo. It is characterized by its role as a meeting place and an arena where many different groups meet. Social workers do outreach work in the area, and are consequentially aiding the police and security personnel in their challenge to keep the area peaceful and safe.

New benches in parks and other public places are made with arm rests so as to ensure that they are not misused as beds or places where one can lie down to rest. Other examples of architectural design with intentions to keep unwanted people away from the public scene are tilted benches, spikes on the pavement outside shops and the transformation of public seating areas into cafes. In the spring/summer of 2015, politicians were subsequently criticized for concealing social deprivation and poverty through marginalization of non-consumer groups by introducing what was called *hostile architecture.*

Some artist have initialized counter-reactions to the hostile architecture by, among other things creating illustrations around garbage bins to make it easier to find bottles otherwise hidden in the garbage.

There are stories of beggars who are denied access to public toilets, even though they pay for the services (10 NOK), and since these toilets only accept credit cards, not coins, its use is automatically limited to people who have access to such cards. This is rather rare amongst homeless or poor migrants. Other examples include poor migrants being denied access to stores even if they have money.

During spring and summer, the activity level in and surrounding Oslo S is particularly high. Beggars find their more or less permanent locations for work, preferably connected to the subway, department stores, cafes or shops. Many play instruments to earn money. A musical playing ban has been introduced during working hours (8 am—5 pm) on weekdays. Violation of the ban can be penalized with a high fine. Unpaid fines over a certain total amount can make grounds for eviction from the country.

Some Oslo citizens engage in claims that the way in which public authorities, such as the police and criminal justice system, prosecute the varied group of people living and working around Oslo S is in violation with human rights.

Kaia Schultz Rønsdal (Oslo)

Murmurs of pastoral care?

> If one observes a crowd attentively at peak times, and especially if one listens to its murmur, one will discern in the apparent disorder currents and an order that reveal themselves through rhythms: accidental or determined encounters, hurried carryings or nonchalant meanderings of people who go home in order to withdraw from the external world, or of those who leave their homes in order to make contact with the outside, […]. The rhythmanalyst thus knows how to listen to a square, a market, an avenue. (Lefebvre/Régulier 2013 [1986]: 95)

Assuming the premises laid out in the present book's introduction, there are spaces that might display a specific quality that one may call hospitality. This chapter will relate to narratives from a specific urban public space in Oslo presented in the preceding pages. Compared to the spaces analyzed earlier, this space has no particular mission or function towards anybody. It is a small intersection, around 50 meters West of Jernbanetorget, which is the large square outside the old railway station marking the start of Karl Johans gate,[1] Oslo's parade street going all the way up to the royal castle. This little intersection is made up of a pedestrian section of Karl Johan and the one-way (South to North) street Skippergata. Skippergata is the second street to cross Karl Johan to the West from Jernbanetorget. This street has a few residences, but is dominated by office buildings, shops, service shops, as well as a few pubs and hotels. Many of the different services directed at street people[2] are also located in, or in the vicinity of Skippergata. This means that there are many street people, primarily substance users that move about in this street, especially in the blocks closest to Karl Johan, and the Oslo Church City Mission's locations two blocks to the South. The four building corners that surrounds the intersection consists of (per Nov. 2011) one fast food restaurant, two clothing stores and a 7/11 store that is open 24/7. The Skippergata stretch from Karl Johan to the North is fairly empty. On the Eastern side of the street there are no shops or restaurants, only a block of stone walls with one or two entrances to offices. The Western side is dominated by the windows of one or

1 Citizens will call the street just Karl Johan, as will be done in this context.

2 Hereby meant by people who spend their daily life in the streets, having them as their main social arena, work place, home, etc. Following Nafstad these areas (and specific groups) offer identity; self-respect; practice of competence and knowledge; and income strategies (Nafstad 2012).

two stores, with no entrances, as well as a night club that is not open until evening. Skippergata to the South of the intersection holds several small stores on both sides of the street, a few entryways to backyards, as well as a pub, a cafe, hotels and the city mission's main office and cafe.[3] The entire intersection is no more than approximately 12 by 12 meters.

It is at first glance neither welcoming and hospitable, nor un-welcoming or inhospitable. It has no religious or secular commitments, in contrast to the other spaces discussed in this book. It may, however, still imbue spaces with a kind of hospitality. In 2011, as part of a multi-departmental attempt (Sentrumsarbeidet, 2012–2015) to dissolve the open drug scene in the area, the Oslo police started a major operation that was to last for minimum six months. The aim was to use a so-called soft approach with the aim of expelling people associated with the drug scene. As the intersection was a central place for the buying and selling of illegal substances, it also became a point of encounter between the street people and the police. The small intersection suddenly became a very interesting space, a location for strange encounters, power demonstration, surveillance, but also a space for surprising encounters, encounters of care, and maybe counter-conduct.

There are traces of hospitality to be discovered in this space, traces to be presented and interpreted in the following. The starting point is that these spaces, both the larger Oslo S area and the intersection, could be interpreted as heterotopic spaces. However, as mode of analysis, Henri Lefebvre's triadic model on the production of space will be used, as this opens the spaces, uncovering more details that may enrich the discussion. Lefebvre's theory of the production of space, states that all spaces are produced, and all spaces can be analyzed on three levels—*spatial practice*, *representations of space* and *representational spaces* (Lefebvre 2007 [1974]: 33). Simplified, one may say that spatial practice is the way spaces are, how they are perceived, and thought. Representations of space are the abstract presentations, the maps, and the construction of spaces, the known. Representational spaces refer to the symbolic aspects of space (2007 [1974]: 37 ff). Lefebvre emphasizes that symbolic refers to ambiguities and complexities that are linked to life (Schmid 2008). The levels, moments or values are intertwined or appear in different relationships in complex dynamics. Sometimes one is prevalent, other times another (2008). In the following the intersection will be analyzed within this framework, in order to see whether the details thus uncovered points to moments of counter-conduct.

3 The street continues South towards the harbor and fortification.

Henri Lefebvre's perspectives—Spatial triad and rhythmanalysis

Like Foucault, his fellow Frenchman and contemporary thinker Henri Lefebvre, was highly influential in pointing out and exploring the dimensions of social spatiality. He too emphasized the impact of linking spatiality to the traditional couple of historicality and sociality. Like Foucault, he was concerned with societal power structures, although his views were based in Marxism.

Lefebvre was concerned with the development of (modern) society through categories of space. To exist in society one needs spatial knowledge and competence. One premise of his spatial theories is his deconstruction and disordering of binary logic, he reinterpreted and recombined center-periphery relations, which he used to understand and critique everyday life, struggles over rights to the city and to be different (Soja 1996). The rejection of binary logic means that two terms are never sufficient, there is always a third. Lefebvre always asserted that this third made either/or choices impossible; a *both/and* logic disrupts the closed categories of the either/or. This assertion has consequences for how a field is seen and what questions to pose. The question of both/and is central to the narratives to be discussed here. Furthermore, his theory on the production of space, with the three concepts *spatial practice*, *representations of space* and *representational spaces*, play the central part in analyzing the intersection.

Lefebvre's aim was to develop a theory of space as "the shared aspect and outcome of all social practices," (Stanek 2008: 63) and his emphasis was on the "processes and strategies of producing space [...]." (Kipfer/Goonewardena/Schmid/Milgrom 2008: 9) The notion of the production of space "integrates the categories of city and space in a single, comprehensive social theory, enabling the understanding and analysis of spatial processes at different levels." (Schmid 2008: 27 f) Lefebvre's contributions are very influential in opening up and exploring the dimensions of our social spatiality, and in arguing for connecting historicality, sociality and spatiality in a balanced and interdisciplinary triple dialectic, an idea that developed through his conceptualization of the relationship between centers and peripheries (Soja 1996; Lefebvre 2007 [1974]).

In Lefebvre's explanations of the three terms, *spatial practice* refers to production and reproduction, "and the particular locations and spatial sets characteristic of each social formation." (Lefebvre 2007 [1974]: 33) Lefebvre also refers to this space as *perceived* space *(espace perçu)* (2007 [1974]). In the words of other thinkers, this level refers to a perception that "comprises everything that presents itself to the senses." (Schmid 2008: 39) Spatial practice "relies on a "common-sense" understanding of space including both the taken-for-granted dimensions of everyday life and the rationalized institutions and urban networks that we pass through in our daily routines."

(Simonsen 2005: 6) Simply put, how social spaces are perceived by people—spaces as we experience them. When Lefebvre initially explains *representations of space*, he points to signs and codes, to representations tied to order or production (Lefebvre 2007 [1974]). Furthermore, he refers to these as *conceived* (*conçu*) spaces of scientists who "identify what is lived and what is perceived with what is conceived." (2007 [1974]: 38) With Foucault, representations of space would be the "dominant *discourses* of space in a given society." (Simonsen 2005: 7) These representations can be images, maps, plans—anything that represent or show a space (Lefebvre 2007 [1974]; Soja 1996; Schmid 2008).

The third level, *representational spaces*, Lefebvre defines as spaces "embodying complex symbolisms, sometimes coded, sometimes not, linked to the clandestine or underground side of social life [...]." (Lefebvre 2007 [1974]: 33) Here, the struggle of "realizing ourselves as "total persons" and bringing into being alternative imaginations of space" (Simonsen 2005: 7) takes place. These are also referred to as *lived space* (*espace vécu*), meaning that these are the spaces that are experienced by "'inhabitants' and 'users'," (Lefebvre 2007 [1974]: 39) "[...] in the practice of their everyday life." (Schmid 2008: 40) According to Lefebvre, these spaces refer to the symbolic aspects of space. So, the spaces of representation refer to something else than the spaces themselves: "a divine power, the logos, the state, masculine or feminine principle, and so on." (2008: 37) "In the third, the material "order" that emerges on the ground can itself become the vehicle conveying meaning. In this way a (spatial) symbolism develops that expresses and evokes social norms, values, and experience." (2008: 37).

> Such spaces, therefore, are not sites as such but temporal situations, events, which occur in particular places that open up the possibilities of resistance within society to certain marginal groups and social classes. [...] Representational spaces are practices associated with places that have their origins in the realities of that everyday life, [...] in resistance to the mundane and alienating features of everyday existence. (Hetherington 1997: 22 f)

As the levels are always interconnected, this means that spaces, according to Lefebvre, must always be understood as all three levels, and the interpretations of spaces are connected to how the relationships are between them—changes happen in the interplay between all the levels of space. All three are always in a dynamic interaction. A space is constantly in motion, always different, being moved forward—the world is moved forward by contrasts, contradictions and tensions.

Another contribution from Lefebvre needed to analyze the intersection from the perspective of the spatial triad, is that of rhythmanalysis. Although rhythmanalysis is mainly a tool for analysis, it may also be understood as a way of seeing, and *being present,* in the urban. The starting point is that Lefebvre observes an urban space from his balcony, "overlooking one of the liveliest streets in Paris […].” (Lefebvre 2013 [1992]: 41) Following Lefebvre, observing from the balcony makes the observer part of the experience, the observed everyday surroundings, and their murmurs. These are experiences of certain groups’ everyday life in the urban, reports of heterotopias. According to Lefebvre there are some criteria for the observation. You cannot just stare, you have to become part of what you see and sense. Lefebvre writes of the rhythmanalyst that she listens. First she listens to her body, “learns rhythms from it, in order consequently to appreciate external rhythms. [Her] body serves [her] as a metronome.” (2013 [1992]: 19) His premise, then, is “that the rhythmanalyst does not simply analyse the body as a subject, but uses the body as the first point of analysis, the tool for subsequent investigations.” (2013 [1992]: 29)

In this context, the narratives to be discussed tell *everyday* stories—not necessarily spectacular ones, but they were disruptions in the general flow. Seen from a specific point of view, they may be interpreted as transgressive. The mundane is much more than what it seems.

Elaborating from Lefebvre’s perspective: “No camera, no image or series of images can show these rhythms. It requires equally attentive eyes and ears, a head and a memory and a heart.” (2013 [1992]: 45) Lefebvre talks about listening to the city; “The rhythmanalyst strolling about perceives more the ambience of a city, rather than the image flattering the eye; more the atmosphere than the spectacle.” (Meyer 2008: 156) His point is that in order to understand a rhythm, and I would say aspects of urban life, one must not only grasp it, one must “have been *grasped* by it. One must let oneself go, give oneself over, abandon oneself to its duration.” (Lefebvre 2013 [1992]: 37) “In order to grasp and analyse rhythms, it is necessary to get outside them, but not completely: be it through illness or technique. A certain exteriority enables the analytic intellect to function. […]. In order to grasp this fleeting object, which is not exactly an object, it is therefore necessary to situate oneself simultaneously inside and outside.” (2013 [1992]: 37)

Although the rhythmanalysis is more linked to time than space in Lefebvre’s development and descriptions, the rhythms are highly spatial. Both rhythms and cycles came to play a role in the observations in the intersection.

Lefebvre’s descriptions of an unspectacular and seemingly ordinary scene from his window in Paris immediately resonated with scenes in the intersection. First of all, he describes his location, and the benefits of seeing from the outside, so to speak: “The situation of the observer in relation to what is observed is constantly kept in mind. The window overlooking the street is not an abstract location from where the mental eye could, so to speak, abstractly grasp what is happening in the street. It is a real location not only *enabling sights but leading to insights. The observer is implicated in what is happening on the street.*” (Meyer 2008: 153, my emphasis) What is noticeable from Lefebvre’s observations, except for his sometimes poetic and fantastic descriptions, is precisely how inextrordinary it is;

> He who walks down the street, over there, is immersed in the multiplicity of noises, murmurs, rhythms (including those of the body, but does not pay attention, except at the moment of crossing the street, when he has to calculate roughly the number of his steps?). [...] On red, cars at a standstill, the pedestrians cross, feeble murmurings, footsteps, confused voices. One does not chatter while crossing a dangerous junction under the threat of wild cats and elephants ready to charge forward, taxis, buses, lorries, various cars. Hence the relative silence in this crowd. A kind of soft murmuring, sometimes a cry, a call. (Lefebvre 2013 [1992]: 38)

Lefebvre emphasizes the importance of the location of the observer. He really favors the balcony and its incommensurable qualities as a lookout post, partly because it also exposes you to the sounds of what is going on. Lacking a balcony, "you could content yourself with a window, [...]." (Lefebvre 2013 [1992]: 38) Or, as the main focus here is related to human activities, where one is implicated and affected, one could immerse oneself on the actual ground level.

Literally going outside to immerse oneself in the space opens it up for new details, experiences and perspectives. Even though the viewer is the reporter of what is seen and sensed the observation is not introspection, it is a phenomenon that is outside of her and this has an impact on the theory.

We uncover a specific lived space, and through rhythmanalysis we find murmurs of something else than just marginality, power and chaos. There are aspects of the narratives that can only take place in this specific public place.

This knowledge is coming from the rhythms of this specific space. The theories are tools needed to point out these rhythms and details, and to discuss the content of the spaces which again challenge these theories.

Presenting the field—The Oslo drug scene

Norway has a relatively high number of substance users,[4] and the area around the station has been populated by substance users for a long time. Being the node of public transportation in Oslo makes it a good meeting place for activities and businesses that are not tied to specific locations—almost any bus, tram, underground or train passes through this point.

Yet, the substance users have not always been here. When substance use became a visible phenomenon and/or problem in Oslo in the 1960s, the people associated with it established a meeting point in the park surrounding the royal castle. After conflicts with the police the first major removal of the substance users happened in 1984 (Brekke/Ziebarth 2000). Their next location was a square connected to the entrance to the subway situated almost right

4 I do not use the terms *illegal* or *abuser/misuser*. Suffice it to say that I mean people whose lives are largely dominated by the use of different substances, both legal and illegal.

between the castle and the central station, Egertorget, where a market for illegal substances developed (Brekke/Ziebarth 2000; Olsen/Skretting 2006). This was a good place, as the subway station provided both easy access and a warm shelter in the colder periods of the year. This area continued to be the main market for illegal substances throughout the 1980s and 1990s.

During the 1990s the heroin supply grew dramatically and the drug became significantly cheaper (Brekke/Ziebarth 2000). The substance users were constantly being chased by the police, and the "business" moved up or down a block. Nearly every corner between Egertorget and Jernbanetorget has at some time been the hangout place of the users and dealers of substances. Finally, in the late 1990s, the drug scene was moved to the area that was a fairly stable location for some time—the grassy area on Christian Frederiks plass, next to Jernbanetorget—popularly called Plata. This area had earlier been inhabited by rough sleepers struggling with alcoholism. As the house and techno culture appeared in Oslo at the same time, new and younger groups were introduced to Plata—groups of "regular kids," not heavy users with multiple problems (Brekke/Ziebarth 2000). It seemed that everyone let the problem rest here, and all kinds of interest groups, organizations, social services as well as the police itself established their operations directed at the drug scene here (Brekke/Ziebarth 2000; Olsen/Skretting 2006). Some of these services are located in Skippergata, like the city mission's main office and cafe.

Several smaller steps have been taken to disperse the open drug scene since then, but none has made a significant impact until 2004, when a thorough and well-planned effort was organized. For two weeks, the substance users of Oslo were invisible, or at least under cover.

However, they soon reappeared in Skippergata. The group became smaller during this time, and the more obvious dealing and use became somewhat less prominent. But the situation soon returned to what it was before in this new location, now also crowding the area outside the subway station at Jernbanetorget. The debate continued, becoming more heated in the late noughties, involving the city manager, the police, the head of tourism, the business community, etc.

Based on the growing challenges related to the open drug scenes, the lack of permanent solutions following the prior operations, as well as documented experiences from actions taken in other cities (Waal/Gjersing/Clausen 2011), the need for collaborate actions resulted in Sentrumsarbeidet. The essential idea, put simply, was that the police should increase their presence in the areas and actively oppose drug-related crimes as well as monitor the individuals. On the other hand, the medical/health institutions should collaborate in establishing easily accessible spaces for detoxification and long-term rehabilitation, while public and private care organizations should establish specific alternatives to roaming the streets. Another goal was that anyone not registered as citizen of Oslo should be sent back to their own district to receive care and assistance there. Undocumented, returnable migrants should also be sent to their place of origin, and the nonreturnable immigrants should be monitored more closely (Oslo kommunes handlingsplan for Sentrumsarbeidet 2012–2015). What distinguishes this plan of action compared to earlier initiatives is the long-term perspective, with a specific action plan established through 2015. The Oslo Police Department's operations were put into action in late Spring 2011.

Because many different projects and activities aimed at the substance users and other marginalized groups are located in Skippergata, many street people roam this street, especially in the blocks closest to Karl Johan and the Oslo Church City Mission's locations two blocks to the Southwest.

After the Sentrumsarbeidet project started, the number of visible and uniformed police increased substantially, with both foot patrols, higher numbers of marked vehicles as well as a police RV stationed at Jernbanetorget every day, seemingly functioning as headquarters or meeting place for the officers.

An inconspicuous intersection[5]

The starting point of the narratives is the area around Oslo Central Station introduced above. They do, however, take place in a very small part of this area—the intersection.

This intersection is not a place written about in guide books. It is a modest intersection. It is also, and especially before the summer of 2011, an intersection between Oslo's parade street, one of the major shopping streets in the capital, and a small street infamous for its social challenges.

As of summer 2011 the modest and seemingly insignificant little intersection was, to the naked eye, a place for just passing through on the way to somewhere else. However, upon taking a closer look and stopping for a while, it seemed that the dealing of illegal substances, although highly fleeting, was substantial in this intersection as well as in the one or two blocks in either direction East of Skippergata. The police was not just strolling through, they were patrolling heavily, hardly leaving the intersection unguarded for even minutes at the time.

An Other intersection

After observing the intersection for hours, days and weeks at end, it became clear that much more was going on than substance users trying to do their business while the police was hunting them down. However, this was not

5 The following is based on fieldwork carried out in July–November 2011 as part of a doctoral thesis project (Rønsdal, 2016).

obvious, rather it was mere glimpses of something surprising. Something suggesting a more complex space as well as a more diversified relationship between the people moving around there. Through observation and rhythmanalysis, short but detailed narratives of the intersection developed. The crucial point is that I, on the basis of rhythmanalysis did more than merely observing from the outside. I dwelled inside this space, bodily experiencing parts of what others there were experiencing, such as being cold, unable to rest, etc. It is inside these other spaces the narratives came to be that may show an unexpected hospitality.

Most of the narratives describe everyday situations that did not tell extraordinary tales of spectacular events, or obvious hospitality, as it is hardly observable. Rather, most narratives are only between five to ten lines and describe events that sometimes lasted less than 5 seconds. Nonetheless, could these narratives point to surprising, transgressive events and actions fit for discussions of hospitality and care? The objective when observing the intersection was to see what appeared when the resulting narratives were analyzed through spatial theories and categories. What kind of space is this? Are there other kinds of spaces in this place? What are they? Who creates and participates in these spaces? What perspectives appear when the intersection and the people there are interpreted within a new framework?

Foucault's notion of heterotopia embraces the *intersection.* Heterotopias are *other spaces*, where the otherness is established through the relations between the difference to others spaces, such that their presence brings either a disturbance in spatial and social relations or an alternative representation of spatial and social relations (Hetherington 1997). They are contested spaces because of the difference to other spaces, the spaces they reflect. "Likewise, but in a different register, heterotopia *makes* differences and unsettles spaces, sometimes exposing the extraordinary in the most ordinary of places. [...]. Heterotopia is a brief exercise in formulating a different 'point of view'." (Johnson 2013: 796) The ideas of "other spaces" and "spaces of others" will both be used here. The first stems from Foucault and specifically regards spaces that hold certain qualities that make them different or other. The second was developed by several thinkers and regards spaces that are specifically characterized by the otherness of the people there.[6] The other also appears other by way of the "other space" (Foucault 1984) in which they appear, are observed, and are often forced to stay.

The narratives uncover, as will be elaborated, murmurs within these other spaces that shines light on other aspects of them. The murmurs are about these spaces being more than they seem. Lefebvre's spatial triad opens up the space and adds to Foucault's notion—there are *practices* within the spaces that expose contradictions and paradoxes in even minute spaces and encounters.

The intersection, through the activities of the substance users, and

6 See, for instance, Wyller 2009.

particularly how they create a breach by using it differently and in unexpected ways, is a place of otherness. The same can be said of the police, as the intersection challenges their role of keepers of law and order, as will be shown. Interpreting the intersection as heterotopic thus opens up a perspective that enables us to point out such alternative representations of these groups.

Other thinkers who build on Foucault's notion of heterotopia focus among other things "on spaces that seem to be both mundane and extraordinary, [...]. Such research focuses on a social or cultural space that is both in place and out of place." (Johnson 2013: 797) The intersection does not seem extraordinary if left un-analyzed. It is not a place that is in any way marked out on a map as a location worthy of a visit. The intersection is in place, it has specific functions to fulfil, but it is also out of place, as certain individuals living on the margins actually live their lives here instead of just passing through. It is a marketplace, a meeting place, a hangout place, both a safe and a risky place. The police also contribute to it being out of place—they are not always playing the expected role as enforcers of pure power and upholding the law. The intersection becomes an extraordinary place, with the sociality that plays out in the encounters between the people present.

The premise then, in the analysis to follow, is that the intersection is interpreted as a *contested* heterotopic space. It is, I believe, possible to point out moments of counter-conduct and hospitality in this heterotopic space using Lefebvre as contributor in the analysis, in order to point out the transgressions and surprises that make it possible to interpret the intersection as a space for possible urban hospitality.

Murmurs, Bodies and Lived Space

The premise for the following discussion is "seeing" the heterotopic spaces in Lefebvre's mode of analysis: "[T]o release and listen to rhythms demands attention and a certain time. In other words, it serves only as a *glimpse* for entering into the *murmur*, noises, cries." (Lefebvre 2013 [1992]: 41) Murmur, as shown in the introductory quote, is interpreted here as what manifests itself as something other than disorder in a busy cityscape, something that may add to a discussion about what is taking place.

At the very root of Lefebvre's theories on the production of space lies the notion that social space "is encounter, assembly, and simultaneity." (Lefebvre 2007 [1974]: 101) The intersection with its activities, here interpreted as a social space, could be analyzed within Lefebvre's dialectical framework of the production of space. "Space is to be understood in an active sense as an intricate web of relationships that is continuously produced and reproduced. The object of the analysis is, consequently, the active processes of production that takes place in time." (Schmid 2008: 41)

As spatial practice or perceived space, the intersection is how people perceive it. This could only be found out by asking, as it presupposes the use of the body (Lefebvre 2007 [1974]), and is thus subjective. For a rhythmanalyst it may be a place to sit down and open the senses to the murmur, to listen and watch intently, "the surroundings of bodies, be they in nature of a social gathering [...] to which it is necessary to listen in order to grasp the natural or produced ensembles." (Lefebvre 2013 [1992]: 30) It is impossible to state how people perceive the intersection as it "comprises everything that presents itself to the senses," (Schmid 2008: 39) but for the sake of analysis these are *some* perceptions.

Considering the intersection as a representation of space, as conceived space, it is the factual layout of it. It can be shown as a map, a drawing, maybe even a photograph. It may at first sight not look like a particularly interesting place as representation. As shown earlier, in the presentation of the intersection, however, new or other details appear when one takes a closer look or takes another perspective. The intersection can, for instance, be conceived in its distance to the subway or to the city mission café. A day or even a week may be planned from the intersection's location with respect to other significant locations. For the researcher, the intersection is mapped, drawn, photographed according to whatever catches one's attention. Who moves there, where do they move, are there patterns, etc.?

As lived space or representational space, on the other hand, the intersection becomes even more. "[...]—a third term between the poles of perception and conception. Socially lived space depends on material as well as mental constructs—and on the body." (Simonsen 2005: 7) It is this level of analysis where the majority of the discussion in this chapter takes place. These are the spaces experienced by "'inhabitants' and 'users'," (Lefebvre 2007 [1974]: 39) "[...] in the practice of their everyday life." (Schmid 2008: 40) These spaces refer to the symbols, the ambiguities and complexities that are linked to life (2008). Maybe one can say that interpreted in this way, one *really* sees what goes on here. Meaning that the intersection is not *only* practice and representation. It is *also* a place where someone lives their lives, a place that is the goal, a social place where people's everyday lives take place, where they struggle for health, sociality, acceptance. It is also a place where someone is doing a job, and one of the goals of this job is to make sure that the space is used as intended—and not for criminal activities or disturbance of businesses.

Through Lefebvre's triadic model it should be clear that the intersection is not either perceived *or* conceived *or* lived; it is perceived *and* conceived *and* lived. Hence, the question "and?" must be asked repetitively through the analysis.

Because the intersection consists of the bodies, rhythms and the space that surrounds them, Lefebvre's method of rhythmanalysis directs focus to these details. Rhythmanalysis "accentuates the centrality of the body to social understanding" (Simonsen 2005: 9) and "raises the question on development of alternative methodologies in order to grasp the more opaque sides of social life." (2005: 9) Therefore, the murmurs and having obtained them through rhythmanalysis become important. The space has to be given substance by actual life, especially since the goal is to look for interpretations of life, and map their significance for the production of space.

The previous pages have presented the perspective on the very street-level where some contrapuntal narratives manifest themselves in a small space. Some analytical key terms that have been discovered are murmurs, body and lived space. The distinctive features of the intersection to be shown are what take place in the intersection as lived space. Small narratives from the intersection where the police and substance users hold front stage are presented. These particular narratives are believed to point to surprising events that add to a discussion about pastoral care.

Contrapuntal Narratives from an Intersection

The intersection and the neighboring area are, at first sight, even when one stops to take a closer look, a cacophony of noises, people, smells and other sensual impressions—in short, chaos. For a tourist or someone just rushing through, one might even fail to take notice of anything in particular at all. Most people in the intersection appear to be inconspicuous unless one takes a closer look and knows what to look for. In areas where dealing with illegal substances is going on, one of the things one may notice is that people move much closer to each other than is customary. Norwegians are not known for their need for physical closeness with strangers (Kiel, 1993). A Norwegian will sometimes even cross the street in order to avoid having to pass someone on a narrow sidewalk. Walking in a substance "market place," however, people are suddenly moving unnaturally close to each other. If you pay attention and listen, you notice that people passing you mumble that they possess specific substances or what substances they are looking for. At times people seem to be standing still having an apparently normal conversation. But the ones moving about are constantly communicating about "merchandise," without stopping, looking up or even turning their heads. Seen from the outside, without noticing the "close walkers," nothing is really going on. Until you see people suddenly changing direction or becoming a group for anything from a few seconds to a few minutes before the group dissolves again.

The area, if not the specific intersection, holds smaller locations that are known for and characterized by undesirable activities and those placed there to control them. An example from a morning in September;

"[...] have been at Jernbanetorget since 09:00, very quiet, very quiet! Just four or five substance users. Just now three constables came, so I guess they are on the way in now. It is 09:53, and the RV just arrived. Before that, at least nine [officers] came in cars, and walked in. Now even more have arrived, one in an unmarked car, now they are (counting) 16. And the mini bus just arrived, so now they will be even more. […]. It is 10:05, […]. By the time all the constables had arrived, they were 23, so it is clear that they have some other strategy today."

During the hour within which these 20 minutes took place, few others were in the area; the area was dominated by police.

Without time and analytical tools it is easy enough to leave it at just that, an area dominated by a high level of police presence. Knowing of the open drug scene, it is easy to imagine that this is for some an area of persecution, and for others somewhere to feel safe. However, one is to look for transgressions and surprises, listen for the murmurs. The idea of the murmur can be tied to Lefebvre's idea of moments, "the attempt to achieve the total realization of a possibility." (Lefebvre 2008 [1961]: 348) According to Simonsen, Lefebvre stated the moment as "decisive sensation implicating a double recognition of the "other" and the "self"." (Simonsen 2005: 8) "Possibility" in the first quote refers to something lying there to be both revealed and performed, and discovering this "possibility" entails a significant action. Combining this with the second quote, the "possibility" may, for this discussion, be interpreted as "the other" and his body's request [or call] for us to act. However, we must search for the present possibility, not turn to *our* own solutions to *our* problem. These are important lives that are taking place in an important space, by which we need to be grasped. This "being grasped" implies that we need to be present in order to be moved into action—whatever action the other body requests of us.

For instance, in an intersection where there are hundreds of encounters between the police and substance users every day, one is likely to assume to know who holds the power and who is always defeated by being arrested, expelled, ransacked or told off. Observing such encounters does not necessarily prove such assumptions wrong. Leaving the narratives at that is possible and could lead to a meaningful discussion about surveillance society or power relations or any range of other important topics. However, looking at the narratives again, there may be a murmur about something else:

"(September 14th)[…], the two on the window sill, they had moved to the 7/11 sill, had fallen asleep, heroin sleep, and two constables came up Karl Johan and touched their shoulder and asked them to leave in a friendly way, well, maybe not friendly, but not stressing either. And all the ones along Skippergata disappeared toward Møtestedet."

This 3-second event took place by the intersection, among hundreds of pedestrians; substance users moving here and there, maybe dealing; police officers ever watching and patrolling. This particular day was a day with a higher number of patrolling officers than most other days, so the assumption was that there would be a more aggressive atmosphere in the intersection.

Observing the approaching officers and the two sleepers, the anticipation was that the encounter would end in some kind of drama. But the actual encounter was something else. Following Lefebvre's *both/and* logic and theory of production of space, this encounter is not about whether the police or the substance user holds the power in this particular space. Rather, asking "and?" and using the concept of lived space, the encounter may embody complex symbolisms linked to the social life this embodies (Lefebvre 2007 [1974]) referring to ambiguities and complexities that are linked to this life (Schmid 2008). There are substance users who are using the space "wrongly," behaving privately in the public sphere, using a window sill for sleeping. And the police are fulfilling their role as guardians of public peace and order, removing disorderly elements. *And*, the encounter is something more. In the cacophony, there is a murmur of something else: It is bodies responding to the other bodies.

Elaborating on the issue of the body, the narrative told of a body touching another body. There is another narrative that tells of a similar, but even more acute embodied response to another human being. This is from November and the temperature outside is approximately 0 degrees C.

> "It is 13:28, the two cops walked toward Møtestedet now. They have stood here quite some time now, chatting amiably with a couple of substance users, very amiably and pleasant, humanly. Not just being buddies, but warming each other. One of the policewomen is rubbing one of the substance users' back. As one would do when helping another to stay warm. Even if it was just a joke—or if it was irony—it was still a physical, bodily, closeness that no one had needed to show the other."

This encounter between the police and substance users lasted for a few minutes. And the encounter in itself was a surprise, as it appeared to be genuinely pleasant, like old friends meeting in the street. It is not possible to tell that it was or that it was not, only what it seemed to be. However, regardless of the intentions behind the pleasantness, the event was a breach, and it was surprising in that everyone behaved differently from what was expected. As representational or lived space, the space between these people challenges the symbolic character of both the police and the substance users, and it becomes highly ambiguous and complex. It is no longer simply an intersection. And it is no longer a space where the marginalized are dominated by expected power persons. Everyone was on the same inside, sharing space. It is the small gesture, the touching, that defines the entire event, that is the unexpected rupture in the rhythms. The encounter is not a site, but it links to "temporal situations, events, which occur in particular places that open up the possibilities of resistance within society to certain marginal groups and social classes." (Hetherington 1997: 22)

The narratives expressing communal co-creation and re-creation of spaces would not originate if it were not for the police and the substance users. These spaces exist only for minutes, if not mere seconds, and they can exist only where they are. When they dissolve, they are no longer there, though they reproduce several times a day, or from day to day. These spaces would not be visible without observing the area over a period of time. People walking too close to you once may be a coincidence, while when people pass too close a hundred times it is a rhythm, and in it may be a murmur. The closeness or presence in these spaces may be described in spatial categories, which carries the narratives.

It is possible to imagine the interaction between the police and substance users as its own space. The substance user is an undesirable neighbor in many ways. First and foremost he or she is a stranger to most. He or she is perceived to be involved in criminal activities, joining others in larger or smaller groups. He or she is drugged, often on unknown substances with unknown effects. He or she may look unwashed with stains of unknown matter on the clothes, have dirty hair and hands. He or she might look seriously ill, pale, with an emaciated face and body, lacking teeth. Whether he or she is a person is not relevant, "[I]n public space, the homeless[7] do not appear as individuals with distinctive identities. […] As a specific mode of embodiment, the homeless body [or that of a substance user] is not an identity but an emergent and contingent condition that traverses and occludes identity." (Kawash 1998: 324) He or she is a body that is threatening. However, this body is obviously suffering. And the suffering is what calls to us. And our bodies respond. And when you share space, it becomes harder to deny the body this response. On the other hand, imagining the other person as only a body, it is also easier to keep a distance, as well as for the politicians (and police) to imagine them as a removable problem. "[…] the production of a homeless body adds another dimension to our efforts to understand the sources of antipathy towards the homeless […]." (Kawash 1998: 325) When a body responds to a body, however, the body becomes a person.

This is why the actual touching in these narratives is of importance. Foucault refers many times to the metaphor of the social body, and Lefebvre also writes of the body, by emphasizing human beings as corporeal and sensuous beings (Schmid 2008). A premise for spatiality and sociality is our relationship with our body, since this body is needed to partake in social practice—hence the first spatial level is the body perceiving its social surroundings (Lefebvre 2007 [1974]). In the context of urban public space, namely the intersection, this becomes relevant as the police keep the public space in order, often by removing bodies: "[…], the body emerges as the stake and the site of the contest over public space." (Kawash 1998: 323) The touching could be said to be a spontaneous, even unconscious response to perceiving a sleeping or freezing body. It is not a calculated action where anyone wins. The people are probably very aware of their roles, where one could be arresting the

7 Although the substance users in Oslo are not necessarily homeless, they are seen and treated as such by many. They could be interpreted as "placeless."

other within the hour or day, but still in the moment, one body responds to another.

In a more dramatic scene, where a substance user is frisked and the officer finds illegal substances on him, he is placed under arrest.

"(September 14th) It was clear that she found something, that she held in her hand. She took out one of those tiny evidence bags. It seems to be an easy tone, they were just standing for a while, and then she took out a small bottle of sterilising liquid, gave him some and took some herself, they both rubbed their hands. Now they are just standing there."

In this tale, the anticipated chain of events—detainment, frisking and arrest—seems to be met. However, in the anticipated, something unexpected occurs. It is a tiny gesture, and substance user who was frisked might not remember it or think about it at all. However, it is nonetheless noteworthy. They are together in this situation. There are thousands of explanations for her sharing the sterilizing liquid. One obvious could be that she knew that she might have to touch his hands. Another could simply be that he asked for some. But seeing the interaction and encounter going on the entire time, this was a breach in what seemed to be routines. These people see each other every single day, they are "human beings who enter into relationships with each other through their activity and practice." (Schmid 2008: 29) They literally share work space. They share the heat or the cold, the smell and noises.

Turning to the concept of heterotopia, Lefebvre also contributes to this notion, as *heterotopy*, although in a slightly different manner, in *The Urban Revolution* ([1970] 2003). He describes it several times, but one concept is particularly significant in this context. Johnson writes: "Historically, it is formulated as the "place of the other" in terms of marginality. [Trade and exchange outside cities]. Such activities are both excluded from and interwoven within the city." (Johnson 2006: 9) Although the intersection is inside the metaphorical city walls, the activities of the substance users in the intersection are outside of society. By this is meant that the intersection is concretely there. Any person can go there and participate in what may be considered ordinary everyday life, it is mapped, it is a place that people probably do not even think about, it is just there. Except for the "common" knowledge of Skippergata being a bit shady, so to speak, most people may not even notice that they are crossing it. It is so close to the center of the capital, so close to many of the attractions on the map, that it could hardly be more inside. However, from the perspective of heterotopia, it is very much on the outside. The quote from Lefebvre refers to trade and exchange outside the city walls, and it is an obvious link to the illegal substance market—however, it is more interesting to connect the perspective to the people, the bodies who live their lives in the intersection. Foucault explains several principles for his heterotopias, among them is how they hold specific functions within different societies, and how they juxtapose "in a single real place several spaces, several sites that are in themselves incompatible." (Foucault 1984: 6) There are several small "societies" in the intersection whose use of it is not that of others. It is, to them, meeting place, market place, safe place, unsafe place, and surely many other things—it is *where* they are going, it *is a place*, rather than more pavement on the road to somewhere else. Although the activities are similar to all everyday activities, the place is "wrong", and the bodies doing the activities are "wrong"—the lives lived at the intersection and the lives passing the intersection are incompatible, making the spaces at the intersection "wrong" too. The inside/outside concept thus adds to the analysis, as such spaces and the people there also direct criticism at society, threatening the general discourse, and challenging it—heterotopia "disturbs and unsettles wherever it sheds its light: [...]." (Johnson 2013: 800). The added value may be that these disturbances, the sense of chaos, can be interpreted as production of space. And furthermore that this production of space holds within it counter-conduct and hospitality.

Chaos or Production?

"The city needs a periphery, an elsewhere, an other and different place. This movement, produced by the urban, in turn produces the urban. Creation comes to a halt to create again." (Lefebvre 2003 [1970]: 118 f) One of the reasons for the relevance of Lefebvre's thoughts thus becomes clear—the seeming chaos and constant movement of the field is not just this, chaos, it is rather production.

"(November 16th) It is 13:34, and suddenly... the ones that have been standing here for a while, maybe ten minutes, six or seven individuals, suddenly there were 25! Complete chaos, with several others approaching from everywhere to join the group. Many just appearing from the outskirts here. Some disappeared around one corner, and others around another and some are still roaming around just outside here. So suddenly things are happening. [...]. 13:38, two new cops came up from Jernbanetorget, and took place here. [...]. Now, the entire cluster from before has dissolved, only one is left, and three more are on their way in from different sides, they appear to be just passing."

Lefebvre presents a theory that makes it possible to understand what is going on as such, as production. These are not insignificant spaces or insignificant people, they are producing space. Space is never finished, as the spatial triad shows. It is processual, always under construction. This was Lefebvre's aim, to develop a theory where one can understand and analyze spatial processes on different levels. Even a very small intersection thus becomes part of the production space, and so do people not partaking in the majority production, as space is "the shared aspect and outcome of all social practices." (Stanek 2008: 63)

"(September 12th) It is 14:02. Police is still there, and they have been since before. I have counted everyone I have seen. 377 substance users. Here, while I have been sitting here, for two hours! I have to check that again, it seems too many. Of those, around 30–40 I have seen more than once, the rest I have only seen once. I think. […] There are some that do not seem to mind being here, while others walk on this side of the road, and never stop here, and some just come in, pick out a person, and they continue together."

The number of substance users in the small area that is the intersection does not simply express a failure in the police operations. It could obviously be seen as such, but then again, the operations had only lasted around 3 months at this time, so no such conclusion could yet be drawn. The high number of substance users, and also their speed and endless circling could, in spatial terms, be a sign of policies changing the geographies of this group. Changing not only how they behave, but also where they behave. And it expresses what Soja calls spatial injustice, where the needs of leading groups literally moves the "less important" somewhere else, to places with inferior conditions and of no use—injustice has spatial consequences (Soja 2010). "And?" In the incessant circling the stress is apparent. Sharing this space for some time, feeling the cold, feeling corporal needs not being relieved, always seeing a twinkle of a police officer's reflective trouser leg at the corner of your eye, the bodies of this space cry for action.

In our discomfort we feel the need to do something—people cannot live like this. But, maybe they can! The people of this contested space are also showing resourcefulness and resilience in their refusal of being forcefully removed from a public area. They do, to a certain degree, play along with the police, as in trying to behave within the accepted framework, attempting not to be caught in a criminal act. However, in their pursuit of survival and to lead their life, they have to be there. Also, in order to lead a life of sociality and normalcy, participating in everyday activities like meeting friends, window shopping, getting a cup of coffee, doing errands, they must come here. Obviously, in this area the chances of being seen as other, or a criminal or a substance user, is greater if you look a little "off" than in other places, due to society's perception of this area as particularly "loaded" by marginality, so the chances of being detained here are greater than elsewhere. Yet, they still come and use the area as they want, and as their own.

Pushing a little further with Lefebvre and his idea that the moment is "the attempt to achieve the total realization of a possibility" (Lefebvre 2008 [1961]: 348), "this idea allowed him to extend the theory of moments from the analysis on everyday life to the understanding of sublime moments of revolutionary fervor." (Simonsen 2005: 8) And with Foucault, this countersite, this space of resistance, challenges the expected roles of the people in this public space. It may be farfetched to interpret this as "revolutionary." It could also be interpreted as there being "no place in the contemporary urban landscape for the homeless to *be.*" (Kawash 1998: 326) "[T]he homeless exist in a perpetual state of movement," (1998: 327) where they are perceived as completely powerless. However, through the spatial analysis, the point is that there is a possibility in these spaces.

This particular discussion relates to spaces where the relations between the powerful and the perceived powerless are challenged by unexpected encounters in unexpected spaces. These encounters could open a discussion about counter-conduct within pastoral power. "[I]n some ways, heterotopias provide an escape route from power." (Johnson 2006: 86) The point is not, however, to "escape" power, but become open to the possibility that power in these heterotopias is more complex and could be discussed from perspectives that challenges the concept to the extent that the powers at play could even be seen as inputs to a discussion on counter-conduct. Lefebvre's perspectives make this possible. Analyzing the intersection through his perspectives makes it possible to point out another version of counter-conduct.

When Lefebvre writes of the lived spaces, he points to "a utopian element in the form of a desire for some form of improvement or change within society." (Hetherington 1997: 23) Some of the events or encounters I refer to in the narratives are maybe such "utopian elements" that manifest themselves in human practice. For instance the sharing of the sterilizing liquid may be such an element, as for a moment there is an improvement and change in this ambivalent space. According to Lefebvre, such spaces of ambivalence and uncertainty, allows them "to offer a vantage point from which the productions of space can be made visible and be critically viewed." (1997: 23)

Conclusion

What has this analysis has brought to the surface? This discussion is a contribution to thinking about a known public space in a new framework, to examining life conditions that are both normatively and ethically significant to everyone, such as everyday, exposed marginality. Lefebvre's spatial rhythmanalysis and concepts allow for a discovery that challenges traditional pastoral power and opens for brotherly love, as it is not simply the powerful exercising power, it is recognizing the other in the shared lived space. This book discusses moments when pastoral power contributes to the recognition of others rather than to their control, pointing out that they then belong to the counter-conduct [and] the pastoral power as hospitality and not as control. In this context we do find traces of hospitality; as interaction between equal bodies, and in seemingly secular spaces. Still it is close to something fundamentally human.

According to the Swedish theologian Gustaf Wingren, human solidarity with the suffering is something given in human existence (Wingren 1995

[1974]). Wingren, building on Luther, was concerned with the concept of vocation, opening the concept, and making it relevant regardless of faith. He points to the universality of being attentive and wanting to respond to the needs of others. He claims that this is universal and given in human existence, it is something that does not require prior knowledge, it is embodied. Following this, what takes place in the spaces of the tales regards every *body* in society. If we do not want to help, this solidarity is something we have to fight to *rid* ourselves of in encounters with this suffering (1995 [1974]). In the narrative of the police woman who rubs some heat into the substance user on a freezing November day. He, as her fellow human being, makes his suffering or embodied need alive for her (1995 [1974])—she just responds. The action, in accordance with Wingren, is latent, lying in waiting, always dormant in human existence and can be executed to exemplary perfection even by an illiterate (1995 [1974]). The police woman is probably not illiterate, but the point is that her body does not need specific training or knowledge to respond to this other body. She may even have received training in acting professional, i. e., *not* being moved by this other person. Wingren, in his work on vocation, helps us see that it does not matter whether our attention and response to the other body is related to the secular or the sacred—everyone can and should serve the needs of the other, and it does not matter what the responder believes, as long as he responds to his neighbour. A piece of bread is, according to Wingren, life-giving for the starving regardless of whether it is given in aversion or in love (1995 [1974]).

Maybe it was, in the narrative with the police woman, a case of her mind slipping and her body stepping in. Are these bodies involved in hospitality? Do we discover traces of an unexpected embodied counter-conduct? Thus, this inconspicuous intersection is an example of a contested, urban space where caring pastoral power and counter-conduct unfold in an absolutely unexpected location.

References

Brekke, T./Ziebarth, U. (2000), Veien til Sjøsida. En rapport om situasjonen i de etablerte misbruker- og rekrutteringsmiljøene i Oslo sentrum sommer 1999, Uteseksjonens Skriftserie NR. 1.2000.

Erdal, B./Reiermark, H. (1999), Når broene er brent…. Rusmiljøet ved Oslo S, Uteseksjonen Rapport

Foucault, M. (1984), 'Of Other Spaces (1967), Heterotopias', in *Architecture/ Mouvement/Continuité*, Oct. 1984

Hetherington, K. (1997), The Badlands of Modernity. Heterotopia and Social Ordering, Routledge, London

Johnson, B. (2006), Unravelling Foucault's 'different spaces,' History of the Human Sciences, vol. 19, No. 4 (2006): 75–90

Johnson, P. (2013), *The Geographies of Heterotopia*, Geography Compass 7/11 (2013): 790–803

Kawash, S. (1998), The Homeless Body. *Public Culture* 10(2): 319–339

Kipfer, S./Goonewardena, K./Schmid, C./Milgrom, R. (2008), On the Production of Henri Lefebvre, in K. Goonewardena/S. Kipfer/R. Milgrom/C. Schmid (Ed.), Space, Difference, Everyday Life. Reading Henri Lefebvre, New York, 1–24

Lefebvre, H. (2003) [1970], The Urban Revolution, trans. R. Bononno, MA

Lefebvre, H. (2007) [1974], The Production of Space, translated [1991] by Donald Nicholson-Smith, Malden, MA

Lefebvre, H. (2008) [1961], Critique of Everyday Life, Vol. II. Foundations for a Sociology of the Everyday, New York. Translated by J. Moore, originally published as *Critique de la vie quotidienne II: Fondements d'une sociologie de la quotidienneté* by L'Arche Editeur, Paris, 1961

Lefebvre, H. (2013 [1992]), Rhythmanalysis. Space, Time and Everyday Life, translated [2004] by S. Elden/G. Moore, London/New York, originally published as *Éléments de rythmanalyse* by Éditions Syllepse, Paris, 1992

Lefebve, H./Régulier, C. (2013 [1986]), Attempt at the Rhythmanalysis of Mediterranean Cities, in H. Lefebvre, Rhythmanalysis. Space, Time and Everyday Life, London/New York. Translated by S. Elden and G. Moore, originally published as *'Essai de rhythmanalyse des villes méditerranéennes'* in *Peuples Méditerranéens*, 37, 1986, 93–106

Meyer, K. (2008), Rhythms, Streets, Cities, in K. Goonewardena/S. Kipfer/R. Milgrom/C. Schmid, Space, Difference, Everyday Life. Reading Henri Lefebvre, New York, 147–160

Nafstad, I. (2012), Et anstendig menneske. Møter mellom rusbrukere og det offentlige rom i Oslo, Doctoral thesis, Det juridiske fakultet [Faculty of Law], UiO, 2012

Olsen. H./Skretting, A. (2006), Ingen enkle løsninger. Evaluering av Tiltaksplan for alternativer til rusmiljøene i Oslo sentrum, SIRUS rapport nr. 2/2006, Statens institutt for rusmiddelforskning, Oslo

PROSJEKT "Trygghet for alle i Skippergata', Prosjekteiere: Oslo politidistrikt/Oslo kommune, Prosjektgruppe: Oslo kommune, Oslo politidistrikt, Kirkens Bymisjon, Frelsesarmeen, Rusmiddeletaten, 2007

Rønsdal, K.D.S. (2016), Calling Bodies in Lived Space. Spatial Explorations on the Concept of Calling in a Public Urban Space, Doctoral thesis, Det teologiske fakultet [Faculty of Theology], UiO, 2016

Schmid, C. (2008), Henri Lefebvre's Theory of the Production of Space—Towards a Three-Dimensional Dialectic, in K. Goonewardena/S. Kipfer/R. Milgrom/C. Schmid (Ed.), Space, Difference, Everyday Life. Reading Henri Lefebvre, New York, 27–45

Sentrumsarbeidet 2012-2015, Det åpne narkotikamisbruket i Oslo sentrum. Oslo kommunes handlingsplan for Sentrumsarbeidet 2012–2015 ("The center work—The open drug scene in the center of Oslo". The municipality of Oslo's plan of action).

Simonsen, K. (2005), Bodies, Sensations, Space and Time: The Contribution from Henri Lefebvre, Geografiska Annaler. Series B, Human Geography, Vol. 87, No. 1 (2005), pp. 1–14

Soja, E. (1996), Thirdspace—Journeys to Los Angeles and Other-Real-and-Imagined Places, Blacell Publishing, Malden, MA

Soja, E. (2010), Seeking Spatial Justice, Minneapolis, MN

Stanek, L. (2008), Space as Concrete Abstraction, in K. Goonewardena/S. Kipfer/R. Milgrom/C. Schmid (Ed.), Space, Difference, Everyday Life. Reading Henri Lefebvre, New York, 62–80

Waal, H./Gjersing, L./Clausen, T. (2011), Open Drug Scenes and Overdose Mortality—What to do? Report from Five European Cities, SERAF rapport nr. 1/11. Senter for rus- og avhengighetsforskning, Det medisinske fakultet, Universitetet i Oslo

Wingren, G. (1995 [1974]), Credo. Den kristna tros- och livsåskådningen, Skellefteå

Wyller, T. E. (Ed.) (2009), Heterotopic Citizen: New Research on Religious Work for the Disadvantaged, Göttingen

Bryan S. Turner (New York and Melbourne)/Kaspar Villadsen (Copenhagen)

Counter movements and Space: The Settlement, Occupy Wall Street and the Tea Party*

Introduction

In this chapter, we examine the relationship between social and political movements, on the one hand, and space, on the other hand. Social and political movements emerge when people collaborate and act together toward a common end, demanding large- or small-scale change in the social order. The direction of such striving can be formulated as incremental changes within the existing order or as utopian images of a completely new society. Schematically, space comes into view in two ways: First, there is the tangible question of how particular social and physical spaces give shape to social movements. Components making up space in this first sense include, for instance, the distribution of wealth, population density, urbanization, demography, ownership of the means of production, religious adherence and the use of communication technology. Here, we speak in terms of *lived space*. Second, there is the *imagined space* that people might dream of establishing in the future or perhaps returning to. There, space exists as a potential reality—just awaiting realization—and hence serves to justify political action. While we give some attention to the tangible role of social-material space, in this chapter we take a greater interest in imagined space. We demonstrate how images of space play a key role in the discursive and social mobilization of social movements. Indeed, the *Settlement Movement*, *Occupy Wall Street* and the *Tea Party* all rely heavily upon particular images of the spaces from which they arise and the imagined spaces toward which they move.

In this chapter, then, we explore the American Settlement movement (its Danish offspring was studied in chapter three) and its lasting influence on social welfare and social policy. Settlements, especially in the United States, are intriguing because they often combined a religious impulse with the idea of sociology as a factual science of society. We also consider the Occupy Wall Street movement, paying particular attention to the ideology of the movement and its approach to space. Finally, we analyze the Tea Party focusing on its antigovernment message and its identity as representing the "little people" of suburban and rural America.

* We Thank Emily Campbel from The Graduate Center CUNY for her field work on churches connected to Occupy Wall Street.

Counter movements, religion, modern politics

In pursuing this theme, we take up a range of issues touched upon in the Introduction to this book, with Michel Foucault being the key reference. Foucault offers a helpful conceptual vocabulary for analyzing social movements which attempt to contest state power and political rulers. While we consider these movements in light of heterotopia, we also find Foucault's rendering of the concepts of counter-conducts, civil society and political eschatology to be very helpful in the following analysis. The possibility of there being social movements that speak up against political governors with reference to certain ideas of "the truth of society" or the community is relatively recent. In Foucault's historical optic, such counter-movements arose as a distinctly modern creation, albeit one that can take on very different political shapes.

As is well known, Foucault describes a major rupture in political reasoning that occurred in the 17th century, from sovereign princely rule over a territory to the government of a living population (2007). Emerging from this rupture was a new opposition between state and civil society, which was particularly theorized by 17th- and 18th-century political philosophy. The incipient idea of "civil society" as an independent reality possessing inherent self-regulating mechanisms inaugurated a tempering of the totalizing aspirations of sovereign rule. It became possible to advice, caution or contest political rulers with reference to the detrimental effects of too much intervention in civil society. Modern political games of power had thus been launched, observes Foucault, insofar as the limits of government were no longer decided one-sidedly but achieved through arbitration, struggle and reciprocal concession. Instead of sovereign command, the fundamental modus of power would be transactions "at the interface ... of governors and governed" (Foucault, 2008, 297). The modern invention of "a civil society" established a new "interface" at which more open-ended games of power could be played out between the governors and the governed.

We should be careful, however, not to read these observations as a univocal commemoration of how the Enlightenment and modern democracy did away with sovereign and authoritarian forms of political reasoning and practice. In fact, Foucault notes, modern-liberal government was accompanied by extreme or utopian political movements that attacked state-centered, and often also democratic, government by invoking the coming of a human community not regulated by the state. Modern antistatist movements shared the imagery of a future where the state would be absorbed by some variant of society, and they included communitarian theologians, utopian socialists, libertarians as well as subsequently Fascism, Stalinism, National Socialism, and ethnic extremism. The result would be a perfect party-state or "people's state."

Foucault used the term "counter-conducts" to describe a variety of historical instances where groups contested rulers or authorities by questioning the truth by which they were being governed. He mentioned five modalities of such "counter-conduct" that emerged within and as opposition to the Christian pastorate from the Middle Ages onwards (Foucault, 2007, 214, 225–226). Here, we regard only two of these counter-conducts. The first rests on the idea of the absolute right to revolt, to insurrection and to breaking all the bonds of obedience. This right is grounded in a message of radical equality or universal equality that may spur different kinds of revolutionary eschatology. Foucault does not posit any direct link between the counter movements associated with the pastorate and modern revolutionary movements. However, there are affinities, especially in their invocation of eschatological themes.

The concept of "political eschatology" appears in Foucault's analyses as a pivotal theme that justifies radical political action against existent governmental structures. Political eschatologies take a religious or quasireligious form, whether or not they have determinate religious content (Crocket, 2011, 102). Eschatology designates the theological study or artistic representation of the dramatic end of the world and its rebirth in a more perfect form, usually according to a divine plan. Eschatological themes are mainly found in religious discourse, but also in some science-fiction writing. Foucault used political eschatology in a rather loose fashion. He mostly employs the term to describe teleological doctrines claiming a predesigned historical process that culminates in a glorious victory, where society is finally unified or perfected (Villadsen, 2015, 14–15). Political eschatology constitutes, on Foucault's account, a quite flexible idiom that can take diverse political forms.

This flexibility becomes evident when we notice how eschatological themes travel from the counter-conducts connected to the Christian pastorate to political movements opposing modern liberal government. In Foucault's account, eschatological themes were reactivated to suspend the "indefinite time" of governmentality (Foucault, 2007, 355). With the emergence of modern reasoning regarding the state—*raison d'État*—in the 17th century, eschatological themes became excluded from political discourse. Modern state reason entailed a fundamentally different historicity, or perception of historical time, than religious, teleological thinking, or "the kingdom of eschatology" (Foucault, 2007, 356). Henceforth, the state would be perceived of as an always unfinished project, propelled forward by the impossible striving for universality. This is why Foucault says that modern state reason rests upon the idea that the state will always be there, and that we now live in an infinite political time that is "not temporally oriented toward a final unity" (Foucault, 2007, 379).

This infiniteness of the state would be challenged by political countermovements that asserted the idea of a rupture and the completion of political time with the coming of a new society:

"Counter-conducts develop that make it a principle to assert the coming of a time when time will end, and to posit the possibility of an eschatology, of a final time, of a suspension or completion of historical and political time when, if you like, the indefinite governmentality of the state will be brought to an end and halted" (Foucault, 2007, 256).

We note that, when political movements adopt the idiom of eschatological promises of sudden transitions from one society to another, they usually do not speak of "the end of the world" or "the end of time." Instead, they tend to use less apocalyptic phrases like "the end of an era" or "the end of x-society," ushering in the coming of a different time and a new society. Often, such quasi-eschatological political idiom relies upon some notion of a major crisis that, to be overcome, requires our entering into a new social order, a new society.

Foucault (2008, 310–311) made cautionary remarks on the adoption of anti-state political eschatology across so diverse contexts as the founding of the American republic, and in the propagation of the Third Estate in France. He also assigns political eschatology to totalitarian movements like Stalinism, Fascism and National Socialism. The Marxist promise of a "withering away of the state" and the fascist nationalist dream of unifying the state and people come to mind. It would be tempting to conclude, then, that political eschatology is a property belonging exclusively to nationalist and authoritarian regimes. However, we must remember that Foucault treated eschatology as a kind of flexible or open-ended political idiom that can be appropriated by very different countermovements and mobilized to spearhead very different political visions. The terrain hence spans such diverse movements as Christian reformists, communist revolutionaries and extreme nationalist republicans.

At moments, it is quite easy to follow Foucault when he expresses sympathy for people who decide to stand up against an overwhelming power, perhaps in the shape of an authoritarian regime. In such events of revolt, the subjectivity of ordinary people inscribes itself into history, "breathing life into it" (Foucault, 1994, 452). Although the outcomes of revolts are always uncertain and hazardous, one must treat revolts as something irreducible, a singularity that cannot be evaluated a priori. People may be driven to revolt by a particular sense of injustice, or their struggle may rest on the axiomatic principle of the equality of each and every citizen. Small groups of the subaltern population may engage in struggles that turn out to have a universal scope and implications. Religion has often carried a particular force in mass revolts by way of its dramaturgical scripts, its demand for sacrifice and its eschatological visions:

"[B]ecause everyone stakes his life, and his death, on their possibility, one understands why uprisings have so easily found their expression and their drama in religious forms. Promises of the afterlife, time's renewal, anticipation of the savior or the empire of the last days, a reign of pure goodness—for centuries all this constituted, where the religious form allowed, not an ideological costume but the very way of experiencing revolts" (Foucault, 1994, 450).

A key component and promise inherent to political eschatology is the triumphant unification of state and society, or the absorption of the state by society. This means that the counter-positioning of the space of the state and the space of civil society is at the core of political eschatology. As we shall see, some political movements may argue that the state has outgrown its limits in its stifling invasion of society, whereas others appeal to the state to surpass a purely legal-punitive function and secure the well-being of the population. We wish to emphasize the question of how movements position themselves, claiming to speak from or to represent particular spaces. We hence seek to pursue the question of the distribution of places and roles in political struggle, that is, the basic issue of who can become legitimate spokespersons for a particular space and determine what should be done in that space. Jacques Rancière succinctly states this perspective:

"In the end everything in politics turns on the distribution of spaces. What are these places? How do they function? Why are they there? Who can occupy them? For me, political action always acts upon the social as the litigious distribution of places and roles. It is always a matter of knowing who is qualified to say what a particular place is and what is done to it" (Rancière, 2003, 201).

The above outline of a conceptual vocabulary for addressing political movements, religion and space leaves us with the following questions: First, how do social movements take up the position of speaking against political rulers by representing "the truth of society"? Second, to what extent do modern social movements invoke eschatological themes, including the theme of the absorption of the state by society and the theme of universal equality? And, third, how do movements imagine space, including the space from which they speak and the space which they aspire to (re)establish?

The modern city

The city is a breeding ground for social movements that engage in the practice of "truth telling" against political governors, invoking different visions of what the city space fundamentally is and which potentials it holds. The social conditions arising in modern, industrialized cities gave birth to diverse kinds of political movements and very different visions of a future society. The city is indeed both a real space and an imagined space.

The city played an important role in the Western imagination—as the site of modernity, as the place of human degradation and as the opposite of community. Unsurprisingly, the city figured large in the evolution of sociology. Out of these diverse responses, one constant is shared by both conservatives and socialists, namely, to reshape and reform city life to make it more livable, albeit in very different ways. These efforts at reform included a romanticism about rural life such as the garden city idea and, at the opposite end, the rise of urban planning as a scientific approach to city development. Another example of urban reformism was the Settlement movement of the late 19th and early 20th century. YES, done!]

Perhaps we can think of the city in terms of interactions between space, religion and politics. For the sake of convenience, we explore these issues in terms of three stages in the development towards modern urban life. The first stage is defined by the idyllic vision of rural communities as integrated, coherent and harmonious. For the sake of convenience, we call this first stage a "Tocqueville space". The second stage encompasses the time of the creation of large cities, the response to urbanization in the Settlement movement and the development of early sociology. Finally, the third and last stage is marked by the development of the Internet as a new medium for social struggle that may redesign the way that social movements mobilize in urban spaces. Occupy Wall Street is situated at this stage and it became emblematic for political mobilization by means of the social media and mass media based coverage. In this last stage, we also find the Tea Party, which can be viewed at least partly as a reaction to the dissolution of cultural certainties and the sweeping process of globalization.

This classification of historical stages is designed to help us think about the interplay between political power and counter movements and religious ideas in modernity through a typology that is obviously artificial but hopefully heuristic.

In each historical stage, we explore how lived space, in terms of the real configuration of particular social and physical spaces, gives shape to social movements. In addition, we reconstruct imagined spaces that groups have dreamt of establishing or returning to. Within this artificial framework we trace real developments in the character of urban space with the growth of the modern city against the background of the idyllic vision of rural communities as integrated, coherent and harmonious. As mentioned, we call the first stage a "Tocqueville space" with reference to Alexis de Tocqueville's vision of American civil society as composed of viable communities in an agrarian society. This was also the view of Thomas Jefferson, who imagined the American republic as a collection of small self-governing communities free from aristocratic control. The antigovernmental vision bears the mark of political eschatologies on the coming of stateless self-governance which is presumably innate to society. This vision still dominates much American political theory of a republican democracy that is largely free of "big government" and burdensome taxation. Noteably, he Pre-Raphaelites in England in the late 19th century had a similar vision involving the revival of rural craftsmanship and the refashioning of architectural forms. This rural utopia of a non-distorted, rural space is still alive today as an alternative to urban congestion. Hence, in the ideology of Tea Party we witness a rearticulation of this space of small self-reliant communities opposed to the state. This entails that the stage cannot be contained to a specific time-period but may re-emerge at moments very distant from its original articulation.

The second stage involved the creation of large cities such as Paris and Berlin that became the most significant form of social and political life. In this stage the city is seen to be a site of potential moral corruption, civil conflict and the threat allegedly posed by a working class devoid of manners and breeding. For socialists, the hope was that working-class solidarity might emerge in the face of urban squalor and factory conditions. A similar vision of reform grew out of the Settlement movement, where the Church and university intellectuals created urban Settlements to help workers find solutions to education and health problems. This phase often combined socialism and Christianity. We call this a "Durkheimian space" which entailed a quest for solidarity, the state as a moral agency regulating urban space and the creation of a civic religion as propagated by the French sociologist Emile Durkheim.

Third and finally, there is now a new space with the global spread of the Internet, involving flexible, elastic social relations, online religion and protest movements that in some cases seek to occupy parks, public spaces and public arenas. The growth of social media has been important in Occupy Wall Street, the Arab Spring, the Umbrella Revolution and similar social movements in recent years. The American Tea Party movement was less reliant on social media but did profit from support offered by Fox News to broadcast their message of the perverse effects of "Big Government." We call this third space "Tardian space" after Gabriel Tarde, a contemporary of Durkheim and the theorist of crowds, crime, imitation and communication.

Stage 1: Tocquevillian Democracy

The urbanization of the Western world is a relatively recent event, occurring mainly in the second half of the 19th century. Perhaps London is the exception in that it was already a relatively large and complex city by the end of the 17th century. The relatively late changes to urban space in France and Germany were flagged in the work of Walter Benjamin (1892–1940) on malls, gas lighting and the *flaneur* in his Arcades Project (Tiedemann, 2002). Most observers (both socialist and conservative) were struck by the dramatic changes to Western society posed by the urbanization process, the rise of capital cities, the decline of agrarian occupations and the deprivation of workers in urban slums. The passage toward industrialization spurred an intense debate between divergent political figures, who spoke passionately about the nature of the urban space, demanding or justifying political action. In the case of

Great Britain, there are the famous accounts of F. Engels (1845) *Condition of the Working Class in England* based on his personal observations of Manchester. The studies of Charles Booth (1902) are also indicative of these changes. At the end of the century we find the famous research by Robert Park and others from the so-called Chicago school of sociology. By the end of the 19th century America had large cities. In his visit to Chicago and New York in 1903, Max Weber (Scaff, 2011) was stunned by the size and dynamism of urban life—all while the United States remained a land of small communities.

The American dream and the myth of participant democracy were based on a Tocquevillian dream of small, self-sufficient, self-governing townships or rural communities outside the reach of big business and big government. We should take note of this utopian rural romance because much of the ideology of the Tea Party in modern America is driven by this nostalgia for an original, undistorted space, which in concrete terms meant a space unregulated by Washington bureaucrats and "big government." Robert Bellah's famous re-examination of the Tocqueville legacy in his *Habits of the Heart* (Bellah, Madsen, Sullivan, Swidler and Tipton, 1985) found that Americans were active in civil society, supported local charities and distrusted Washington politics. Tocqueville's civil society depended on mutual trust, local chapels and shared values. It was also an open space as yet not pervaded by large populations, transport systems or industrial sites. Frederick Turner's "frontier thesis" underlined the fact that the white settler societies had ample space—provided they could either ignore or kill the indigenous inhabitants. Why is this frontier myth still so important? Why has it continued to fuel a conservative critique of capitalism?

In the English case, perhaps the best example is the work of the philosopher Roger Scruton in such books as *England: An Elegy* (2001) and in the American case perhaps the continuing popularity of the novels of Mark Twain and the epic *Last of the Mohicans* (Fenimore Cooper, 1995), not to mention the political and social theories of Henry David Thoreau (1871–1862), who, as a member of the Transcendentalist movement, placed his faith squarely in nature. In *Walden* (1854) and *Maine Woods* (1988) Thoreau gave a lasting expression to a solitary life in the wilderness beyond the reach of government and the city. In the 20th century the poetry of Robert Frost (d. 1963) with his nostalgic view of New Hampshire celebrated a rural idyll of small farms and cozy communities. Rural space is homogeneous, ample, unmarked by strangers and essentially secure. The squalor, violence and poverty of the Bronx are hidden from view. Perhaps the shortest poem in America literature is by Ogden Nash:

The Bronx?No thonks!

Stage 2: Durkheimian Social Solidarity

While sociology as a discipline can be dated from 1824 on the basis of the correspondence of Auguste Comte, a more realistic date might be Durkheim's *The Division of Labour in Society* (1893). Durkheim was primarily concerned with answering the question: How can large, urban, complex societies hold together? He proposed several different answers. Here, let us summarize his response by saying, first, there has to be a state that will intervene to regulate the tendencies of crises inherent to modern society; the role of the state is to act as a moral guardian to direct and regulate a rapidly modernizing society prone to anomie. Second, there has to be something like a civil religion to replace more traditional forms of religious sentiment. Third, we need to avoid virulent forms of nationalism (this was his critique of German nationalism prior to the First World War). Furthermore, some division of labor to integrate society is expected to arise because, with occupational specialization, individuals can no longer be completely independent and autonomous. Finally, rather like both Saint Simon and Auguste Comte, Durkheim thought that sociology had an important role to play in analyzing the causes of the crises of modernity. For example, the rising rate of suicide in urban society among young unmarried men was indicative of the underlying malaise. Durkheim is often described as a conservative (Nisbet, 1967). However, his prognosis for managing industrial society was to look toward the state as a regulating agency, to encourage the occupational guilds as an emergent source of solidarity, to limit the power of the Roman Catholic Church and to support beliefs that might coalesce into a civil religion. Durkheimian space is thus quite unlike Tocquevillian space—it is urban, complex, individualistic, secular and dependent on the state for some degree of moral regulation. Durkheim looked toward the possibilities of solidarity and sociability within urban working-class industrial spaces, and in that sense Durkheim's solution was essentially socialist.

The Settlement Movement

The Settlement House movement had its origins in England among intellectuals in the 1860s—John Ruskin, Thomas Carlyle, Charles Kingsley and so-called Christian Socialists, who sought to create a colony of learning and enlightenment in the new industrial slums. The problems they sought to remedy were vividly described in the social novels of Charles Dickens. They were alarmed by urban poverty, the division between social classes and the brutal routinization of work. This drive for reform spurred various philanthropy groups, with the Settlement movement spearheaded by Jane

Addams as probably the most influential one. The Christian socialism of the Settlement movements was, like Durkheim's socialism, concerned with the possibilities of fellowship and cooperation.

The early Settlement experiments took place in university towns where the idea was to bring together undergraduates (from privileged backgrounds) and working-class people who had no education. The early Settlement movement (again like Durkheim) was based on the idea of bringing science to bear on social problems and to create opportunities for solidarity across class divisions. It required a union of "sympathy and science." (Villadsen and Turner, 2015: 7–8).

The first US settlement, Hull-house, was founded in 1889, by Jane Addams and Ellen Gates Starr, Hull House in Chicago. By 1910, a total of 413 social Settlements were active in the US, and the National Social Workers Exchange was created in 1917. Following these developments in England and America, Settlement houses were established in many urban industrial societies. For example, Settlements were created in Finland in 1884, and the first Citizen Hall was founded in Helsinki in 1890. A similar history of Settlement can be told from Copenhagen, Denmark (see chapter three in this book).

In the English case, we can date the emergence of the movement to 1867 when the young Oxford graduate Edward Denison settled in Stepney, offered free education for local children and organized the community to improve health and sanitation. A more enduring contribution was associated with Arnold Toynbee, who in 1875, working with the Vicar of St Judes Church, opened a center for education in Whitechapel in the East end of London. In 1884, a group of Toynbee's followers created Toynbee Hall in Whitechapel and, under the auspices of both Oxford and Cambridge universities, it became a model for other Settlements in England and the US. The Settlement movement in Britain peaked around 1920.

The values behind these Settlement movements were diverse, but perhaps the most common theme was to create an enlightenment or colony of culture and learning as a common center where working-class people could benefit from education, recreation and advice regarding health and hygiene (Davies, 1984). The students lived in the Settlement and they sought to establish collaboration with local organizations, chapels and workers. Settlement workers thought of themselves as good neighbors rather than benefactors. The movement was based on the idea that friendship and mutual contact were essential to overcome class division.

At the same time, similar movements developed in the United States, but the challenge in American cities was posed not only by social class, but also by race and ethnicity, and the many changes brought about by the waves of migration. The American movements were more closely connected to the churches and became influenced by the Social Gospel movement of the late 19th century, thereby setting the stage for the Progressive Era (MacLean & Williams, 2012). US Settlement leaders were shocked by the corruption of urban politics and by the struggles between the parties. The initial emphasis on "cultural uplift" soon gave way to more practical goals—education, healthcare, better homes and secure working conditions.

The US experience was in many ways very different from the European one. Settlement houses in the US were important in assimilating foreign migrants. They also played a major role in assisting black migrants from the South to settle in northern cities after the Civil War. In regard to this issue, churches—such as the Roman Catholic Church and the Missionary Society of the Methodist Episcopal Church South—were important, but the idea to work for social amelioration inside the poor neighborhoods was also connected to the growth of black American evangelical chapels. Yet another important function of these Settlements was providing opportunities for women to fill leadership roles in societies that were decidedly patriarchal. A significant female reformer was Lillian Wald, who founded New York's Henry Street Settlement.

Jane Addams (1860–1935) was a key figure in the US Settlement movement and regarded as the first major female sociologist. She was closely associated with the Chicago school of sociology that produced major works on urban America, migration, city structures and transient workers. Along with Ellen Gates Starr, she started Hull House in Chicago in 1889 after visiting Toynbee House in 1888. In 1892, Addams laid out the program and mission of Settlement sociology in a speech entitled "On the Subjective Necessity of Social Settlements" at the School of Applied Ethics in Plymouth, Massachusetts, in 1892. She argued that democracy had failed to eradicate poverty, class distinction and ignorance. The Settlements were a place where workers could enjoy cultural activities and they provided opportunities to congregate and organize. She also saw the Settlements in the light of the Social Gospel as offering the prospect of a "certain renaissance of Christianity" (quoted in Davies, 1984, 27).

However the Settlements knew nothing about doctrinal orthodoxy. They were to remain inclusive, flexible and secular. Addams shared with the Toynbee Hall leadership a desire to turn Christian values into practice, putting "spirit into action" (Villadsen and Turner, 2015: 13). The aim was less the saving souls for the afterworld than principally about bettering their living conditions and welfare in the real world. Addams's view of Christianity and social work were somewhat contradictory. While she was associated with the rise of social work as a secular and scientific endeavor, she worked in a milieu in which there was no obvious clash between sociology and Christianity (Lengermann and Niebrugge, 2007, 99). Notably, in *The Objective Value of a Social Settlement* she said that the chief value of the Settlement was to act as an "interpretation bureau" in relation to the poor immigrants (1893, 5–7). Thus, Addams wanted to distinguish the Settlement movement from traditional forms of Christian charity and philanthropy. The problems surrounding poverty and lack of education were not the result of the moral failing of individuals, but a consequence of the objective organization of society.

The ambition to document the actual conditions of poverty intensified during the first years of the US Settlement, and the members would soon describe themselves not as philanthropists, but as social scientists (Lengermann and Niebrugge, 1998, 68). It has often been observed that the Settlement workers were pioneers in generating a factual, sociological knowledge about social issues. It is indeed tempting to view the Settlement workers as early sociologists spurred by a quest to free the facts of human misery completely from religious and moralistic assumptions. The attempt to produce a field of factual knowledge about problems arising in an industrial city—solely produced by human activity—without making any reference to transcendent agencies or a divine plan certainly supports such an interpretation. In light of this emphasis, the Settlement movement could readily be inserted into Foucault's overall analysis of governmentalization, a process establishing new relations between political rulers and those agents claiming to speak the truth about society. Addams and her coworkers were carving out a space of factual social knowledge insofar as society would now be represented as made of social activities and regularities. They could be said to undertake a kind of early social statistics mobilized to direct politicians' attention to issues of child labor, work accidents and polluted neighborhoods. The Settlement movement can be said, then, to be emblematic of the movement from transcendentalism to pragmatism in American social reform (Greenstone, 1979). In brief, the space of the industrial city invoked by the Settlement would seem to be purely social.

We should, however, point out that the Settlements did not break entirely with all religious and quasi-religious ideas, evident in their assumptions about the human subject, brotherhood and the community. Addams did not believe that instructions for how to act in a poverty-ridden industrializing city could be derived from theological debate. Neither did she accept the libertarian image of society as a space founded on natural rights, nor did she subscribe to socialists' vision of a collectivized social body. Rather, her vision of society was of a different complexion: It arose from her particular blend of inspirations coming from Social Darwinism, feminism and reformist Protestantism.

Addams believed that the fast-paced industrial urbanization had created a society in which individuals had become dependent upon each other to an unprecedented degree. She also believed that this development had outpaced the ethical standards that, in most areas, were still tied to the previous, traditional, patriarchal order based on individual status and heritage. It was, however, possible to detect the emergence of a new ethics, which Addams termed "social ethics," across the key institutions of society. By studying new forms of organizing and conflict arising within employment relations, the family, philanthropy and more, Addams extracted the incipient emergence of a new social ethics. The main source in this regard is her book *Democracy and Social Ethics* (Addams, 1907). Addams' discovery of a new social ethics corresponded to her social evolutionist view that society was itself generating norms beneficial and timely for its further development. This strategy of "reading norms from facts," of extracting ethical standards from observable behavioral patterns, resonates with contemporary social thought inspired by social Darwinist ideas, including Durkheim's view of society as a social organism.

The fast-paced social-material development had uprooted existent social and moral bonds, granting individuals more freedoms. At the same time, the increasing social interdependencies meant that individuals had become fundamentally more dependent upon the societal order. Addams (1907) reasoned that this situation had rendered inadequate the old ethics based on loyalty to one's closest family and patriarchal relations between employer and employees as well as between the head of the household and servants. There were some grounds for optimism, since Addams detected the emergence of a new social ethics which responded to the challenges of the times by creating novel forms of cooperation in industrial relations. The practices of the new social ethics entail the reconfiguration of the giver-receiver relationship in philanthropy and the establishing of alternative ways of educating or disciplining the youth.

The capacity of the social body to develop such responses cannot merely be explained from Addams' inspiration by a social-evolutionist perspective, but can also be derived from certain assumptions that Addams held about human subjects. Humans were essentially driven by a desire for sociability, and they had a propensity for kindness—innate characteristics termed "the neighborly paradigm' (MacLean and Williams, 2012, 241). Addams and her associates did not subscribe to the idea of "American exceptionalism," which posits the American society as something special inasmuch as it was the place where religious and secular sources would eventually converge in the Kingdom of God. This idea was prevalent among other contemporary, Christian-inspired movements such the Social Gospel. In the Settlement movement, less eschatological terms like neighborly love, brotherhood and a Christian renaissance played a unifying role in movement.

For the Settlement founders, the big industrializing cities were spaces pervaded by contradictory forces. On the one hand, there were the negative forces—an encroaching, consumerist capitalism, increasingly brutal industrial disputes and an American administration exerting a purely legal-punitive role instead of caring for the population's welfare. All of this can lead to a fragmentized, unequal and conflict-ridden society. On the other hand, there is evidence of emergent social ethics, new forms of social collaboration, and the potential entailed in imbuing the public sphere with female values. Addams (1895, 186) reasoned that women's maternal instinct and "family affection" prepared women for practicing and promoting values of caretaking at the level of the society at large, encapsulated in the notion of "city housekeeping" (Lengerman and Niebrugge, 1998, 89 n6). If female values are allowed to infuse into the public and political space, the existing legal-punitive order would be challenged and potentially reinscribed with values of collaboration, care and friendship. It is tempting to say, then, that, for Addams, society was a space of struggle between the forces of good and evil.

In the context of the Settlement, Christianity figures neither as a set of doctrines to be followed nor as a missionary impetus. For Addams, Christianity was rather a potentially transformative force, evident in her view that Christianity should make it possible to construct a society of collaboration and care instead of an agglomeration of selfish individuals (1911). Despite her emphasis on factual knowledge of poverty, Addams' Protestant experience had given her an inspiration essential for her determined work for social change (Villadsen and Turner, 2015: 6). Yet, a strict adherence to religious doctrine would certainly have been a stumbling block for the pragmatic politics she and her associates were practicing. The most significant trace of inspiration from Christianity in Settlement thinking is perhaps the idea of fostering a community of "fellowship", collaboration and mutual care (Maclean and Williams, 2011).

Addams's and her collaborators' political stance is not easily categorized, and it has been assigned both libertarian, conservative and social-democratic traits. The difficulty in understanding the Settlement project from a present-day vantage point is that it does not lend itself to conventional political reasoning concerning state/civil society, the social contract and formal institutions. Ideals of furthering "friendship between the classes," "brotherhood" and "neighborly care" do not easily translate into modern (ideological) political rationalities. Instead, these ideals had a key source in a common premise among people with a Christian upbringing, namely, that, in the final instance, what could keep the community together was a divinely inspired spirit of kindness.

This implicit Christian message is distinct to the Settlement as a counter-movement that carried out pragmatic work to influence political power-holders. There were other ways of looking at industrial society that went in a different direction such as the liberalism of Herbert Spencer (1820–1895), for whom social planning could only interfere with the evolutionary development of societies. We can also compare the Settlement's social critique with more optimistic and celebratory views of city life, for instance, Hart Crane's *The Bridge* (1930), a lyrical reflection on Brooklyn Bridge. Here, urban space acquires a different religious intensity. The message of the poem is that, despite the Civil War and racial conflict, America remained a land of ample spaces and soaring individual opportunity.

In summary, the Settlement movement reflects some of the underlying assumptions of 19th-century sociology: the need for new or revived foundations of social solidarity; a new pattern of civic ethics; measures to overcome urban anomie; and a state that could provide some moral steerage. We have called this tradition Durkheimian. Jane Addams' thinking was nevertheless quite distinct in its blend of inspirations from Social Darwinism,

Feminism and reformist Protestantism. This mixture made it possible to speak at the same time of a society capable of generating new social norms, the need to bring female values into the public-political space and of an inherent community spirit of neighborly love awaiting its embodiment.

Stage 3: Gabriel Tarde and network-based sociability

Perhaps one of the most interesting disputes in late 19th-century French sociology was that between Emile Durkheim (1858–1917) and Gabriel Tarde (1843–1904). Tarde was a brilliant statistician and criminologist who rejected the biological deterministic view of crime championed by Lombroso. Against Durkheim, he developed a theory of imitation-suggestion to explain crowd behavior. Society rests on an imitative foundation—imitation is the foundation of society as a flow or network of imitation-suggestion, he argued in *The Laws of Imitation* (1890). Tarde's way of thinking about sociology had an important impact on the study of social media and modern forms of connectivity and dis-connectivity (Borch, 2012).

If we are to think about the sociology of spaces, we should keep in mind that one great fear of the 19th century concerned the role of the mob or crowd as an aspect of social and political instability. Crowds occupied a space of irrational contagion. The irrational impact of imitation undermined habit and the moral fabric. Similarly, mob behavior in the modern city is often directed against migrant workers invading the space of the host community. In 2013, the "mob" is still an aspect of strategies to invade or protect space. A mob in Moscow attacked undocumented migrant, primarily Asian, workers; a mob in Sydney fought the police in public spaces over alleged insults to the Prophet; a Japanese mob attacked Korean workers in Tokyo. Fears about crowd behavior may explain the current revival of interest in Tarde's contributions to criminology and the psychology of the crowd (Tarde, 1969).

The Settlement movement was at its most creative between the1880s and 1920s. If we take a look at our contemporary world, it becomes evident that it provides a different context for countermovements. It is possible to point at a range of social, political and spatial transformations.

As rental costs rise, there has been an exodus of workers from city centers with the middle class becoming suburbanized and the working population marginalized—thereby causing them to commit much of their income to travel to and from their workplaces. There is, for example, currently an exodus of workers from Manhattan where few can afford to live without two incomes. At the same time, shops and malls are closing as online shopping becomes more widespread. Only establishments providing services to the body are thriving—nail shops, hairdressers, coffee shops, restaurants, massage parlors—and brothels.

There has been a decline of the working class with the erosion of manufacturing, outsourcing, overseas investment, the growth of service industry, the decline in the size of productive processes, computerization of manufacturing and legal constraints on union activity. The result is a significant drop in "union density," that is, the number of workers with union membership. Income inequality has grown, although social class as a form of *Gemeinschaft* or communal identity has largely disappeared in advanced economies. These changes are also associated with the fact that electoral victories are increasingly won by center-right parties (with recent elections in Greece and Spain being exceptions), and political debate has been dominated by populist appeals to the disaffected electorate in opposition to the increase in migrant populations. Thus, many European societies now have influential right-wing populist movements such as UKIP, the English Defense League, Gold Dawn, the Northern League in Italy and Pegida in Germany.

In ethnic, cultural and religious terms, cities in Europe are now far more diverse and divided. In many societies, we have "parallel communities" or separate enclaves with little connection to the wider society. However, the evidence of social exclusion is mixed. There is some evidence (in the United States particularly) of an increasing pattern of interracial marriage, Jewish assimilation and religious tolerance (Putnam and Campbell, 2010). Yet communities are deeply stratified into what sociologists have called "housing classes" (Rex and Moore, 1967) as an effect of income inequality, unequal access to mortgages, casualization of employment and the absence of "credit worthiness." Most cities are confronted with the absence of "affordable housing."

We have seen that the churches were important in the Settlement movement in both Europe and the United States. While many sociologists are critical of the secularization thesis, there are also sociologists who detect a move away from organized religion to a more individualized form of spirituality. In her book *Religion in Britain since 1945* Grace Davie (1994) made famous the notion of "believing without belonging." There is also the growth of religion online and finally a general increase of people who claim no religion at all (the "nones"), who number between 22–25 % in most societies, being drawn mainly from people under 25 years of age. Bryan Turner and his associates have emphasized that religion can serve as a source of inspiration and a medium of contemporary political struggle (Campbell, Torpey and Turner, 2015).

Given the neo-liberal revolution in economics, the modern state assumes less and less responsibility for steering society. With Thatcherism, many state functions were privatized and public spaces were increasingly put in private hands. This development was famously summarized by Thatcher: "There is no such thing as society ..." As the tax base of the state shrinks, it has privatized public utilities and withdrawn support for pensions, health, education and commitment to full employment. With the dominance of "market fundamentalism" (Sommers, 2008), most governments are reluctant to invest in the infrastructure that is necessary to maintain the modern city.

What are the consequences for counter movements?

Tardean Monads: Occupy and Tea Party

Tarde, following Leibniz, was interested in monads. For sociology we can translate this idea as meaning that modern forms of interconnectivity allow people to participate in social networks online as more or less isolated individuals. In the isolation of the home, individuals can in principle be connected to everybody. The internet has been underresearched in urban sociology because modern communication means that social and economic services can be decentralized and dispersed across space. For example, online shopping can bypass the local store, so that production storage and final delivery of commodities can be far removed from customers. New technologies such as Google's experimentation with drones may even remove human labor from the delivery of services and commodities from the city. Currently, we are witnessing social movements unfolding through novel social media technologies, evident from Occupy to the Tea Party movement (Agarwal, Barthel, Rost, Borning, Bennett and Johnson, 2014).

We can contrast this situation with, say, the civil rights movements in the US, which mobilized whole communities rather than individuals. Contemporary sociology understands social movements as mobilizing otherwise isolated and disconnected individuals through the social media. Many contemporary social movements—Occupy, Arab Spring, Indignados, the Umbrella Revolution—depend heavily on social media; they are not community based, they tend not to have permanent structures or leadership, they employ similar tactics (occupying parks, plazas, squares, creating short-term "villages"), and above all they are *movements of individuals.* They recruit heavily from the young, the educated and the middle class. The crisis in Egypt after the Arab Spring and the tensions remaining in Turkey are on a different scale, but they share some characteristics with Occupy—the mobilization of disaffected young people in public spaces for protest. Contemporary protests against austerity packages in Greece, Spain and Italy have similar characteristics.

Occupy Wall Street had a significant impact in late 2012 especially on the Obama campaign by effectively mobilizing around the slogan "We are the 99 %." The movement rejected organization and leadership, had obvious anarchist tendencies, recruited mainly from young white constituencies, and had very limited connections with churches, trade unions or political parties. Accordingly, opinion is divided over the following question: Has Occupy Wall Street disappeared? Some supporters of the principles of Occupy Wall Street argue that this model of protest is now diffused across a range of movements. Occupy Wall Street is a model for organizing and assembling large gatherings for protests on a range of issues—typically of concern to the young whose expectations have been dashed by the on-going crisis of capitalist economies. For example "International People's Assembly: Detroit October 5–6" claims to have been inspired by Occupy Wall Street. The Detroit agenda is very diverse—mainly aimed at banking, but several items relate to our interest in cities and spaces. A key claim voiced by these urban movements, which are concentrated on a moratorium on mortgage foreclosures and foreclosure-related evictions, is that housing is a basic right.

A key characteristic of Occupy Wall Street was the hitherto unseen use of space, insofar as occupancies at public squares and in parks were choreographed, photographed or filmed and then circulated as emblematic sites of insurrectional democratizing practices. The movement's founders have explained that before any political concepts or arguments could be formulated a sustained daily presence at the heart of the capitalist order was needed (Creech, 2014, 467). They needed to occupy spaces that symbolized the constant flow of capital, thus choreographing the occupancies by counter positioning crowds of peaceful protestors with cooperate capitalism and its protectors represented by the police force. By this retaking of city streets and squares Occupy sought to create a new language suited for articulating the existence of lack of freedom, of inequality and of exploitation. Occupy Wall Street gained momentum when it became attached to a wide range of popular protest movements—Occupy Binghamton, Occupy USA, Occupy Portland, Occupy Boulder Flood Relief, the latter of which was inspired by the efforts of Occupy Sandy. The choreographed and social media-born movement seemed to have inaugurated a novel kind of political struggle.

More critical views argued that Occupy Wall Street "fizzled out" after the short-term occupation of parks. Once the occupiers left their parks, it was unclear what they had actually achieved. Critics like Robert Reich and Larry McDonald pointed to lack of focus on a single mission, disorganization and lack of leadership. Similarly, Todd Gitlin (2012), in *Occupy Nation,* noted that the lack of connection to communities, unions and churches meant that a movement of individuals could not survive effectively over time. Despite the mass appeal of Occupy Wall Street and similar movements, a widely held conclusion is that they failed to generate sustained political changes because they lacked the unity, coherence, leadership and organization needed to effectively carry out such changes.

A more positive view of the potentials of new social movements mobilized around social media may be found in Michael Hardt and Antoni Negri's collective work (2000; 2012). From their viewpoint, the lack of institutional embedding can alternatively be evaluated as the very strength of the Occupy movement, insofar as they take into account the new reality of the Empire. In fact, commenting on the Occupy movement, Hardt and Negri related it to the need for a whole new form of democratic agency, that is, the need for constructing "new constitutional figures that can open avenues to again take up the project of the pursuit of collective happiness" (Hardt and Negri, 2012). In their grandiose analysis, "the Empire" is described as a loosely connected, all-inclusive and expansive circuit of exchanges that contains certain novel potentials of resistance. The open, network-like character of globalized capitalism makes it more flexible and difficult to locate, but also turns it vulnerable to acts of circumvention, blockage or sabotage. On this basis, Occupy Wall Street could be viewed as a decentered knot in the worldwide circuit where videos, photos and blogging could circulate. The Occupy movement that swept across the US and parts of the globe was a loose alliance consisting of essentially disparate actions of occupancy of public spaces and protest connected via social media.

It has been argued (Swyngedouw, 2014) that Occupy Wall Street was a reaction to situations of depolitization and the prevalence of identity politics in contemporary liberal-capitalist society. The first implies the "disappearance of the political" by including different opinions or demands as long as they do not contest fundamentally the existent neo-liberal political and economic order (Swyngedouw, 2014, 123). This "postdemocratic" situation entails that social space is saturated by a police order in which a technocratic-managerial expertise turns any kind of challenge into an issue of expert administration. Politics thus disappear in the management of a presumably inevitable neo-liberal order. By invoking principles of "good governance," in tandem with an economic oligarchy the administrative elite increasingly occupy "the spatiality of the political" (Swyngedouw, 2014, 124). Occupy indeed succeeded in repoliticizing the existing order by completely rejecting the system of representation and refusing to formulate demands that could be accommodated by the system. The movement broke decidedly with conventional notions of what constitutes the spaces appropriate for political processes, such as parliaments, council chambers and negotiations between employers and labor unions.

Occupy has also been viewed as a reaction to a situation increasingly dominated by identity politics. The progressive potential herein is that individuals can be granted rights according to ethnic, gender and sexual identities. The downside is that identity politics can negate itself if identities become instruments in political-administrative programs that fragment groups, disarming collective action. It has been argued that the situation in the 1990s in the US was marked by "a more or less complete demobilization of the social movements" (Blunden, 2014, 430). Identity politics that reconfigure, for instance, a shared "female identity" to become "minority rights" poses serious obstacles for collective action.

"(O)nce an individual counts themselves as part of something according to the possession of an admittedly inessential attribute, then the logic of identity politics is in place. On the one hand, an individual is subjected to forms of discrimination according to a socially constructed stigma based on an inessential attribute, and on the other hand, granted recognition and inclusion by virtue of this or that attribute. There is no end to the inessential attributes of a person, which can be the basis of a claim for justice and recognition" (Blunden, 2014, 429).

It could be argued that the Occupy movement succeeded in a kind of repoliticization exactly by way of its inclusive and open character. Occupy Wall Street and related movements invoke a decidedly universalizing logic. Although they would admit to constituting a minority in number, they nevertheless claim to speak for "everyone," for "the majority," or to give voice to "the 99 %." These slogans express a strife for transcending the particularism of the local issues of poverty, debts, home evictions and labor struggles and to insert them in an overall political spectacle.

There is a striking difference in the staging of political struggle between the Settlement and Occupy Wall Street. Compared to Addams and the Settlement workers' mundane pragmatism, resting on the belief that it was better to achieve something small than not to achieve anything at all, Occupy Wall Street staged a dramatic spectacle. The goal was not to engage in any kind of participatory governance, but rather to disrupt the field of vision of the political, including the distribution of spaces where discontent can be voiced and where the workings of the liberal-capitalist order unfolds. Occupy Wall Street and its offshoots would eventually place themselves into the order of spectacle, as "they have an aesthetic dimension and are often dramatic," in that they "dramatize key issues in a given society" (Kellner cited in Creech, 2014, 463).

Occupy Wall Street's attempt to disrupt the political ontology of representation could be seen as an intervention with eschatological connotations, insofar as it carried the message that politics as we know it will henceforth be impossible. It promises, as it were, to halt the infinite governmentality of constitutionalism and ushers in a new world.

"A democratic government derives its just power from the people, but corporations do not seek consent to extract wealth from the people and the Earth; and that no true democracy is attainable when the process is determined by economic power. We come to you at a time when corporations, which place profit over people, self-interest over justice, and oppression over equality, run our governments" (Occupy Wall Street General Assembly cited in Creech, 2014, 466).

Occupy Wall Street came to signify popular protests that revealed a world order where cooperate capital corrupts and misuses the state apparatus to suppress the expression of popular will. Banks and big corporations were posited as the absolute antitheses of collectivist, truly democratic politics. Occupy manage to dramatically stage cast a battle between the forces of good and evil. The two-headed monster of abusive corporate capital and the undemocratic political elite was confronted with the mass of protestors united merely in the axiomatic presumption of equality.

Of course, left-leaning youthful protests are not the only new movements of protest to have appeared recently. We can contrast Occupy Wall Street with the Tea Party, which has a very different base—mainly elderly, white, retired Americans with strong connections to evangelical Protestantism (Williamson, Skocpol and Coggin, 2011). They have stronger and more obvious connections with community and chapels. They were also connected to organized politics, namely, the right-wing of the Republican Party, and they received considerable support in both material and symbolic terms from various lobby groups and thinktanks such as Americans for Prosperity, Freedom Works, the Heritage Foundation, and Friends of Liberty. They also had the backing of Fox News.[elaborate?]

While Occupy Wall Street was a new development in social movements—and certainly the most significant criticism of financial capitalism in recent years in New York—there are of course well-established religious groups, institutions and churches that have played an important role in caring for the poor and offering alternative spaces to the homeless and the marginalized.

How then did the Christian Churches in Manhattan respond to the more general problems of inequality, racial discrimination, poverty and homelessness over a longer period of time? After all, Occupy Wall Street was more an event than a long-term contribution to the city's problems, and the churches of all denominations have in some sense been involved in the provision of welfare services and sanctuary for the homeless and the downtrodden. The statement below offers one reflection on the more general problems facing inner-city churches confronted by declining membership and the rising needs of the local community:

> The time of famine has intensified for many clergy and for their dwindling congregations, making it imperative to switch directions. The old organizing model had churches bringing their internal parish strength to external community action. This model wrongly equated the strength of congregations with the "number" of people in the pews who could be convinced to hold a protest sign. Now, it is time for a model that embodies mutuality. We clergy and congregations need the community's help. We need the community's energy to assist parishes so that parishes may assist communities. We need the outer to touch the inner. That shift in direction is happening of necessity, due to the extraordinary pressures on parish clergy. It could also happen by design and improve us all.[1]

Judson Memorial Church is located at the south end of Washington Square Park in Greenwich Village, New York City. The church was founded in affiliation with the American Baptist Church in 1890, the mission being to

1 Shaper, Donna. "Why A Shift?" From http://www.judson.org/Occupy Wall Street-Occupy-Wall-St. Retrieved 8 November 2015.

serve the Lower East Side's Italian immigrant community. Today, in the 21st century, the church continues its longstanding mission of furthering progressive politics. Now an "open and affirming" (as in LGBTQ-embracing) member of the American Baptist Church and the United Church of Christ, Judson is a site of worship, artistic expression and activism. A walk around the Italian Renaissance-style building, complete with stained-glass detail and campanile tower, reveals banners advertising current programming, among them: The Bailout Theatre, a "populist art and food program" serving free meals and offering art entertainment once a month; the GYM at Judson, the Church's creative arts group; and Magic Time, their playwright development program. Their letterboard outside, where service times are traditionally listed, offers the message, "Ban the bottle, take back the tap for water" as well as listing the number of American troops serving, injured and killed in Iraq and Afghanistan, alongside the number of civilian casualties in each country.

Sunday morning services are held at 11AM and reveal the broad-minded and actual reach of the Church. Their service is structured by prayer, hymns and a sermon, offering an "open-mic" style invitation to church attendees at the beginning and the end, for community announcements and general expressions of joy and criticism. These include a wide range of concerns, such as messages to "thank a veteran" and remember their suffering, prayer requests for a safe transition in Burma after elections, thanks to participants and supporters of the Black Liberation Theology of Disability Symposium event, among more personal requests such as prayer for the sick.[2] A look at the "This Week @ Judson" calendar on the service bulletin reveals the dynamic use of the church space, which is open seven days a week and hosts two to three events and meetings daily, centering on spirituality, the arts, activism and service.

Among them, Judson hosts and facilitates weekly Excess Anonymous meetings, a twelve-step program for persons struggling with addiction, as well as Kit Parties, where safer injection kits for intravenous drug users are assembled. The 2,500 kits prepared annually are distributed nearby at the Lower East Side Harm Reduction Center, a nonprofit organization offering counseling and syringe exchange, among other health and education services. At Judson, the Kit Parties are advertised as a time to have fun and laugh alongside other church members, while simultaneously serving the community.

Judson continues their longstanding tradition of work around immigrant rights as well. In 2007, they helped found the New Sanctuary Coalition of NYC. They explain the goal of the group on their website, contrasting themselves to early sanctuary movements for Central American migrants in the 1980s. "Instead of hiding them, however, the New Sanctuary Movement proposed to publicize their stories, to put a human face on the issues, raise public

2 Ethnographic field notes. 8 November 2015.

awareness of their plight, and encourage legislative reform."[3] The website profiles two families currently sponsored by Judson: a Haitian father and business owner who has been in the US for over 17 years, and a Chinese man, father to three American citizens, who has lived and worked in the US for over 10 years, seeking political asylum out of fear of religious persecution. Currently, members of Judson serve the New Sanctuary Accompaniment program, where volunteers offer moral and physical support to persons dealing with immigration and deportation hearings by attending alongside them. This, they believe, encourages ethical treatment of the individuals as well as offering company and solidarity throughout the process.

During the Occupy Wall Street protests, which began in lower Manhattan's Zuccotti Park on September 17, 2011, Judson's clergy and church members were highly visible and involved in the protests. When asked about their participation with Occupy Wall Street, Rev. Donna Schaper explained, "When it looked like people wanted to do something about the issues of the 99 %, who can't afford to live after working not to mention the genuinely poor who can't even get a job and are dependent on the welfare state, we knew the hardship of our own community, and we said, 'Oh great! You guys want to put a megaphone on this, we're with you.' So, we almost felt like they were joining us, rather than we joining them."[4]

Judson's contributions to the Occupy Wall Street protests were both material and symbolic. They offered space during and after the eviction, allowing protesters to use their bathrooms during the encampment and later housed several hundred protesters for months like other churches in the area. They organized the march giving the golden calf the name "Greed" and assembled weekly at Zuccotti Park, garnering press attention. Occupy Faith, an interfaith group and a subset of Occupy Wall Street, was originally facilitated by Judson. Though membership of that group did spread to beyond their walls, they continued to use the Judson Memorial Church space to hold meetings. It is unlikely that Judson's work will stop anytime soon, as their programming and mission are both productive and responsive to the society and community within which they are embedded.

The reference to "sanctuary" in the New Sanctuary Movement is an important reminder of how the Christian churches provide space for outsiders and the dispossessed to find some security and protection in a harsh social environment. In the megacity, churches are finding new ways to serve the poor by refashioning and reasserting the sanctuary.

The Tea Party was also a critical response to the economic problems of modern America, albeit clearly from a very different standpoint and ideology. If the

3 "Immigrant Rights". From: http://www.judson.org/ImmigrantRights. Retrieved 8 November 2015.

4 Schaper, Donna. Interview with E.B. Campbell on July 17, 2012.

Photograph taken by E.B. Campbell at the Judson Memorial Church on November 8, 2015

modern sanctuary can be said to be forward looking, in many respects the Tea Party was an old-fashioned form of populism. Its very name looks backward to the American colony and the war of independence. It appeared in 2009 and can be seen as a reaction to, or countermovement against, a set of socioeconomic and cultural changes. These included economic stagnation accompanied by job loss and indebted families, sustained secular challenges to religious identities, for instance, in the debate on same-sex marriages, and the election of the first African-American president. According to national surveys, Tea Party supporters had a disproportionate high participation of white (80–90 %) men (55–60 %) over 45 years old (70–75 %) (Williamson, Skocpol and Coggin, 2011, 27). Their views were generally of a conservative and libertarian orientation, marked by a "less Big Government agenda" and often connected to evangelical movements or congregations. The movement particularly gained supporters from lower middle-class Republicans from rural or suburban areas. It is tempting to view the Tea Party as a reactionary countermovement insofar as it attempts "to defend and retain traditional identities and statuses based on race, patriarchy and hetero-normativity that have been under assault by late modern 'network' society (Langman, 2012, 469).

The Tea Party had a significant impact on the political agenda of the Republican Party, especially by attempting to underline and block "Obamacare" during 2013. It is well represented in the states where the Republican Party is dominant—Texas, Oklahoma, Arizona, Mississippi and North Carolina. It was behind the attempt to close down the government and prevent raising the government debt ceiling. While the Tea Party's agenda failed on October 17, 2013, and while many observers, including senior Republicans, believe the Tea Party has done significant damage to the election of any future Republican Senate and to a future Republican Whitehouse, the Tea Party is not going to go away any time soon.

Space may come into view in two ways with respect to the Tea Party movement. First, it has been suggested that the material and social conditions of rural and suburban America provide a space conducive to conservative viewpoints. This space, says Thomson, "possesses certain social and structural characteristics that can shape styles of moral cognition that in turn lead to conservative predispositions within the personality structure of the individual" (2012, 511). Suburban and country side space tends to entail constrained forms of socialization fostering a dogmatic moral attitude, fear of change, and conservative or new conservative worldviews. Historically, it is also a space populated by small rural merchants and farmers who have sustained distrust to the national government.

Space also figures as an imagined, almost mythical space that has been invaded and needs to be recovered, namely, the original white, rural and Christian America. This conservative vision is invoked variously across the Tea Party movement. Christian conservatives found in the Tea Party a confirmation of their longstanding convictions about the theological signification of the founding of the American constitution and of American exceptionalism (mentioned above). The lasting value of this juridical-theological foundation of America has been jeopardized by misguided politicians and big-city cultural decay: "Indeed, there has been a long tradition in which the conservative, 'idyllic' countryside where people are more 'authentic' and 'virtuous' has counterpoised the nefarious cosmopolitan city with its toleration of diversity, sophistication, and above all, decadence and sites of transgression" (Langman, 2012, 473).

The invocation of the lost space of "real America" makes it possible for the movement to confirm that it is in fact nonpartisan. This follows from the premise that the movement's demands simply reinstate the Founding Fathers' intentions and the divine plan for "God's own country." Underpinning the Tea Party's vision of recovery or reinstatement "is a consistent set of identifications that link the founders -and the particular forms of fiscal and moral probity they are understood to exemplify—with contemporary Tea Party conservatism" (Wilson and Burack, 2012, 182). Taking the role as defenders of the original constitution also makes it possible to represent other political programs as violating the constitution, for instance, President Obama, whose socialist, collectivizing impulses are allegedly checked only by one impediment: "Mr. Obama's problem is that the Constitution of the United States stands in his way" (Wilson and Burack, 2012: 183).

The Occupy Wall Street and Tea Party share a discourse on representing "the people" against the central political system, sometimes termed "big government." They can also be compared in terms of their quasi-eschatological visions, which do not exactly promise the "end of time" but rather the end of a certain period of time, namely, the end of life as we now know it, and the beginning of a new time. In both cases it is the idea of a major crisis that brings an end to current reality and ushers in a new social order, or, in the case of the Tea Party, makes necessary the recovery of the lost reality of "real America."

There is nevertheless also an important contrast between Occupy Wall Street (young, educated, mobile, white, urban, secular, East coast, connected by iPhones, Twitter, Facebook) and Tea Party (elderly, retired, white, lower middle class, rural , South, evangelical Protestant). In short, they occupied and used space in very different ways, though perhaps the contrast is too simple. The Tea Party also used modern means of communication very effectively. Perhaps the explanation of the Tea Party's success in mobilizing Christian conservative Americans is that they were rooted in communities, they had organization and leadership, they were well connected to elites and funding, and they used the Internet and social media. The failure of Occupy was perhaps that it never established an institutional support structure.

Conclusion

We simply do not know what the long-term consequences of the Internet will be in terms of setting new conditions for countermovements. Perhaps social capital will become eroded as a consequence of "bowling alone" (Putnam, 2000). However, recall that Addams argued that the main function of the Settlement movement was to disseminate useful information. Obviously modern communication technologies are far superior in storing and delivering information than were the intellectuals and students working in Settlements. Surveillance cameras may also be more effective in achieving neighborhood security. Therefore, the consequences of this Tardean revolution in space are mixed. To some extent, the media create a "Fifth Estate," namely, a space in which professionals, corporations and governments can be made accountable and transparent to an online clientele.

The distinct approach of the Settlement was that it eschewed institutionalizing itself as a political actor centered on the key tropes of the party as an adequate organizational form and of the proletarian as the privileged political subject to represent and struggle on behalf of. The Settlement was in a sense a countermovement against traditional philanthropy and corrupted political institutions. Recently, we witnessed another upsurge of countermovements that do not take class, party and state as the key arenas of struggle. Instead, Occupy Wall Street revolved around the belief that the present situation requires a reimagination of the space and means of political struggle. The movement was constituted by occupancies rapidly shifting between different insurrectional sites united by broad notions of equality in the face of political-economic monopolization. The universal messages of equality, solidarity and revived democracy gave, along with the proclamation of a whole new form of politics, the Occupy Wall Street movement an almost eschatological tenor.

The Occupy Wall Street movement, the Tea Party and The Settlement movement emerged in civil society, which Foucault presented as an "interface," where, in principle, indeterminate games of power could be played out between the governors and the governed. Occupy Wall Street and Tea Party shared the attempt to interrupt the "infinite governmentality"—if we can use this term to designate the modern governmental practice of continuously integrating oppositional actors in policy processes and decision-making. The difference was, schematically speaking, that Occupy Wall Street envisioned incipient politics beyond the ontology of representation, whereas the Tea Party aspired to reinstitute original American traditions defined by the founders and American exceptionalism.

We have suggested that all of the countermovements discussed here evince elements of political eschatology, insofar as they articulate religious idioms (leaving aside whether or not they have determinate religious content). Foucault was attentive to, perhaps even fascinated by, the specific transformative force of religion as a medium of political struggle. But does he offer any resources for ascertaining the potentials and risks of the modern countermovements under consideration here? Foucault said (1994, 453) that one should never condemn a priori a mass in revolt, but rather always "be respectful." Yet, this is also the moment at which one should be alert of the risk of a sudden descent into violations of rights and the persecution of opponents. He hence termed his own theoretical ethic "antistrategic." It rested on a dual requirement

> "to be respectful when a singularity revolts, intransigent as soon as power violates the universal. A simple choice, a difficult job: for one must at the same time look closely, a bit beneath history, at what cleaves it and stirs it, and keep watch, a bit behind politics, over what must unconditionally limit it" (Foucault, 1994, 453).

The statement could be thus read: Although countermovements, revolts and revolutions can certainly breathe new life into our history, that same history shows us the precarious realities that may swiftly emerge when universal norms are contested and overcome in the quest of a different universality. Political spirituality should be spurred not only by a utopian vision, but also be tempered by a measured and historically informed interrogation of all political projects that claim to speak for everyone, promise to guarantee our ultimate freedom or to fulfill human history.

References

Addams, Jane (1893) *The Objective Value of a Social Settlement.* Available at: http://www.swarthmore.edu/library/peace/DG001-025/DG001JAddams/objvalue.pdf

Addams, Jane (1895) The Settlement as a Factor in the Labor Movement, in: *Hull-House Maps and Papers.* New York: Crowell, 183–204.

Addams, Jane (1907) *Democracy and Social Ethics.* New York: Macmillan.

Addams, Jane (1911) The Social Situation: Religious Education and Contemporary Social Conditions, *Religious Education*, 6(2): 147–48.

Agarwal, Sheetal D.; Barthel, Michael L.; Rost, Caterina; Borning, Alan; Bennett, W. Lance; Johnson, Courtney N. (2014) Grassroots organizing in the digital age: considering values and technology in Tea Party and Occupy Wall Street, *Information, Communication & Society*, 17(3): 326–341.

Bellah, Robert, Madsen, Robert, Sullivan, William M. Swidler, Ann and Tipton, Steven M. (1985) *Habits of the Heart. Individualism and Commitment in American Life.* New York: Harper & Row.

Blunden, Andy (2014) Forms of Radical Subjectivity, *International Critical Thought*, 4(4): 418–432.

Borch, Christian (2012) *The Politics of Crowds. An Alternative History of Sociology.* Cambridge: Cambridge University Press.

Booth, Charles (1902) *Life and Labour of the People in London, Volume 1–2.* London: Macmillan and Co.

Campbell, Emily; Torpey, John and Turner, Bryan S. (2015) Religion and the Occupy Wall Street Movement, *Critical Research in Religion* (August)

Cooper, Fenimore (1995) [1826] *The Last of the Mohicans. A Narrative of 1757.* Jackson: University Press of Mississippi.

Crane, Hart (1984) [1930] The Bridge, *Complete Poems*, New York: Bloodaxe Books, pp. 63–110.

Creech, Brian (2014) Digital representation and Occupy Wall Street's challenge to political Subjectivity, *Convergence: The International Journal of Research into New Media Technologies*, 20(4): 461–477.

Crockett, Clayton (2011) *Radical Political Theology: Religion and Politics after Liberalism.* New York: Columbia University Press.

Davie, Grace (1994) *Religion in Britain since 1945, Believing without Belonging*, Oxford: Blackwell.

Davis, Allen F. (1984) *Spearheads for Reform: The Social Settlements and the Progressive Movement, 1890–1914.* New York: Oxford University Press.

Durkheim, Emile (1960) [1893] *The Division of Labor in Society.* Glencoe, IL: The Free Press.

Elliott, Anthony and Turner, Bryan S. (2012) *On Society.* Cambridge: Polity Press.

Engels, Friedrich (1958) [1845] *The Condition of the Working Class in England.* Oxford: Blackwell.

Foucault, Michel (2008) *The Birth of Biopolitics: Lectures at the College de France 1978–1979.* New York: Palgrave Macmillan.

Foucault, Michel (2007) *Security, Territory, Population: Lectures at the College de France 1977–1978.* Basingstoke: Palgrave.

Foucault, Michel (1994) Useless to Revolt? In: James D. Fabion (ed.) *Power: The Essential Works of Foucault 1954–1984, Vol. 3*, pp. 449–453. New York: The New Press.

Gitlin, Todd (2012) *Occupy Nation. The Roots, Spirit and the Promise of Occupy Wall Street.* New York: Harper Collins.

Greenstone, David J. (1979) Dorothea Dix and Jane Addams: From transcendentalism to pragmatism in American social reform, *Social Service Review*, 53(4): 527–559.

Hardt, Michael and Negri, Antony (2012) The fight for "real democracy" at the heart of Occupy Wall Street, *Foreign Affairs* (January 11, 2012).

Hardt, Michael and Negri, Antony (2000) *Empire.* Cambridge: Harvard University Press.

Rex, John and Moore, Robert (1967) *Race, Community and Conflict: A Study of Sparkbrook.* Oxford: Oxford University Press.

Langman, Lauren (2012) Cycles of contention: The rise and fall of the Tea Party, *Critical Sociology*, 38(4): 469–494.

Lengermann, Patricia M. and Niebrugge, Gillian (1998) *The Women Founders: Sociology and Social Theory, 1830–1930.* Boston: McGraw-Hill.

Lengermann, Patricia and Niebrugge, Gillian (2007) Thrice told: narratives of sociology's relation to social work, in: Craig Calhoun (ed.) *Sociology in America. A History.* Chicago and London: The University of Chicago Press, pp. 63–114

MacLean, Vicky M. and Williams, Joyce E. (2012) Ghosts of sociologies past: Settlement sociology in the progressive era at the Chicago School of Civics and Philanthropy', *American Sociologist*, 43: 235–263.

Nisbet, Robert A. (1967) *The Sociological Tradition.* London: Heinemann Educational Books.

Putnam, Robert D. (2000) *Bowling Alone: The Collapse and Revival of American Community.* New York: Simon & Schuster.

Putnam, Robert D. and David Campbell, David (2010) *American Grace, How Religion Divides and Unites Us,* New York: Simon & Schuster.

Rancière, Jacques (2003) Politics and Aesthetics: An interview, *Angelaki*, 8(2): 194–211.

Scaff, Lawrence A. (2011) *Max Weber in America.* Princeton and Oxford: Princeton University Press.

Scruton, Roger (2001) *England: An Elegy.* London: Pimlico.

Sommers, Margaret (2008) *The Genealogies of Citizenship and the Right to have Rights.* Cambridge: Cambridge University Press.

Steensland, Brian and Wright, Eric L. (2014) American Evangelicals and Conservative Politics: Past, Present, and Future, *Sociology Compass*, 8(5): 705–717.

Swyngedouw, Erik (2014) Where is the political? Insurgent mobilisations and the incipient "return of the political," *Space and Polity*, 18(2): 122–136.

Tarde, Gabriele (1969) *On Communication and Social Influence: Selected Papers.* Chicago: University of Chicago Press.

Tarde, Gabriele (1962) [1890] *The Laws of Imitation.* Gloucester: Peter Smith.

Thompson, Michael J. (2012) Suburban Origins of the Tea Party: Spatial Dimensions of the New Conservative Personality, *Critical Sociology*, 38(4): 511–528.

Thoreau, Henry David (1854) *Walden or Life in the Woods.* Boston: Tickner and Fields.

Thoreau, Henry David (1988) *The Maine Woods.* New York: Penguin.

Tiedemann, Rolf (ed) (2002) The Arcades Project. New York Belknap Press.

Tocqueville, Alexis de (2004) [1834 and 1840] *Democracy in America.* New York: Library of America.

Villadsen, Kaspar (2015) Michel Foucault and the forces of civil society, *Theory, Culture and Society* (published early online): 1–24.

Villadsen, Kaspar & Turner, Bryan (2015) Tracing the roots of social citizenship: Jane Addams' thought between formal rights and moral obligation, *Citizenship Studies* (published early online): 1–18.

Williamson, Vanessa; Skocpol, Theda and Coggin, John (2011) The Tea Party and the remaking of Republican conservatism, *Perspectives on Politics*, 9(1): 25–43.

Wilson, Angelia R. and Burack, Cynthia (2012) Where Liberty Reigns and God is Supreme: The Christian right and the Tea Party Movement, *New Political Science*, 34(2): 172–190.

Hans-Joachim Sander (Salzburg)/
Kaspar Villadsen (Copenhagen)/ Trygve Wyller (Oslo)

Conclusion

A heterotopian grammar of hospitality

Researching the heterotopic

In the Introduction to this book we stated: "This book argues that hospitality and space are inextricably connected. Hospitality is not necessarily something we possess as an inner quality or as something disconnected from others. Rather, this is one of the main ideas in this book, it is practiced in specific ways in in particular spaces. The thesis is that we have to look for the characteristics of hospitality in "the other spaces" that Michel Foucault once called *heterotopias*" (p. 9).

So the question is now: What are the major findings described in the five case studies with respect to the dynamics of power and counter-conduct and the ensuing heterotopia characteristic?

This conclusion looks at whether it is possible to reconstruct a distinct heterotopian grammar of hospitality. The chapters included in this volume span five rather heterogeneous spaces, yet they all "display a specific quality, something one might call *hospitality.* Thus, our intention was to research whether one could expand the understanding of the heterotopia as a way to discover what hospitality might mean today.

We respond to this by, first, defining six characteristics related to social order, social issues, power structure, secular counter conduct, juxtaposition of power and powerlessness, space dimensions. On this basis we present a short outline of what we call a "heterotopian grammar of hospitality." It seems that the five heterotopian spaces cast new light on what practices of hospitality might be. This grammar involves contesting the normal order, transforming the persons involved, challenging both the secular and the religious order as well as the sharp distinction between them, and finally giving new representation to the power of the powerlessness. All of these perspectives come from the cases illustrated and show that the heterotopian approach can indeed help us to develop focused discussions on hospitality in a time so desperately in need of more of it. So we start with the basic: the contestation of the normal order.

I. The heterotopias dispense with the normal social order

In all spaces we have looked at in this book people are caring for other people who do not belong to their own religion, social class, cultural background and existential situation. This is not surprising, as this is part of the normality of religious convictions or human solidarity. One should treat others as human beings like oneself in order to follow the Christian idea of loving one's neighbor or to follow the social progressivist idea of "brotherly love"—or to follow simple human feelings for the basic needs of those living on the margins of society. Usually this is described as a face-to-face situation, from one individual to another. The Gospel story of the Good Samaritan forms the role model for this sort of religious activity.

Such activity can also be expressed by a sort of formal diaconal organization that provides official places of basic care. But, if so, then the normal form of pastoral power will be established. This means that disciplinary practices and divisions are established that bring order to a sort of social, existential or political chaos. This process lies at the core of the secularization of caring activities that, in the end, leads to the modern welfare state. It creates a sort of "disciplined hospitality," which has a normalizing effect on the lives of all involved in this system. Universal notions of care and equality are merged with disciplinary mechanisms.

To some extent all the spaces we have dealt with start in the context of such a merging. The Garden of Religion belongs to a monastery that follows a sort of spiritual diaconia for other religions. The Gothenburg Parish Clinic belongs to the pastoral goal of a community taking care of people living in this part of the city. The Settlement House in Vesterbro belongs to a movement that aspired to bring the future elite of a society into direct contact with people from the underclass. For the Oslo intersection and for Occupy Wall Street, such a value of human compassion is not that obvious. Yet, the police present in the intersection in Oslo are professionally following a line of duty that is looking out for the security of *all* people in the area of the station, so they cannot simply kick the substance user out at will. They too are part of the society and should be treated as citizens as long as they behave as such. And Occupy Wall Street was oriented toward forms of civil disobedience that respect the elementary rules of political behavior in the public arena, even though the goal was to overthrow the political order. Open violence must be avoided as long as possible.

So far, the five places seem to follow the "normal order," like normalized practices. Yet, there is a fracture in the picture. In all these cases, the ruling order is being contested and modified in favor of other people and their order of things. The spaces do not, then, display the implementation of an already fixed program or rationale, rather they open ground for an alternative order of things present in the social activity. In this heterotopian process, "the others" with their other realities can introduce their particular ideas for social, economic and religious life. They certainly do not have the power to implement them in a revolutionary process so that they can rule the normal order. But they provide a hint of a different order—and the people who are organizing the spaces are invited to take the best aspects of this order into their own agenda. So it is up to the people who are provided with hospitality to create a sort of "other hospitality." This hospitality is unable to dominate the space where it emerges, but it does have the power to bring the owner of the space, the agents of the relevant activity and the rulers of the scene, to realize that there is an alternative in social, political, cultural and religious terms. The roles in traditional forms of hospitality are flipped.

This other form of hospitality does not simply imply caring for other people. Rather, it implies that the helpers have become different persons by taking care of them. A kind of change of change of identity is introduced, and this process gives shape to a different form of hospitality. This other hospitality then entails embodied experiences for the people involved, which affect and shape them. This brings us to the second perspective.

II. The heterotopias shape people and social issues

The people and the social issues this book has dealt with are bound to specific spaces. One may even say that the people and the issues can be described solely within the framework of these spaces. Both the clients and the volunteers in Copenhagen have roles because they are part of the heterotopic Settlement project. They cannot be identified only by their personal biographies or by their specific goals in life. They have a sort of "spatial identity" because the innovative practices and roles they perform belong to the very spaces they live in. For that reason, these spaces are not only socially constructed like all spaces are; they are not only contexts of social activities like all places are; they represent not only social constellations like all fields are. The persons involved in the Gothenburg project explicitly reported being deeply influenced by the space through achieving a specific dignity there, a fact that applied to both the volunteers and the visiting undocumented persons. In general, the spaces have a major impact on the people who are acting within them, whether they have been invited to join them or if they are just visiting these spaces. This impact does not necessarily happen to them because of some explicit decision or the stated intention of the project leadership; instead, one could speculate whether the impact comes from the heterotopic grammar they are part of.

In Foucault's analysis of "other spaces," heterotopia and utopia are inextricably linked to each other. Some heterotopias even start out being utopias but then turn into the otherness of a socially alienating grammar when the utopian expectations are tempered or fall apart. This is evident in the spaces discussed above. Bringing fundamentally incongruent components of our reality together at a specific space can generate new visions and solutions. The juxtapositions that characterize "other spaces" can de-familiarize each component, revealing their arbitrariness and hence opening up a plethora of virtualities and possible reinterpretations. Furthermore, the analysis of localized spaces can render contingent broader cultural assumptions, such as the premises underpinning the economy, the welfare state and religions.

The Altenburg Garden forces the monks to become involved in the social struggle about respecting other cultures. The Garden transforms the monastery from being a major symbol of the dominant religion in Austrian society to becoming an innovative place in a globalized civilization in which Catholicism is only one of a variety of religious options—where the issue of left or right political theologies has been surpassed. The Gothenburg clinic forces the parish to move beyond institutionalized social rights and criteria of eligibility of the Swedish state. It does so by pushing the Church of Sweden to stand on the side of those who have no place in a welfare system that claims to be inclusive and premised on universal notions of welfare. And the clinic forces the volunteers coming from the official health system to recognize that they can provide better help in such a clandestine place than in the context of their professional positions. They are forced to come to terms with their authorized professional codex as well as the limits and risks entailed in its legal premises.

The Oslo Central Station and its surroundings force the public and its policing authorities to accept people using it as a clandestine marketplace for illegal transfers. As a result, these spaces become a domain of precarious and temporal rest as well as repetitive and circling social movements. These transitory spaces expose the fact that, despite the overall economic success of Norway, such a space of "urban hospitality" continues to exist and be necessary. The Copenhagen Settlement House forced the Settlement Movement to look for other places for enacting its original fervor of religious opposition to an unjust economic system—and it pushed them to reach out in favor of marginalized people beyond the traditional class division. The Occupy Wall Street movement radicalized the critique of the prevailing capitalist system by insisting that incremental reform is simply not enough. The movement articulated its identity as the "disempowered majority" to justify its distinction between the present and a future world, its unifying "no" to the political-corporate capital alliance and its loosely defined demand for a new economic-political order. Anyone who is deeply ingrained in these places has to overcome or at least temper his or her utopias, including the great utopias of the community, the movement or the Church once believed to be worth struggling for.

Yet, at the same time, all the aspirations, contradictions and obstacles that formed at these spaces have an innovative dimension that spurs ideas of a fundamentally different world. The people involved here are to some extent avant-garde in articulating progressive ideas, yet in their articulations they also depend on those people or phenomena they are offering hospitality to. Their "avant-gardeness" can then be said to be secondary to their experiences of the marginalized and excluded. All our spaces are illustrative examples of the passage from utopia to heterotopia Foucault asserted in his comments on heterotopias. They are avant-garde by being situated within spaces, not by way of departing from those spaces. At the same time, as they renew how we can conceive of these spaces, they do not primarily spur a transformation of discourse on a broad scale. Rather, such transformative effects arise from small, locally established, almost invisible counter-conducts carried out in order to ameliorate the systems they oppose. It is not that utopias simply fall apart, but rather that their expectations are challenged by people or realities invited into or attracted by the utopian aspirations that belong to at these places.

On Wall Street the never-ending quest for profit has priority. This quest rests on the idea of the market as indefinite series of transactions without finitude. By contrast, the Occupy Wall Street movement brought a sort of secular eschatology into the very heart of modern capitalism. Occupy succeeded, at least momentarily, in repoliticizing the existing order by completely rejecting the political system of representation and by refusing to formulate demands that could be accommodated by the system. The movement decidedly broke with conventional notions of what constitutes the spaces appropriate for political processes, such as parliaments, council chambers and organized labor disputes. Although Occupy never mobilized around a defined political program, the movement expressed the loosely defined hope of instituting a completely new political order. This hope could be termed eschatological insofar as it relied upon the promise of the coming of a new time that would disrupt linear time and institute a society of fundamental equality. Occupy Wall Street served as a vehicle for claims that the state should be fundamentally restructured in order to minimize the power of corporate capital and institute true democracy for all. This reconfiguration of the grammar of Wall Street may potentially give the place much more importance for our global civilization than its prior emblematic symbol of profit-making.

All of the places we have looked into here demonstrate how hospitality toward people in need of care embody and modify utopian expectations. These expectations spur forms of counter-conducts that do not break down the systems they are targeting, but on the contrary they induce gradual transformations on the basis of the spaces. In this respect, the spaces we have explored challenge the conceptual side of heterotopia: These other spaces form the loci of a specific pastoral power that takes a hold on those who are practicing it. This is, of course, not true for all heterotopias, but as soon as a space becomes the locus of pastoral power, it tends to push the agents to become involved in issues that reach beyond the original framework of the activity. This pastoral power simultaneously structures the possible positions and relationships that the involved individuals can occupy, and it incites them to reach out beyond what was immediately within the realm of the possible. They are spurred to look for the impossible, so to speak, and this quest for the impossible incites them to accept a higher demand of self-sacrifice and self-discipline than in all other institutionalized spaces organized around issues of need and hospitality.

The improvements these people have in mind extend beyond the tangible improvements possible in the spaces and institutions they are situated in. Often, they include religious motivations into a secularized domain or secular notions of rights and respect into a religious space. This leads us to consider two more perspectives of the heterotopian grammar, both linked to the tension and traditional distinction between the secular and the sacred. Again, the heterotopian grammar opens up to important reinterpretations.

III. A heterotopia impacts a religiously established power structure

In several of the preceding chapters we observed counter-conducts opposed to the established institutions of pastoral power. In Sweden, as in all similar national contexts, the historical origin of the welfare state can be traced back to the doctrine that the church must provide care for its baptized members, in this case fellow Lutherans. This means that a space becomes heterotopic when a secular counter-conduct intertwines with and contests the entrenched doctrines of pastoral power. In effect, these kinds of heterotopias also contest religious discourse and practices. They are created and organized on the basis of a type of secular counter-conduct toward the religious values inherent to these spaces.

In the study of the Garden of Religions in the Altenburg monastery, the internal debates between the monks as well as the public political debates they partake in as organizers of such a garden demonstrate the fundamental problem that religious plurality precipitates in open societies. Here, the usual divisions between the secular and the sacred collapse. Another formula is needed not only to mediate between secularization and religious tolerance, but also to introduce an alternative aspect into the internal life of such a religious community. The monks cannot simply stick to the Benedictine Rule to institute the hospitality that they have invented by this Garden. Any monastery that opens a Garden of Religions becomes in effect a champion in welcoming interreligious dialogue and in instituting respect toward all people and ideas with foreign cultural backgrounds. It is not simply a common religious affair to establish such a garden; there are tensions one has to creatively transform in order to sustain the progressive potential of this

Garden. The religious garden claims a religious counter-conduct on those administering it as a garden of multiple religions.

In other cases, the risks of challenging the existing order are of a more tangible nature. The Gothenburg clinic demonstrates the kinds of risks present in all phases of a migration, in particular, when it happens illegally. These risks are not some "adventure" welcomed by all participants. Rather, they push everyone involved into a higher level of attention and social awareness of how different life can be and how fast normal orders may simply fall apart. People have to take care of their bodies differently if they have to live illegally in a public space, so if need be they have to seek treatment outside of the well-ordered welfare system. Developing a heterotopian body means entering a matrix of mutual hospitality that cannot be guaranteed by anybody involved. This hospitality is fragile, and it can fall apart at any moment. It is only possible to practice this hospitality on the basis of mutual trust and by securing anonymity. The particular overlapping and merging of public space and religious space cannot be expected to function in many other contexts than the clandestine clinic. It would seem that it is only within the secure walls of such a parish place that this kind of clinic appears as a possible practice. So, the place of healthcare, counseling and the recycling of clothes can function only if it remains hidden. Yet, seeking protection behind the walls of recognized religious spaces, i. e., the parish church building, in this case does not mean partaking fully in the religious order of this place. The walls do not protect religion but instead protect *against* secular powers not belonging to the place. The parish itself becomes a locus of counter-conduct with respect to what is expected to take place there.

In the Oslo intersection we observe a similar picture: As soon as people no longer use an intersection just for passing but also live there and do clandestine, risky things, the question of being welcomed becomes an urgent issue. The substance-users are not welcomed where they are, and they cannot hope to be welcomed for what they are doing there. But exactly because they are not welcomed, to use the intersection as they do they are put in desperate need of basic hospitality. Only the intersection can give them hospitality simply by being open for constant circular motion. It provides the space for a counter-conduct that one can become aware of only by closely observing the whole scene. Nobody offers hospitality here to the substance-users, yet the whole intersection space is rendered hospitable as a result of their practices of counter-conduct. And then, under special circumstances, in specific social constellations and at very rare moments, even the police become involved in these spatial practices of counter-conduct. The hospitality of the place turns the intersection into a heterotopian place urging all people involved to concede a sort of hospitality that the intersection was not intended to offer.

By its very nature the Christian Student Settlement in Copenhagen was "an impossible idea" that tried to bring together social change and Christian conversion in a working-class neighborhood. Right from the beginning, it was a dual form of counter-conduct. It rendered practical and social the Christian message of brotherly love, and it introduced respect for those who are normally not respected because of their poverty. For that reason the Settlement was placed at the center of tensions between social classes and between religious and secular ideas. Overcoming prejudices, opposing exclusion mechanisms and—nowadays—assisting the marginalized in their contact with the welfare system is still an ongoing process for the Settlement. Spearheading social citizenship in a neighborhood described as the "dark continent of the poor" was spurred by Christian utopian values of human equality, which themselves were transformed by being put into action. The new space impacted the established religious power structure also in this context.

Counter-conducts have developed and become institutionalized in all spaces studied, and at the same time these spaces have been transformed and propelled forward by the ambiguous dynamics of the heterotopic. Foucault linked the emergence of counter-conduct to the crises of pastoral power—we in turn can link counter-conduct to spaces that provide a form of hospitality in the face of crisis in the secularized offspring of pastoral power and in traditional religious authority.

IV. Religious utopias spur counter-conducts in the secular

Using the first perspective of heterotopia as spaces of contestation of the normal social order, we observed that individuals within heterotopic spaces learn to identify themselves in distance to the notions, divisions and institutions of "normal society." This distance is experienced by these people by way of the spaces to which they are bound. Hence, the counter-conducts described arise from, and are shaped by, particular spaces. Even the police at the Oslo intersection sometimes develop minor practices that can be interpreted as counter-conducts to normal society. Similarly, the Garden of Religion in Altenburg incites the monks to respond to the divisions established by power structures differently than tradition would prescribe The monks are impacted not only by the classical religious hierarchy, but they are also impacted by the spatial influence of the garden and its profile. This counter-conduct is a *secular* counter-conduct in relation to the normal arrangements in the welfare state, including the ways in which social issues are tackled traditionally and is expected in the established Church-State relations. However, it also constitutes a counter-conduct that challenges normal religious practice and discourse, which traditionally were part of a Benedictine monastery. It is at the same time disturbing entrenched religious and secular conventions.

In all the places discussed in this book the intention of the people involved is to improve the situation of society, of the Church, of the marginalized or of contemporary democracy. In some cases, the protagonists do not strive for a complete revolution to institute a new social order structuring a completely different form of grammar. In these contexts, the actors are working toward quite modest goals of improving the conditions for specific people. In the case of the Gothenburg clinic, for instance, the efforts were guided by the need to provide essential health and social services for the undocumented who have nowhere else to go.

In other cases, the activity was initially spurred by utopian aspirations, though these were tempered and shaped by what could actually be accomplished in the context. This applies, for instance, to the Settlement project in Copenhagen, where the activities were continuously shaped by changes in the surrounding neighborhood and by the relationship to the municipal welfare system. By contrast, the Occupy Wall Street movement mobilized around utopian visions of the birth of a new society. The utopias were not tempered by pragmatic and practical concerns, probably because the relatively open and undefined messages were essential to the capacity of these movements to mobilize broadly and align quite diversified support groups. So far, at least, what was hoped for has not yet been tempered by what can actually be done.

In this book, several of the chapters explored a crucial relationship between the secular world and the religious part of it, in short the relationship between the Secular and the Sacred. This is a relationship built through real spaces where people motivated by religious ideas organize hospitality for other people or for other religious beliefs in need of respect or health and social care. Religious motivations, faith-based convictions, spiritual identifications and sometimes even theological considerations have a constitutive impact on these places—they are integral to them. Yet, at the same time, particular social developments, such as migration and globalization, shape these spaces, including the move toward multiculturalism in many regions on the planet, the irruption of economic hardship and crisis in specific localities, thorny problems regarding limits to the institutionalized solidarity of the national welfare state, the demands posed by broken lives of all kinds, unsolved political issues and major catastrophic events like financial breakdowns. All of this brings an urgency to organizing "other spaces."

The intricate relationship between the Sacred and the Secular is one of otherness and of mutual dependency. In the spaces of hospitality explored in this book, this relationship is mitigated anew, sometimes with the result that pastoral power assumes new forms. An example is the Settlement, where the notion of redemption transfigures personal conversion to social redemption. It is an illustration of how pastoral techniques may fundamentally transform under the impression of new social predicaments and urgencies. The trajectory of the Settlement also reflects the much more broad process in which pastoral power begins to proliferate and lend itself to secular institutions and practices.

Our studies demonstrate, however, that this process is not simply one in which the rationalities of pastoral guidance of consciousness and care of the community become rationalized in welfare institutions. Pastoral power constitutes a flexible resource that can be (and in fact has been) mobilized in counter-conducts opposing religious as well as secular authorities. This form of power supports counter-conducts in the social field—and sometimes within the political sphere. The disciplinary elements of pastoral power are in effect turned toward the Secular so that the Sacred attains a sustained impact on the ways social issues are addressed in modern and contemporary contexts. The extension of caring for the marginalized into the mundane and secular areas of human life, as displayed by the Settlement movement, resonates with Jesus' commandment to walk with the poor wherever they go. Perhaps this move can be associated with the principle of the old doctrine of the pastorate, which implied that the shepherd should be ready to sacrifice himself for the herd. We witness how agents of pastoral power turn the usual conduct of religious communities into a new sort of care organized around the needs of "the flock."

This transformation creates different forms of hospitality, which are not organized on the basis of traditional religious communities but on a sort of religious/secular motivation not rooted in the traditional order of the Sacred. It is here where other forms of counteractions arise than the ones we know so well from the public sphere, like demonstrations and rebellion. Instead, other forms of embodiments of ideals of care, political resistance and spiritual tolerance come forward. At these moments, we begin to see the emergence of a spatial grammar overriding the Secular and the Sacred.

So, it is not enough to simply observe that there are agents in these spaces offering help and people seeking help. Rather, one must go further and explore the specific relationship of these agents to these spaces and the relationship that marginalized people have to these places. One has to dig into the locality of these spaces to grasp the different modes of practice and the unexpected inventions. Here, on the ground, one cannot avoid being confronted by activities of hospitality that extend beyond any structure of social welfare provision. One cannot help being struck by the enactment of deep-rooted respect for the otherness of people and their realities, which go far beyond traditional truth claims of religious convictions. Particular spaces come into view where we find both secular articulations of the Sacred *and* rearticulations of the Secular by means of a sacred grammar. We see that in the Gothenburcg case where a classical secular project is part of the explicit church space.

Several of the places studied in the book are pervaded by deep-rooted religious convictions that, however, move far beyond dogmatic formulated Creeds as they become profoundly shaped by secular needs. For that reason, spaces such as the Garden of Religions in Altenburg, the clandestine Clinic in the Gothenburg parish, the intersection near the Oslo Railway Station, the Settlement House in Copenhagen and the occupied park in the financial district of Manhattan have a twofold nature. At first glance, they are simply distinct physical localities: a garden, a parish, an intersection, a house, an occupied area. But on second glance, these spaces display concerns that reach beyond their specificity and symbolize something more generally significant, "above and beyond" the existing order: religious plurality without resentment, provision of healthcare irrespective of nationality and rights, caring for substance users without disciplinarity, respect for people without regard to class, the promise of an alternative to corporate capitalism.

The spaces we have explored constitute spaces of transformation. They must be understood not simply as embodiments of predetermined religious or welfarist ideas. Instead, they are precarious spaces, constantly in a process of change. This can very easily create a situation by which these places can be closed down, abandoned, left behind or appropriated by other agencies, which [what?] entail the loss of the original goals. This calls for analytical attention to the ideals, symbols, narratives and utopias that urge the involved people to carry on. Future research is needed to explore questions like: Is it possible to identify contemporary spaces where long standing ideas, like religious convictions, are rearticulated and begin to spur social change? And how can we better understand the interplay between religious traditions and secular institutions—as an open-ended interplay in which religious values serve to contest secular realities but where none of the two are viewed as primary? This book has begun addressing these tasks.

V. The heterotopias reorganize the juxtaposition of power and what is powerlessness

In all of the case studies included in this book, we observe that the motivation for organizing alternative spaces results from experiences of irrefutable predicaments, powerlessness or social urgencies. In Copenhagen, it was the miserable social situation manifested by the working poor; in Gothenburg, it was the intolerable situation of clandestine migrants in need of healthcare; in Oslo, it was the deplorable situation of substance users targeted by the police and threatened by the aspiration for "public order"; in the case of Occupy Wall Street, the defining event was the breakdown of the financial markets with the associated hardship for those subjected to market forces; and in Altenburg, the challenge was the exclusion of other religions and members of non-Christian religious communities. But these experiences belong not only to those who are offered hospitality, but also to those who provide it. We may speak in terms of a sort of spatial solidarity mechanism emerging in these contexts. In the six spaces power and powerlessness, powerful regimes and powerless people are coming together. Powerlessness is changed into a sort of authority in hospitality that cannot overcome the power regimes but can create a space to grow beyond these regimes. Powerless people find themselves empowered to find a different sort of goal in their lives and spaces dominated by power have to open an other space for this empowerment. This gives hospitality a political impact on all sort of aspects in public life.

VI. A heterotopian grammar of hospitality

The spaces discussed in this book challenge the usual understanding of heterotopia, which was inherited from Foucault and which today circulates in the commentary literature. They are not heterotopias of themselves but heterotopias out of hospitality practices. These practices do not create the heterotopias but they produce spaces, which then are turned into other spaces. It is a twofold process and not a linear genetic development. We recognize our indebtedness to Foucault, who initiated the contemporary stream of research on "other spaces" or heterotopias. This is why the spatial perspective is fundamental to all case studies in this book. Nevertheless, we think that we need to emphasize heterotopia as a second level in spatial production zones—and as a phenomenon that influences the space in return. Our hypothesis was that we can discover traces and aspects of what hospitality might mean if we address both the physical spaces in their own right and the spatially formatted otherness and innovative practices reconstructed in our analyses. This is why all five case studies in this book addressed "spaces of the others" and not only "other spaces".

In this regard, several of the case studies in this book implicitly or explicitly follow Lefebvre's insistence that one also needs to include what he called the lived space (*l'espace vécu*), in other words: giving attention to the spaces of the others. In this attention hospitality is an important factor that can result from religious but also from secular practices. So, departing somewhat from both Foucault and Lefebvre, when we chose to study religiously inspired (or religiously relevant) spaces of the others we finally were linked to secular practices and vice versa. Our intention has been to research and discuss whether hospitality could be understood as a spatially embedded and shaped phenomenon. This is why we visited the undocumented in Gothenburg, the monks in Austria and the Settlement in Copenhagen, and this is why we included the Occupy movement in New York and the Oslo intersection as well. So, the final question is: Is it possible to reconstruct a heterotopian grammar of hospitality?

Hospitality is a word and a practice rooted in religious traditions but it is at the same time a secular practice within public spaces. It is an important challenge in itself to consider whether such a word, framed by strong and not always freedom-seeking religious traditions, could still be meaningful today. The shift from the perspective of the other space to the spaces of the others is, in our view, a helpful starting point for offering informed responses to the challenged possibility of a distinct heterotopian grammar of hospitality We use the grammar terminology with no linguistic pretentions. But the term implies that we are looking for some basic components that are developed in and through the practices we have studies. The heterotopian grammar is not a system we apply to the lived world, but it develops out of experiences, analyses and interpretations in the lived world itself. It comes out of a rationality within hospitality binding together the people involved, the spaces involved and the unsolved social problems involved. The people and the problems are productive for the hospital spaces by binding them together to a counter conductivity present in the hospital spaces.

In this way it is a basic assumption in this book that hospitality is needs to be experienced in the lived world. In the counter conductive powerlessness that can be observed at the relevant spaces But the grammar terminology also suggests that we think needs to be reflected also in a more systematic way. Then we can see some of the grammar of a contemporary hospitality that needs to be reformulated again and again with a practical, empirical context.

It is possible to establish a connection between the original (heterotopian) space and the significance experienced by "the other" people in the space. The other spaces, such as the monastery, the clinic, the intersection, the Settlement house and its projects, are governed not only by the original initiators, Instead, the other spaces become spaces of the others insofar as "the others'" presence, significance and impact upon the space increase. This is an important element in the heterotopian grammar of hospitality. Hospitality is an experience rooted in the transformation of the space first structured by its founders, organizers or some kind of authority. Governing (pastoral power) is not only about receiving and expressing gratitude. The spatial transformation integral to the heterotopian grammar can be conceived of as practices and social arrangements that allow the "subaltern to speak." The heterotopian grammar of hospitality redistributes power and authority because the space is also given shape by the presence of the others.

This first issue of a heterotopian grammar of hospitality is hence deeply connected to the second issue: Heterotopias are places of hospitality for marginalized people, ideas or practices that can only be given a place and a voice through at least some minor form of counter-conduct. The bodies that figure in these spaces represent essential human needs or elementary forms of social discipline. The particular discourses developed on the specific sites introduce local issues that seemingly concern marginal aspects of social life into contact with universal themes. The localized discourse opens up to problems, ideas and challenges pertaining to religion, politics and the economy, which are of much greater importance than the problems these spaces revolved around in the first place. For that reason, all of the spaces included in this book represent counter narratives of religiously motivated hospitality or secular grounded solidarity, which move beyond or even distort the normalizing discourses of our societies. They present open questions, destructions and unfinished experiments in the realms of politics, welfare and the economy.

The third issue in the heterotopian grammar is connected to the intertwinement, or entanglement, between the secular and the sacred. We have seen in many of the above case studies that traditional distinctions between what is secular and what is sacred are becoming less and less clear-cut. The people in the Oslo intersection act in a very typical public context. Nevertheless, some of the acts they perform could be reconceived as emerging from within a religious discourse. The monks in the Altenburg monastery might have started the Garden for interreligious dialogue for purely religious reasons. The result is, however, that they have to take part in all kinds of secular, political events. Conversely, the religiously motivated Garden also becomes a secular event, which challenges and reframes the monastery itself and the monks' self-identity.

These recent intertwinements and entanglements of the Secular and the Sacred are obviously spatially embedded. To repeat the main point in the heterotopic grammar, this kind of spatial intertwinement or entanglement may increase the space for hospitality. Some people might find the religious articulations and resonances we have observed to be archaic and something of a weakness. But instead, the use of religious or quasi-religious idioms in the spaces and projects examined might be one of the basic components in a new heterotopic grammar of hospitality. The spatial *mélange* between the Secular and the Sacred is, in this view, neither obstructive nor conserving. It is rather an opening up to the enactment of hospitality.

The grammar of hospitality, then, seems to lead to a reconstruction of received lines of division so central to our Western context. The Gothenburg case shows this explicitly. It is not the policy of the official Church of Sweden to invite all people of other confessions to become visible and significant "partners" inside their church buildings. But this is what is happening in the congregation in Gothenburg. Such an invitation—such a form of hospitality—was spurred by an irresolvable problem arising in the secular Swedish welfare state, that is, the existence of undocumented immigrants who were not being adequately cared for by the welfare system. We noticed how this problem impacts and reconfigures the inside of the building, the internal structuring of the community and even the inner part of the belief system of the community.

In other words, the heterotopic grammar of hospitality develops when spaces reconfigure and extend their specific locations. Hospitality does not belong to the one or the other part of the religious/secular binary. Hospitality challenges the binary and leads to embodied experiences that are most likely more essential to the people who take part in this grammar than the abstract religious/secular binary. When the police constable in the Oslo intersection rubs the substance user's shoulder to warm it, everything in the context is secular. But the embodied experience of respect and dignity that occurs at these moments clearly resonates with parallel experiences in spaces defined by religion. We suggest that it belongs to the heterotopic grammar of hospitality to expand and criticize—from the perspective of lived experiences—the traditional spatial binary of religion and secular. We propose, then, to see hospitality as an emblematic *third space* that is both connected to the secular and the religious but renews them by spurring new spatial arrangements. These spaces give new shape to what hospitality can mean in the present context—one that is neither religious nor secular but both at the same time.

List of Contributors

Johs Bertelsen
Leader of Frivilligt Forum, Landsforeningen for de frivillige sociale organisationer 1996 – 2012: Leader of Kristeligt Studenter-Settlement
Johs@frivilligtforum.dk

Pater Michael Hüttl, OSB
Nosta-Aetate Garten, Altenburg. Prior, Pfarrer von Maria Dreieichen, Verantwortlicher für den Bereich Kultur.Tourismus, Socius des Novizenmeisters, Delegierter zum Generalkapitel
p.michael@stift-altenburg.at

Hilde Kirkebøen
Deacon Østre Aker og Haugerud menighet
Former project leader for 'Rom for fattige tilreisende' (Spaces for Poor Visitors), Church City Mission, Oslo.
HK848@kirken.no

Kaia S. Rønsdal
PhD candidate at Faculty of Theology, University of Oslo.
She has published articles on marginality, urban and spatial theory, Christian social practice and citizenship theory.
k.d.m.s.ronsdal@teologi.uio.no

Sander, Hans-Joachim
Univ.-Prof. for Dogmatics
Faculty of Catholic Theology at the University of Salzburg
Hans-Joachim.SANDER@sbg.ac.at

Anne Sjögren
One of the founders of the medical network Rosengrenska in 1998. Registered nurse (1974), specialised in district since 1983. Employee of the Swedish Red Cross since 2008
anne@sjogren.info

Bryan S. Turner
Presidential Professor of Sociology, Department of Sociology ,The Graduate Center CUNY, USA; Professor of the Sociology of Religion The Australian Catholic University Melbourne Australia; Guest Professor Department of Sociology Faculty of Social Sciences Potsdam University Germany
BTurner@gc.cuny.edu

Kaspar Villadsen
Professor with special responsibilities, Director of the PhD program, Department of Management, Politics and Philosophy, Copenhagen Business School.
k_villadsen@yahoo.com

Trygve Wyller
Professor (Christian Social Practice) Faculty of Theology, University of Oslo. Honorary professor, School of Philosophy, Religion and Classics, University of Kwazulu-Natal, South Africa Editor of the journal Diaconia. Journal for the Study of Christian Social Practice.
trygve.wyller@teologi.uio.no

Index of Topics

Altenburg Garden 101, 103–106, 108, 176
American exceptionalism 155, 167, 169
American Settlement movement 16, 143
American traditions 169
Anormality 102
Arab Spring 149, 159

Benedictine monastery 16, 79, 90 f., 180
blind spot 109
bodies 13, 64, 130 f., 134–140, 179, 185
brotherly love 21, 29, 32, 45–48, 139, 174, 180
Buddhism 16, 83, 92, 98

capitalism 41, 150, 155, 160, 163, 177, 183
Catholicism 93, 96 f., 176
charitable 26, 34, 37 f., 43
charity 15, 26, 30 f., 35, 37, 39, 62, 75, 153
Christianity 12, 23, 25 f., 38–40, 43, 45, 89, 92, 96, 149, 153, 156
Christian philanthropy 34 f., 40
Christian reformists 146
Christian socialism 152
church 5, 14 f., 25 f., 34, 37, 39 f., 51, 54 f., 59–62, 65–70, 74–76, 82, 89 f., 92–97, 99, 107, 110 f., 121, 128, 143, 149, 151–153, 158–160, 163–165, 176, 178–182, 186
citizen 12, 29, 53, 71, 120 f., 127, 146, 152, 165, 174
clients 44, 67, 175
communication technology 143
communist revolutionaries 146
community 28, 31, 34, 37, 41, 44, 46, 60 f., 65, 72, 76, 82 f., 86, 89, 91 f., 96 f., 99, 103, 127, 144, 147, 152, 154, 156 f., 159, 163–165, 174, 176, 178, 182, 186
Compassion 9, 14, 17, 61 f., 174
conceived space 91, 131
contemporary liberal-capitalist society 161
contested 9–11, 17, 31, 45, 68, 94, 96, 99, 103 f., 106–109, 129 f., 138, 140, 144, 169, 174
Copenhagen Settlement House 176
counter-conduct 11, 13–15, 17, 35 f., 47, 59, 63, 76, 89, 106 f., 109, 113 f., 122, 130, 137, 139 f., 144–146, 173, 177–180, 182, 185
countermovements 145 f., 157, 168 f.
counter-sites 10, 31, 68
cultural uplift 153

debts 162
democratic agency 161
democratic politics 162
dialectical framework 130
disciplinary normalization 29
disciplinary practices 32, 174
discipline 5, 12–15, 24, 29, 36, 48, 59, 63, 71, 89, 105, 107 f., 112, 151, 185

ecclesiology 75 f.
embodied presence 64, 76
empathy 59, 63–67, 69, 71, 75
empowerment 90, 96, 184
enactment of hospitality 186
eschatological representation 114
eschatology 13, 106, 109, 111, 114, 145 f., 177
ethnic 65, 144, 158, 161

evangelical Protestantism 36, 163
extreme nationalist republicans 146

faith 16, 26, 37, 56, 84 f., 94–99, 102 f., 111, 140, 150, 165, 181
firstspace 90 f., 94, 103
freedom of religion 95

Garden of Religions 16, 79, 81, 83, 85 f., 89–94, 98 f., 102, 178, 182
gender and sexual identities 161
globalized capitalism 161
Gothenburg Parish Clinic 174
Governmentality 11 f., 145 f., 169
governmentality of constitutionalism 162

Heterotopia 9–11, 14–17, 31–34, 38, 42, 45 f., 59, 62, 67–72, 76, 86, 94–97, 104 f., 109, 113, 125, 129 f., 136 f., 139, 144, 173–175, 177–180, 183–186
heterotopian grammar of hospitality 17, 173, 184 f.
Heterotopia of Compensation 38, 67, 69–71, 73 f., 76
heterotopic 9–11, 13, 15–17, 33, 42, 45, 47 f., 59–62, 68–74, 76, 93 f., 130, 173, 175, 178, 180, 186 f.
heterotopic requirement 59
heterotopic space 11 f., 16 f., 59, 66–72, 75, 122, 130, 180
Hinduism 16, 83, 92
historicality 123
home evictions 162
homeless 9, 42, 54, 119 f., 135, 139, 163
homogeneity 103 f.
Hospitality 5, 9, 11, 14–18, 36, 54, 59 f., 62, 65–67, 70–72, 74, 76, 79, 84, 90, 92, 95 f., 99 f., 107, 112–114, 117, 121 f., 129 f., 137, 139 f., 173–175, 177–187
housing 27 f., 30, 40, 43, 158, 160
Hull-House 170, 172
human dignity 56, 61, 100
human right 53, 61 f., 64, 97, 120

identity politics 161
imagined space 143, 147 f.
Indignados 159
industrial city 154
industrial urbanization 154
inequality 158, 160, 163
institutionalized spaces 178
interreligious dialogue 10, 85 f., 92, 99, 104, 178, 186
intersection 10, 16, 117, 121–125, 128–140, 174, 179, 183, 185

Jernbanetorget 121, 127 f., 132, 137
Judaism 16, 83 f., 92
Judson Memorial Church 24, 163, 165
juxtapositions 32, 48, 176

Kingdom of God 26, 39, 155

labor struggles 162
lived experiences 187
lived space 10, 81, 86 f., 91, 124, 126, 130–132, 134, 139, 143, 148, 184
Lutheran congregation 10, 15, 51, 74 f.

marginalization 120
marginalized people 67, 101–103, 105, 107 f., 112, 176, 182, 185
modes of practice 182
monastic garden 10, 14, 16, 79, 108
murmurs 121, 125 f., 129 f., 132 f.
Muslim 61, 66 f., 69, 83
mutual hospitality 179

narratives 17, 63, 111–113, 121, 123, 125 f., 128 f., 132–135, 139, 183, 186
neo-liberal 158, 161

Occupy Binghamton 160
Occupy Boulder Flood Relief 160
Occupy Portland 160
Occupy Sandy 160
Occupy USA 160
Occupy Wall Street 10, 16, 143, 148 f.,

159–163, 165, 167–169, 174, 176 f., 181, 183
Oslo central station 16, 119, 128, 176
Oslo intersection 174, 179 f., 184, 186 f.
otherness 5, 11, 63 f., 74, 90 f., 104, 129 f., 175, 181 f., 184

parallel communities 158
participatory governance 162
pastoral authority 114
pastoral guidance of consciousness 182
pastoral power 11–15, 35 f., 59 f., 63, 65–67, 73, 76, 94, 106–109, 113 f., 139 f., 174, 177 f., 180–182, 185
pastoral techniques 181
perceived space 91, 123, 131
Phenomenology 64
police 15, 27, 56, 63, 66, 117, 120, 122, 126–128, 130, 132–135, 138, 140, 157, 160 f., 174, 179 f., 183, 187
political elite 163
political eschatology 144–147, 169
political ontology of representation 162
political resistance 182
political spectacle 162
political sphere 106, 182
political struggle 35, 147, 158, 160, 162, 168 f.
poor relief 30, 34 f.
postcolonial 60, 72, 72, 77
poverty 9, 21, 23, 34 f., 38 f., 120, 150 f., 153 f., 156, 162 f., 180
powerlessness 15, 17, 89, 96, 99, 102, 107, 109 f., 173, 183–185
Protestantism 36, 96, 154, 157

quasireligious 36, 145

racial discrimination 163
Reformation 13 f., 25, 97
religious 9–14, 16 f., 23, 25, 28, 36, 41 f., 46 f., 61, 69 f., 74 f., 84, 89–106, 109, 111–114, 119, 122, 143, 145–148, 151, 154–156, 158, 163, 165 f., 169, 173–176, 178–187
religious communities 83, 89 f., 96 f., 100 f., 106, 108, 110 f., 182 f.
religious discourse 145, 178, 186
religious institution 111
repoliticizing 161, 177
representational space 122–124, 131
representations of space 122–124
Republican Party 163, 166
revolution 106, 111 f., 136, 149, 158 f., 168 f., 181
rhythmanalyst 121, 125, 131
Rosengrenska 51, 53 f., 59–76

sacred 45, 71, 74, 140, 178, 181 f., 186
sanspapiers 61 f., 68
secondspace and thirdspace 90, 103
secular 9, 11 f., 14 f., 17, 36, 39, 43, 45, 47, 92–94, 97, 101–103, 109, 111–114, 122, 139 f., 151, 153, 155, 166, 168, 173, 177 f., 180–184, 186 f.
secular institutions 31, 36, 182 f.
secular power 114, 179
secular practices 184
self-discipline 13, 178
self-identity 186
Settlement 15, 21, 23–25, 27–32, 34–48, 90, 143, 149, 151–156, 162, 168, 174 f., 179–181, 183–185
Settlement movement 15, 23, 29 f., 34, 37, 40, 143, 148 f., 151–158, 168 f., 176, 182
social 6, 9–13, 17, 21, 23–31, 33–48, 60 f., 63, 68 f., 74 f., 81 f., 85, 90 f., 94–96, 99–106, 108–111, 114, 119–121, 123 f., 127–132, 134 f., 137, 143, 146–159, 161, 165, 167 f., 173–176, 179–183, 185
social body 135, 154 f.
social citizenship 15, 30 f., 180
social classes 24, 30, 124, 134, 151, 180
social cohesion 34 f.

social critique 21, 29, 31, 40, 43, 47, 156
social media 148 f., 157, 159–161, 168
social mobilization 143
social movement 28, 143 f., 147–149, 159–161, 163, 176
social organism 155
social project 29 f., 46
social transformation 32, 47
space 5, 9–11, 13–17, 21, 30–33, 36, 38, 41–45, 47 f., 59–63, 67, 69 f., 72–76, 81, 86, 89–114, 117, 119, 121–127, 129–140, 143, 147–151, 154–165, 167 f., 173–187
spaces of transformation 183
spatial identity 175
spatial justice 100
spatial political theology 89, 100, 114
spatial production 91 f., 184
spatial solidarity mechanism 183
spatial theology 70
spiritual hospitality 99
spirituality 13, 66, 85, 94–98, 101 f., 105, 158, 164, 169
spiritual tolerance 182
substance users 16, 117, 121, 126–129, 132–136, 138, 183

Tea Party 16, 143, 148–150, 159, 163, 165–169
the city 15, 23, 25, 27, 85, 93, 100, 122 f., 125, 127, 131, 136 f., 147–150, 159, 163, 174
theory of hospitality 59
the other 9 f., 12, 16 f., 31 f., 35, 42 f., 46, 48, 59 f., 62–64, 67, 69 f., 72, 75 f., 89, 92 f., 99, 102, 107 f., 110, 122, 127, 129, 131, 133–136, 139 f., 143, 155, 162, 173 f., 184–186
third space 10 f., 149, 187
Toynbee Hall 23, 29, 36, 152 f.
triadic model 122, 131

undocumented migrants 10, 15, 51, 53–56, 59–61, 68
unthinkable spaces 45
urban hospitality 94, 130, 176
urban movements 160
utopia 10, 15, 29 f., 32–34, 39, 43, 45–48, 71 f., 76, 86, 89, 91, 95–99, 102–105, 110, 112, 139, 143 f., 149 f., 169, 175–177, 180 f., 183

volunteers 17, 21, 23, 26 f., 54, 56, 61, 63, 65–67, 69, 71, 74, 165, 175 f.

welfare 11 f., 27, 29, 31, 43–45, 47 f., 54, 68, 143, 153, 155, 163, 176, 179–182, 186
welfare state 5, 9, 11 f., 21, 45 f., 48, 65, 68, 101, 105, 111, 165, 174, 176, 178, 180 f., 186

youth 24, 28, 31, 44, 120, 155

Zuccotti Park 165

Index of Names

Addams, J. 152–156, 162, 168
Agamben, G. 71 f., 109
Agarwal, S. D. 159
Andersson, R. 73
Andraschek-Holzer, R. 91

Barrett, D. B. 89
Barthel, M. L. 159
Bellah, R. 150
Bennett, W. L. 159
Bertelsen, J. 23, 29 f., 44
Blasi, A. 89
Boedeltje, F. 71–73
Booth, C. 150
Borch, C. 157
Borioni, P. 38, 40, 44
Borning, A. 159
Brekke, T. 126 f.
Bundesen, P. 34, 37, 42–44
Burack, C. 167

Calvo, A.M.M. 59, 76
Campbell, E. 24, 158, 165
Campbell, D. 171
Campese, C. 77
Caroll, M.D. 77
Casanova, J. 94
Clausen, T. 127
Coggin, J. 163, 166
Cooper, F. 150
Crane, H. 156
Creech, B. 160, 162
Crockett, C. 109

Davidson, A. 13 f., 106
Davie, G. 152 f., 158
Davis, A. F. 170
Deleuze, G. 18
Derrida, J. 73, 76
Donzelot, J. 34
Dumm, T. 32
Durkheim, E. 149, 151 f., 155, 157

Ehrkamp, P. 18
Elizondo, V.V. 70–72
Elliott, A. 170
Engels, F. 150

Foucault, Gabriel, K. 5, 9–14, 16 f., 31–33, 35 f., 38, 42, 45, 60, 62 f., 68 f., 71, 74, 76, 86, 104, 106 f., 113, 123 f., 129 f., 135–138, 144–147, 154, 169, 173, 175, 177, 180, 184

Gärtner, C. 89
Gitlin, T. 160
Gjersing, L. 127
Goonewardena, K. M. 123
Greco, M. 12
Greenstone, J. D. 154
Groody, D. 60, 71

Hardt, M. 160 f.
Henriksen, L. S. 34, 37
Hetherington, K. 124, 129, 134, 139
Hill, L. 18
Hoffman, M. 106
Hopkins, P. 18
Hunt, L. 103

Jespersen, H. 49
Johnson, B. 32 f., 42, 89, 129 f., 136 f., 139, 159
Jørgensen, A. 25, 37

Kahl, S. 49
Karlsen, M. P. 18
Kawash, S. 135, 139

Keul, H. 97
King, R. 72 f.
Kipfer, S. 123
Knott, K. 10 f., 14, 94
Kong, L. 18
Kurian, G.T. 89

Laclau, E. 46
Langman, L. 166
Laratta R. 19
Lefebvre, H. 10, 14, 16 f., 90 f., 95, 103, 121–126, 129–131, 133–139, 184
Lengermann, P. M. 153 f.
Lindhardt P. G. 49
Losonczi, P. 109

MacLean, V. M. 152, 155
Mahmood, S. 72 f.
Manemann, J. 109
McLean, G.F. 94
Mehring, R. 109
Metz, J.B. 109–111
Meyer, K. 125
Milgrom, R. 123
Moore, R. 158

Nafstad, I. 121
Nagel, C. 18
Nassehi, A. 89
Negri, Niebrugge, G. A. 160 f.
Nisbet, R. A. 151

Olsen. H. 141
Olson, E. 18

Laneth, P.F. 28
Pohl, C. 18
Pollack, D. 89
Putnam, R. D. 158, 168

Quandt, J. B. C. 36

Rancière, J. 147
Régulier, C. 121
Reinders, R. C. 40
Rex, J. 158
Rissing, M. 109, 116
Rissing, T. 109, 116
Rosol, M. 18
Rost, C. 159
Rousmaniere, J. P. 38, 43

Sanchez, L.A. 60
Scaff, L. A. 150
Schmid, C. 122–124, 130 f., 134–136
Schmitt, C. 109–111
Schüssler Fiorenza, F. 109
Scruton, R. 150
Simonsen, K. 124, 131, 133, 138
Skocpol, T. 163, 166
Skretting, A. 127
Snyder, S. 60
Soja, E. 5, 10, 14, 123 f., 138
Sommers, M. 159
Spivak, G. 71, 73
Stanek, L. 123, 137
Steensland, B. 171
Swyngedouw, E. 161

Tarde, G. 149, 157, 159
Taylor, C. 94
Thompson, M. J. 172
Thoreau, H. D. 150
Tiedemann, R. 149
Tocqueville, A. de. 148, 150
Torpey, J. 158
Tremel, M. 109
Turner, B. S. 5, 16, 143, 150, 152 f., 156, 158

Valverde, M. 12
Van Leeuwen, M. H. D. 49
Van Wyk, T. 77
Vanhoozer, K.J. 89
Vásquez, M.A. 94
Villadsen, K. 6, 9, 15 f., 29, 34 f., 41, 143, 145, 152 f., 156, 173

Waal, H. 127
Ward, G. 76
Warner, M. 89
Weber, M. 150
Westhelle, V. 70, 74 f.
Wille, J. 39
Williams, J. E. 152, 155 f.
Williamson, V. 163, 166
Wilson, A. R. 167
Wingren, G. 139 f.
Wright, E. L. 171
Wyller, T. E. 6, 9, 15, 59, 91, 129, 173

Zahavi, D. 64, 66
Ziebarth, U. 126 f.